"David Madden's approach to the teaching of writing is both practical and inspiring. The evidence he gives of how and why successful writers revise their work, extending their imaginative vision, is fascinating and persuasive. This is a book for both beginning and experienced writers. I recommend it highly."

—Robert Pack
Director, Bread Loaf Writer's Conference,
Middlebury, Vermont

"REVISING FICTION is a thoroughly useful and often inspired guide for writers of all levels, but particularly so for professionals. David Madden presents provocative questions about the essential techniques of fiction that are especially helpful in these days when authors can count on their publishers more for lunch than for line-editing. As an agent I recommend it unreservedly to my clients."

—John Pickering
Pickering Associates, Inc.
Literary Agents

"This is a nuts-and-bolts approach to the craft of composition that reminds us nonetheless of the magic in the enterprise, the music in the gears. Produced by a practitioner who knows whereof he writes, and how he writes, and why he writes—and with examples culled from the wonderful warehouse of fiction. For apprentice authors at every stage of our common apprenticeship, a first-rate work of words."

—Nicholas Delbanco
Author and Director, M.F.A. Program
University of Michigan, Ann Arbor

REVISING FICTION

DAVID MADDEN is the author of *Bijou, The Suicide's Wife,* and other novels, short stories, plays, poetry, critical studies, and textbooks. He has conducted workshops in creative writing for over twenty-five years, and has taught writing at Louisana State University since 1968.

Books by David Madden

FICTION

The Beautiful Greed (1961)
Cassandra Singing (1969)
The Shadow Knows (1970), Short Stories
Brothers in Confidence (1972)
Bijou (1974)
The Suicide's Wife (1978)
Pleasure-Dome (1979)
On the Big Wind (1980)
The New Orleans of Possibilities (1982), Short Stories

NONFICTION

Wright Morris (1964)
The Poetic Image in Six Genres (1969)
James M. Cain (1970; reissued, 1987)
Harlequin's Stick, Charlie's Cane (1975)
A Primer of the Novel (1979)
Writers' Revisions, with Richard Powers (1980)
Cain's Craft (1984)

EDITED WORKS

Proletarian Writers of the Thirties (1968)
Tough Guy Writers of the Thirties (1968)
American Dreams, American Nightmares (1970)
Rediscoveries (1971)
The Popular Culture Explosion, with Ray B. Browne (1972)
Nathanael West: The Cheaters and the Cheated (1973)
Contemporary Literary Scene, with Frank Magill (1974)
Remembering James Agee (1974)
Studies in the Short Story, with Virgil Scott (1980; sixth edition 1984)

REVISING FICTION

A Handbook for Writers

David Madden

A PLUME BOOK

NEW AMERICAN LIBRARY

NEW YORK AND SCARBOROUGH, ONTARIO

NAL BOOKS ARE AVAILABLE AT QUANTITY DISCOUNTS WHEN USED
TO PROMOTE PRODUCTS OR SERVICES. FOR INFORMATION PLEASE
WRITE TO PREMIUM MARKETING DIVISION, NEW AMERICAN LIBRARY,
1633 BROADWAY, NEW YORK, NEW YORK 10019.

Copyright © 1988 by David Madden

All rights reserved

PLUME TRADEMARK REG. U.S. PAT. OFF. AND FOREIGN COUNTRIES
REGISTERED TRADEMARK—MARCA REGISTRADA
HECHO EN CHICAGO, U.S.A.

SIGNET, SIGNET CLASSIC, MENTOR, ONYX, PLUME, MERIDIAN
and NAL BOOKS are published *in the United States* by NAL PENGUIN INC.,
1633 Broadway, New York, New York 10019,
in Canada by The New American Library of Canada Limited,
81 Mack Avenue, Scarborough, Ontario M1L 1M8

Library of Congress Cataloging-in-Publication Data

Madden, David, 1933–
    Revising fiction: a handbook for writers/David Madden.
        p. cm.
    ISBN 0-452-26088-4
    1. Fiction—Authorship.   I. Title.
PN3355.M215 1988
808′.02—dc19

First Printing, June, 1988

1   2   3   4   5   6   7   8   9

PRINTED IN THE UNITED STATES OF AMERICA

"The art of writing is rewriting."
—Sean O'Faolain

ACKNOWLEDGMENTS

I am very grateful to Peggy Bach whose practical intelligence steered me away from a major misdirection and whose insights guided me every step of the way.

Robert Pack's faith and generosity enabled me to test some of this material at Bread Loaf Writers' Conference.

Albert Daub of Scarecrow Press and Charlyce Jones Owen of Holt, Rinehart and Winston, college department, were kind enough to permit me to use, in greatly modified form, passages from my earlier works.

My thanks to John R. May, chairman, for providing assistance from Louisiana State University's English Department in the preparation of the manuscript; to Gloria Henderson, Claudia Scott and Erica Babin for much of the typing; to Ben Bryant for his assistance in tracking down sources of revisions.

CONTENTS

THE USES OF
THIS HANDBOOK

Drawing upon my experiences as a reader, writer, teacher, and editor in the genres of poetry, fiction, playwriting, literary criticism, and imaginative nonfiction—with a heavy emphasis on fiction—I have accumulated a checklist of problems I encounter in fiction as I read, in my own writing as I write, in works that I teach, and in manuscripts I encounter as editor and teacher.

You have probably already noticed, with a hot prickle along the scalp and a sinking feeling in the pit of your stomach, the great swarm of revision questions, all in the negative, in the extensive table of contents. I hope you will concur with my assumption that the achievements of your first draft are thrillingly in evidence, while their effects depend critically upon your identifying the negative elements and dealing with them.

I am assuming then that "yes" answers to some of these negative questions are cause for celebration, not despair. To identify and deal with a mistake in judgment or execution is an achievement. Consider, as another cause for celebration that in the solving of one problem you are very likely to imagine and create some elements that you would not have otherwise conjured up. But an ongoing problem writers always face is this: in the very act of solving one problem, you can only *try* to avoid creating another.

This handbook is an organized compilation of technical questions that short-story writers and novelists sometimes, or often, but not always, ask themselves throughout the various stages of the revision process as they reimagine their fiction. These questions represent guidelines and possibilities, not inflexible how-to-do-it rules. I hasten to stress that failures to follow these guidelines have produced some of the finest moments in fiction.

The questions of technique raised in this handbook are not posed abstractly, but derive from what writers are on record as having actually done in the revision process.

Why another book on the writing of fiction? This is *not* another of the types of books already in print; this is the first of a type, one that writers have always needed. There are no predecessors. Wallace Hildick, who pioneered this approach in *Word for Word* and *Writing with Care*, comes closest to this book, with John Kuehl, offering a quite different format in *Creative Writing and Rewriting*, not far behind. However, *Revising Fiction* is much more a practical handbook than are the works of Hildick and Kuehl.

This handbook is intended for writers at every stage of their development, working alone; for agents and editors; and for teachers and students in creative-writing workshops. Teachers and students in literature courses will also discover uses for it.

The purpose is to provide a reference source that offers questions, explanations, and examples of the range of techniques writers use in the revision process.

The table of contents and the Index of Techniques are themselves designed to be used as checklists. The first is composed of the questions posed in the text; the second lists key terms alphabetically. The key terms also reappear as running heads in the text.

As you approach the revision process, wondering, even as the most experienced and accomplished writers continue to wonder each day, "What do I do *now*?" you may review these questions and terms to identify those that apply most pertinently to the particular problems you have created for yourself in the first and subsequent drafts.

You may then return to the body of the handbook, where explanations of technical concepts and examples of revisions from the works of published writers, with commentary, are given in the entries.

To benefit from the examples of revision that I use, it is not necessary to have read the works from which they are taken. Of course, the examples will be more effective if you have read the works; time taken to read parts or all of those works that seem to relate promisingly to your own personal revision problems is time well spent.

A major effect the examples are intended to have is to show a range of possibilities that will liberate writers from a sense of entrapment in their first and subsequent drafts. Where I have been unable to search out an example, I have made one up out of my own experience as a fiction writer.

I have included examples of my own handling of many of these techniques as they came up in the revision of my story "The Day the Flowers Came," first published in *Playboy* and reprinted in several anthologies. Marginal comments on my revisions offer a kind of preview and review of key techniques. Those comments are cited in a good many of the entries.

This practical handbook is a distillation of all that I have written and planned to write about the creative process of revising fiction. I am convinced that it is in the revision process that the various techniques of writing fiction may be most effectively learned and recalled daily for practical use.

You probably know that very few editors or agents today (or yesterday) know enough about the craft of writing to help you in the revision process. Forget what you've heard or read about Maxwell Perkins and Thomas Wolfe or (if you're willing to wait until you're dead) Edward Aswell and Thomas Wolfe. Perkins is a legend because he was virtually unique; very few editors ever knew, and even fewer today know, how to help you specifically. "Most editors generally can't recognize bad writing when they read it," said publisher Alfred Knopf. "Nor do they try very hard to learn to recognize." Mark Harris's editors told him his first novel needed revision. "Whereas they were correct in believing the book needed revision they had no idea how a book was revised, for they had never done it, and neither did I, for the same reason." It's best to go on the assumption that agents, editors, and friends cannot help you. An understanding of how techniques of writing work in the revision process *can* help you.

This book has evolved over the past thirty years out of my classes in creative writing and in literature, including summer workshops at Bread Loaf and other places, and from my study of revisions of all kinds of writers in all genres.

If I sound pontifical, consider that in any attempt to tell another writer anything about writing, that tone is unavoidable and, I hope, forgivable.

INTRODUCTION:

Revision Is an Act of the Technical Imagination

Virginia Woolf wrote to Clive Bell, one of the friends whose approval she most wanted, about her first novel-in-progress *The Voyage Out*, "When I read the thing over (one very gray evening) I thought it so flat and monotonous that I did not even feel 'the atmosphere': certainly there was no character in it. Next morning I proceeded to slash and rewrite, in the hope of animating it; and (as I suspect for I have not re-read it) destroyed the one virtue it had—a kind of continuity; for I wrote it originally in a dream-like state, which was at any rate, unbroken. . . . I have kept all the pages I cut out; so the thing can be reconstructed precisely as it was" (*The Letters of Virginia Woolf*).

Five years after her ninth revision had produced her first published novel in 1915, Virginia Woolf recorded mixed reactions in her diary: "The mornings from 12 to 1 I spend reading *The Voyage Out*. I've not read it since July 1913. And if you ask me what I think I must reply that I don't know—such a harlequinade as it is—such an assortment of patches—here simple and severe—here frivolous and shallow—here like God's truth—here strong and free flowing as I could wish. What to make of it, Heaven knows. The failures are ghastly enough to make my cheeks burn—and then a turn of the sentence, a direct look ahead of me, makes them burn in a different way. On the whole I like the young woman's mind considerably. How gallantly she takes her fences—and my word, what a gift for pen and ink! I can do little to amend, and must go down to posterity the author of cheap witticisms, smart satires and even, I find, vulgarisms—crudities rather—that will never cease to rankle in the grave."

But the American edition gave the now more mature writer another chance, and Woolf revised the novel extensively once more. For many writers, the creative process is continuous and unending. The fact that

Henry James, William Faulkner, F. Scott Fitzgerald, Gore Vidal, John Fowles, and numerous other writers revised *after* publication dramatizes the importance of revision in the writing process.

In "that solitary room," wrote Virginia Woolf, "processes of the strangest kind are gone through" and life "is subjected to a thousand disciplines and exercises." The author of seven novels was as immersed in the process of revision of her eighth novel as she had been for her first. "And I have just finished . . . the last sentence of *The Waves*. . . . But I have never written a book so full of holes and patches; that will need rebuilding yes, not only remodeling. I suspect the structure is wrong . . . unlike all my other books in every way, it is unlike them in this, that I begin to re-write it, or conceive it again with ardour, directly I have done." "I finished my retyping of *The Waves*. Not that it is finished—oh dear no. For then I must correct the re-retyping . . . no one can say I have been hasty or careless this time; though I doubt not the lapses and slovenliness are innumerable" (*A Writer's Diary*).

I hope that many users of this handbook will have already learned most of the techniques illustrated here. If I am not teaching creative writing in this manual, I am providing practical suggestions within the context of the most practical phase of writing: revision.

Many teachers and writers, even teachers of imaginative writing who are also writers, question whether creative writing can be taught. My experience is that there are certain techniques of writing and elements of style that can be discussed, analyzed, learned, and used. By "techniques," I do not mean *rules*. "There are three rules for writing the novel," said W. Somerset Maugham. "Unfortunately, no one knows what they are." *Talent* cannot be taught, but techniques of writing can be shared and thus stimulate whatever talent a writer already has. My experience has been that one of the most effective ways to teach the techniques of writing is to compare the different early versions of a writer's published work. The pertinent question should then be: Can the techniques of revision be organized for practical use? This handbook attempts to answer that more relevant question.

Most beginning writers have so much trouble finding or imagining—that is, *seeing*—something to write *about* that the problem of rewriting or revision seems remote. But many writers who have earned their reputations through hard work agree that one writes at first just to have something to rewrite.

An examination of the various versions of a story develops one's understanding of the effects of writing techniques—what they do to the reader and how they do it. I urge you to study writers' revisions beyond this handbook. For instance, half a dozen books about Faulkner's revisions show comparisons by setting versions of them side by side. Wallace Hildick, a novelist who is also a scholar of revisions, knows from his examination of numerous revisions that "the alteration of a single word can transform completely one's view of a character." Hemingway reminded his publisher that "the alteration of a word can throw an entire story out of key." My assumption is that what one learns from studying the revisions of a particular work—a Hemingway story, for instance—may apply to the revision of one's own stories from time to time.

In the revision process, from moment to moment, ask yourself, What effect did I want to have on the reader? Have I achieved it? If not, how may I revise to achieve my purpose?

Among writers, there are a variety of approaches to and attitudes about revision. "The best reason for putting anything down on paper," says Bernard De Voto, "is that one may then change it." Robert Penn Warren feels differently. "The idea of writing a first draft with the idea of revising the first draft is repugnant to me . . . I have to play for keeps on every page." William Styron seems to agree. "I seem to have some neurotic need to perfect each paragraph—each sentence, even—as I go along," an average of three pages a day.

Christopher Isherwood revised "a great deal. What I tend to do is not so much pick at a thing but sit down and rewrite it completely. Both for *A Single Man* and *A Meeting at the River* I wrote three entire drafts. After making notes on one draft I'd sit down and rewrite it again from the beginning. I've found that's much better than patching and amputating things. One has to rethink the thing completely." D. H. Lawrence took a similar approach in writing three different versions of his Lady Chatterley story (all now published). Wishful writers should know that few writers use that approach.

Robert Penn Warren, who does, of course, revise, argues the importance of a writer's conscious awareness of technique. "People deeply interested in an art are interested in the 'how.' " "I try to think a lot about the craft of other people. . . . When it comes to your own work you have made some objective decisions, such as which character is going to tell the story." ". . . nothing can permanently please, which does not contain in itself the reason why it is so, and not otherwise." W. H. Auden might have had the revision process in mind when he said, "The innocent eye sees nothing." Daphne du Maurier, a more commercial writer, is ruthless in revision. "No sentimentality about this job," she said, describing her work on her first novel, *The Loving Spirit*. "I was ruthless, I crossed out passages that had given me exquisite pleasure to write."

As with most literary terms, there is some confusion about the precise meaning of "revision" and how (or whether) it ought to be distinguished from "rewriting." Referring to *The Way of All Flesh*, Samuel Butler seems to be making a distinction when he says that he had "always intended to rewrite it or at any rate revise it," but his usage confuses more than it distinguishes. Having declared about *The City and the Pillar*, "I have rewritten the entire book," what expectations does Gore Vidal raise? "I have not changed the point of view nor the essential relationships." What exactly *did* he do to his novel twenty years after its first publication? Did he "revise" it or did he "rewrite" it? What does James A. Michener, describing his general practice, mean when he says, "I rewrite every sentence, and often times I go to five or six revisions of certain parts. But there's a sense of real accomplishment in getting words to behave"?

Henry James once said he made a distinction between revising and rewriting but he could not make clear even to himself what it was. "What I tried for is a mere revision of surface and expression," he said, concerning what he had done to *Roderick Hudson*. One of the last things he said on the subject was this: "What rewriting might be was to remain—it has remained for me to this hour—a mystery." In the novel he most thoroughly revised, *The American*, he did not add or omit major characters, restructure the novel significantly, or change the forces that cause the resolution of the conflict. "Revision" may, even so, be the most useful word for what writers do; we might simply say that James did only some of the things one may do in revising.

If the writer who was more articulate than any other about the craft of fiction could not define the word to his own satisfaction, Henry James could express in telling phrases what *happens* in revision. He stressed that for him the imagination came fully into play in the process; to revise was "to live back into a forgotten state, into convictions . . . credulities . . . reasons of things . . . old motives." Revision is a "renewal of vision," it is a "process of re-dreaming."

For the great reviser Henry James, "revision," says poet-critic R. P. Blackmur in his introduction to James's *The Art of the Novel*, "was responsible re-seeing." Revision: re-seeing. That is the meaning of the term as I use it in this handbook. As with many literary terms, the several meanings may be used interchangeably, and so when I say rewrite, I mean revise. Attempts to distinguish the two would only cause confusion.

What Are the Sources of Ideas?

In *Journal of the Fictive Life*, Howard Nemerov says that the reason why it takes him "so long between one fiction and the next" is "not not 'having an idea,' but having ten or twenty ideas, and having to wait as patiently as possible for the relations among them to reveal themselves. . . . the mind, unable to bear the richness of consequence entailed upon one idea, forthwith produces another instead."

"Where do your ideas for fiction come from?" writers are often asked. Here are a few typical answers:

1. My own direct experience—what I have done or what has happened to me. (At work here is the autobiographical impulse, which sometimes becomes a compulsion.)
2. Experiences of strangers or friends that I have only observed, or have been told about as stories.
3. Actual events reported in newspapers and sometimes on television.
4. Notions or concepts or images for stories that my reading in fiction and poetry, or my viewing of movies and plays, stimulates.
5. Experiences that well up suddenly out of my subconscious.
6. Experiences that I willfully and deliberately conjure up out of my imagination—experiences that I see and feel only in my imagination. (Beginning writers have great trouble imagining stories.)
7. Publisher's ideas—a novel about white collar crime, for example.
8. Ideas from my friends and relatives.
9. Ideas suggested by dreams.
10. Possibilities posed by a new or different technique. (One then imagines uses of that technique.)

Once a writer has a story, he may make a short note, file it away, turn it over to his creative subconscious, and wait for the day—perhaps five years later—when the compulsion to tell that story takes possession of him. "It was in that room that I learned not to think about anything that I was writing from the time I stopped writing until I started again the next day," wrote Hemingway. "That way my subconscious would be working on it and at the same time I would be listening to other people and noticing everything. . . ." The subconscious is constantly revising.

Revision begins in the mind. On paper, revision begins in the note-taking stage. The crucial function of notes is suggested by one Henry James made for the serial version of *The Portrait of a Lady*: "After Isabel's marriage there are five more installments, and the success of the whole story depends upon this portion being well conducted or not. Let me then make the most of it—let me imagine the best. There has been a want of action in the earlier part, and it may be made up here. . . . The weakness of the whole story is that it is too exclusively psychological— that it depends too little on incident; but the complete unfolding of the situation that is established by Isabel's marriage may nonetheless be quite sufficiently dramatic. . . . There is a great deal to do here in a small compass; every word, therefore, must tell—every touch must count." F. Scott Fitzgerald and William Faulkner found their original notes useful as guides in various stages of the revision process. See the Bibliography for the notebooks of Henry James, Thomas Wolfe, and others.

Outlines come next for many writers; they too undergo numerous revisions. The outline, along with several chapters, of *The Heart Is a Lonely Hunter* won a Houghton Mifflin Fellowship for Carson McCullers. "This book is planned according to a definite and balanced design. The form is contrapuntal throughout. . . . There are five distinct styles of writing—one for each of the main characters who is treated subjectively and an objective, legendary style for the mute. . . . This book will be complete in all its phases. No loose ends will be left dangling and at the close there will be a feeling of balanced completion" (*The Mortgaged Heart*). Outlines, too, often continue to guide the writer in long, involved revision processes.

What Happens in the *First Draft*?

Usually, the fallacies or mistakes a writer commits in the first draft are consequences of failing to control point of view. So the one technique you should decide upon before starting to write is the point of view from which you will tell the story. Interrogate your story, asking, Should I tell it in the first person, from Ann's point of view, or John's, from Bill's? In the third person, confined to John's point of view, or Ann's, or Bill's? Or should I tell it from the godlike, omniscient point of view?

Write the first draft in a kind of trance, usually very fast, with little awareness of the techniques of writing you have learned and know and have employed in earlier stories. Of course, after years of writing, you use techniques as unconsciously as you swim—even in the first draft. Katherine Anne Porter boasts of having written "Flowering Judas" spontaneously in two hours. That story is a remarkable achievement—attributable, I am convinced, not to her having written it spontaneously in two hours but to her having spent many years consciously evaluating the techniques of fiction, her own and that of other writers.

"When you start to write," said Hemingway, "you get all the kick and the reader gets none." The first draft is for you the writer; simultaneously, you are also your own first reader. But the final draft is for the others—those strangers numbering from one to one million who will read your story. "Spontaneity belongs in the first jet of writing," said Anaïs Nin, "but some disciplined selectivity and cutting should follow in editing."

And yet we hear a lot of writers who say they hate to revise, that the real fun is in the heat of creation, that cold revision is torture. "Yes," said Dostoyevsky, "that was and ever is my greatest torment—I can never control my material." Reluctant writers *do* use, both consciously and unconsciously, various techniques, and that's how they are able, finally, in the revision process, to complete the work that they find so boring. "Usually when I begin a new book," said Tolstoy, "I am very pleased with it and work with great interest. But as the book work goes on, I become more and more bored, and often in rewriting it I omit things, substitute others, not because the new idea is better, but because I get tired of the old. Often I strike out what is vivid and replace it by something dull." The author of *War and Peace* said, "In a writer there must always be two people—the writer and the critic." Tolstoy seldom reread his published work. "But if by chance I come across a page, it always strikes me: all this must be rewritten; this is how I should have written it," he said.

Cherish inspiration, but don't trust it beyond the first draft. Create a routine, a discipline for yourself—so many hours writing, each day, at a certain time, under similar conditions, even if for only an hour. "During the revision period I try to keep some sort of discipline," says John Fowles, author of *The French Lieutenant's Woman*. "I make myself revise whether I like it or not; in some ways, the more disinclined and dyspeptic one feels, the better—one is harsher with oneself. All the best cutting is done when one is sick of the writing." In *Writing a Novel*, John Braine used his critically acclaimed, and best-selling, first novel,

Room at the Top, to illustrate his points. He concluded, "A novelist's vocation is like any other; discipline and technique are infinitely more important than inspiration." One critic has said that for Henry James "revision was not a matter of choice, but an immediate and absolute necessity. That is, it was a moral act of the highest kind."

What Is the Role of the *Imagination*?

I have emphasized the imagination because I think today it is perilously neglected when we talk about the creative process and especially the revision stages.

"Write about what you know" is the most misused piece of advice ever pontificated upon young writers. "What you know" can be a rich world created out of your imagination—rather than simply what it's like to grow up in a middle-class suburb, for instance. "By refusing to write about anything which is not thoroughly familiar," said Saul Bellow, "the American writer confesses the powerlessness of the imagination and accepts its relegation to an inferior place."

Imagination is more important than experience and inspiration. I don't want to give a faithful report on real-life incidents, I want to *transform* them in my imagination so that the story itself becomes the event; it isn't just an authentic report referring to something outside itself. When my son was a child, he didn't want me to *read* a story to him; he urged me to "make up a story." He wanted to experience the process itself, to feel my imagination at work inventing. The imagination at work is a form of play—play that involves a fusion of intellect and emotion. There is far more to the imagination than the popular notion allows.

It's while looking closely, imaginatively, at every word in the revision process that the imagination suddenly soars—sees larger possibilities.

Think of the imagination as working in these four ways:.

1. In the imagination, characters and their story are created. The source of creative energy here is often an *inspiration.*
2. In the imagination, in the revision stage of the creative process, characters and their story are reshaped many times, in many possible ways. When the *reshaping imagination* is at work, the source of creative energy is almost always the *techniques* of writing themselves.

3. We do not often discuss a third, very important way the imagination works. I call it the *technical imagination*. Often I have had the inspiration to see the characters and their stories in my imagination, but I cannot see *how* to tell the story. I must wait for a *technical* inspiration. Or I must willfully imagine a technique for telling this story. A thrilling inspiration dies very quickly, but the imagination continues to conjure techniques and devices to solve problems raised in the first draft.

4. Unconsciously in the first draft and consciously in the revision stage, the *stylistic imagination* is at work. The imagination does not work simply on the larger elements of plot and character and in the realm of technique, it works line by line in the style.

To paraphrase Socrates, the unimagined, unexpressed life is not worth living. It is a mistake to separate imagination from more intellectual functions. With strict logic, ask yourself: If *this* happens, what might happen as consequence? As you ask that logical question, your imagination is stimulated to explore your raw material to produce all kinds of images.

Wright Morris has said that talent and raw material are useless without imagination. The raw materials are drawn from nature and human society. The author must be true to nature and to life in his society even as he reconceives and recreates it in his imagination. The imagination is a recombining agent that makes a new perspective or vision occur. Even when it must operate within the strictest externally or internally imposed limitations, the quality that holds a reader is the author's imagination, and his techniques for conceptualizing that which he imagines will make the reader feel his imagination at work.

As you read stories and novels, determine to what degree the authors stimulate the imagination of the reader. Which stories seem most "made-up," the product of the author's imagination—as opposed to reporting on life pretty much the way it is?

What Are the *Stages* a Writer Goes Through in His Mastery of Revision?

One of the most important lessons a writer learns—through practice—for no amount of theorizing can convince him—is the absolute *necessity* of rewriting. The real breakthrough comes when he discovers the rhapsodic *elations* of rewriting.

If when you scrutinize your first draft you find that you've committed all the fallacies and ineptitudes on the checklist, do not despair. Help is on the way. From within yourself—that is, *if* you are convinced that revision is the most important and exciting stage in the creative process. For every general principle I offer in this handbook, there are exceptions, some of which I will cite. It was in *The Crack-up*, appropriately enough, that F. Scott Fitzgerald said that "the test of a first rate intelligence is the ability to hold two opposed ideas in the mind at the same time, and still retain the ability to function." The writer engaged in passing Fitzgerald's test (a lifelong but exhilarating ordeal) will see immediately that my approach here only *appears* to be negative: a good writer knows he can, with an inspired leap of the imagination, transform any of these fallacies or errors into a unique achievement. Nothing is more encouraging for a working, disciplined writer than the realization that he is consciously coping with problems that obstruct the free flow of his creative energy.

Once the first draft is down, once the writer has captured on paper what he has seen in his imagination, he begins to resee to rewrite—the process of *revision* begins. Sometimes it takes a long time for his imagination to see again and again and again, every aspect of a story, from the plot to a comma. Three poets express the problem succinctly: "We must labour to be beautiful," said W. B. Yeats. "Beauty is difficult," said Ezra Pound. "It is not every day," said Wallace Stevens, "that the world arranges itself into a poem." It never does. Only the writer can do that.

What happens in the revision process? The writer, to put it as simply as possible, cuts this, adds that, substitutes this for that, and relocates this from here to there, in small or large units, thus contracting or expanding the work. He often reorganizes large elements. The writer, says Robert Louis Stevenson, "must suppress much and omit more." About his first novel, *This Side of Paradise*, Fitzgerald said he "wrote and revised and compiled and boiled down." "I've never had a sentence turn up in the final form," says Evan S. Connell, "as it was in the beginning."

For a new edition of his novel *A Place on Earth*, Wendell Berry described in the preface the history of writing that novel: "I began writing this book on January 1, 1960, and continued to work on it in such time as I had available until its first publication in 1967. Especially in the earlier parts, it was a halting, doubtful procedure. I began to learn what I was doing somewhere in the middle, too late to define a formal principle that could have told me what belonged and what did not.

"With the wise help of Dan Wickenden, my editor at that time, I cut a great many pages from the typescript and made other changes. That taught me more. But the full lesson was learned slowly, after publication: the book was clumsy, overwritten, wasteful. And yet I continued to like it. I liked the idea of it, the characters, many of the episodes.''

Then Berry describes his revisions for the new edition. His only rule ''was to do the work as far as possible by cutting. I have cut words, sentences, paragraphs, whole passages, all the cuts together amounting to perhaps a third of the text of the first edition, and I have made in the process many small changes of punctuation, diction, and phrasing. My additions, scattered throughout, are small and relatively few. The present edition, unlike the first, has chapter titles.

''This, then is not a new book, but a renewed one . . .''

My experience convinces me—and my study of the revisions of all kinds of writers convinces me—that writers make the same mistakes all their lives. Each day, they learn how to write all over again. But the process gets faster.

In *Word for Word*, Wallace Hildick shows, with examples of revision and comment, that D. H. Lawrence went through three stages within five years, from ''raw young writer'' to ''experienced but still not fully competent writer'' to ''inspired, experienced and technically accomplished author'' (p. 52). In his or her development, the writer goes through four stages in the matter of revision, and you may recognize where you are.

1. He makes a mistake, but fails to see it.
2. He makes a mistake, he sees it, but doesn't know how to fix it—or reimagine it. He hasn't learned enough about the techniques of fiction.
3. He makes a mistake, he sees it, he has learned how to fix it, because he has learned some of the techniques of fiction, but he just can't do it.
4. He makes a mistake, he sees it, he knows how to fix it, he fixes it—and by now he has learned that solving technical problems in the creative process is just as exciting as writing the first draft. (Then book reviewers come along and tell him he only *thinks* he's fixed the problems.)

How many revisions are necessary really to finish a story? ''Thirty-seven,'' S. J. Perelman replied promptly when asked. ''I once tried doing thirty-three, but something was lacking. . . .'' That was Perelman's way of saying that the question is one for which there could not possibly be an answer. In the first, and last, place, one never really finishes a story; as a writer once said, one must finally abandon a story. Even after a story is published and honored in some way, the rewriting does not end for some writers. In *Writers at Work*, the interviewer asked Frank O'Connor, "Do you rewrite?" O'Connor replied, "Endlessly, endlessly, endlessly. And keep on rewriting, and after it's published, and then after it's published in book form, I usually rewrite it again."

Many beginning writers tell me, "After the first draft, I lose interest. I can't force myself to rewrite." A knowledge of techniques and of when and how to imagine their use will give a writer the fresh starts he needs, day after day, in the long, hard, but exhilarating revision process.

I POINT OF VIEW

1 | Considering the experience you want the reader to have in this story, have you used a point of view that is *ineffective*?

All the reader's experiences flow from the point-of-view technique you employ. When the point of view is gratuitous, the writer loses control of other elements. Because it most directly affects the choice and use of all elements, point of view is the most important technical choice. Because the choice of an ineffective point-of-view technique produces so many other problems, it is the only technical choice you need to make *before* plunging into the first draft.

In the revision process, you may ask yourself:

What is the best point of view for the effects I want to have on the reader?

How does the point of view affect style, characterization, conflict, theme, structure?

What is the psychological effect on the reader of presenting this story through the mind of the main character in the third person as opposed to letting him tell it in his own voice?

What are other possible points of view for this story and what are their particular effects?

The major fallacy, from which all other fallacies spring, is the point-of-view fallacy. If the writer uses poor judgment in his choice of the point of view through which the elements of the story are presented, or if he mishandles the one he chooses, he sets up a chain reaction that demolishes most of his carefully prepared effects. A story told in the third person will differ radically—in style, content, even structure—from the same story told in the first person.

The reader must feel that the point of view through which all elements reach him is the inevitable one for this story. In every story, the reader responds to a voice of authority as the source of everything—words, phrases, sentences, etc.—presented in the story. The writer creates that voice: sometimes the voice is the writer's own voice; sometimes he lets a character tell the story in the first person; sometimes he filters the story through the mind of a character, using the third person. For both writers and readers, point of view is the most difficult concept to understand and keep in focus.

"The whole question of the point of view," said Mary McCarthy, ". . . tortures everybody." Choosing the most effective point of view, as we can see in *The Notebooks for "Crime and Punishment,"* tortured Dostoyevsky. "The decision on narrative point-of-view," said Ross Macdonald, "is a key one for any novelist. It determines shape and tone, and even the class of detail that can be used."

The major point-of-view techniques are described in the next three sections; Questions 2–5.

There are some excellent articles and books by novelists on point of view: see. Wallace Hildick's *Thirteen Types of Narrative*; James Moffett and Kenneth McElheny's *Points of View*; and Eudora Welty's "How I Write," in Brooks and Warren's *Understanding Fiction*.

See "The Day the Flowers Came," p. 283–84.

2 | If you have used the *omniscient* point of view, have you realized all its potentials?

In the omniscient point of view, the author narrates the story in the third person, although he may speak now and then in this own first-person voice. The all-knowing omniscient narrator is godlike, for he sees, hears, feels, knows all; he may move from one character to another; he may move anywhere he wishes in time and space, giving the reader objective views of his characters' actions, or subjective views of their thoughts. The roving, omniscient narrator strives for a balance between interior and exterior views of his characters. He has a godlike control of all the elements.

You may get a very good sense of the characteristics of the omniscient point of view by reading the opening passages of novels using that technique. Charles Dickens's novels exhibit the entire range from extremely remote from, to close to a character. In the opening of *Bleak*

House, a metaphor pervades, like the creator's own consciousness, the scene.

> London. . . . Fog everywhere. Fog up the river, where it flows among green aits and meadows; fog down the river, where it rolls defiled among the tiers of shipping, and the waterside pollutions of a great (and dirty) city. Fog on the Essex marshes, fog on the Kentish heights. Fog creeping into the cabooses of collier-brigs; fog lying out on the yards, and hovering in the rigging of great ships; fog drooping on the gunwales of barges and small boats. Fog in the eyes and throats of ancient Greenwich pensioners, wheezing by the firesides of their wards. . . . Chance people on the bridges peeping over the parapets into a nether sky of fog, with fog all round them, as if they were up in a balloon, and hanging in the misty clouds.

Now, to see the range of characteristics of the omniscient point of view, read, in order, the openings of Dickens's *The Life and Adventures of Martin Chuzzlewit*, *Our Mutual Friend*, and *The Life and Adventures of Nicholas Nickleby*. The openings of Dickens's chapters in these and his other novels also demonstrate the range of omniscience.

Each type of point-of-view technique allows the writer its own particular freedoms and imposes its own particular limitations. The omniscient narrator is the freest, but his freedom may lead to excess, lack of focus, loss of control. The reader may feel that the omniscient narrator, because he sees and knows all and can go anywhere, ought to tell all, that he should not withhold information (arbitrarily, it sometimes seems), that he should not fail to render a scene which the reader knows he can render.

The omniscient narrator is free to speak directly to the reader, to tell him what he will or will not do in a particular story. Or because he speaks in his own voice, he may so ingratiate himself with the reader that he is not reproached for withholding information or for failing to present an expected scene. And he knows that the reader knows that he cannot, after all, tell everything. The omniscient narrator may use his freedom to manipulate the reader intellectually or emotionally; he may intrude to make explicit authorial comments, to analyze, philosophize, to render judgments on his characters. He may tell about his characters in generalized commentary or summary narrative passages, or he may show them in dramatic scenes.

Authorial commentary can provide relief from dramatic pacing, and it can perform many other functions, such as enabling the author to cover a great deal of important but nondramatic territory through panoramic narrative, enlivened sometimes with the author's own distinctive first-person voice. Henry Fielding's "Farewell to the Reader," after 750 pages of *The History of Tom Jones, a Foundling*, gives an impression of the engaging personality of the author, of which the reader is almost always conscious:

> We are now, reader, arrived at the last stage of our long journey. As we have, therefore, travelled together through so many pages, let us behave to one another like fellow-travellers in a stage-coach, who have passed several days in the company of each other; and who, notwithstanding any bickerings or little animosities which may have occurred on the road, generally make all up at last. . . . As I have taken up this simile, give me leave to carry it a little further.

Modern writers, critics, and readers generally object to commentary direct from the author because it shatters the illusion that real people are involved in real events; unity is also shattered when a reader must reorient himself with each shift from dramatic scene to panoramic narration, conveying a sense of events happening now, not told as having happened in the past.

To solve the problems of classic omniscient narration, and to achieve dramatic immediacy, some writers create an objective narrator. The author is invisible; his voice is silent or neutral. As much as is humanly possible, he does not take sides with one character against another; he is impartial, impersonal, disinterested. He refrains from expressing attitudes about every passing controversy or social issue. The reader feels as if there were no narrator, as if he were watching a play or a movie. This camera-eye objectivity can never be total, of course; words have too many uncontrollable connotations. Ernest Hemingway's "The Killers" sets the scene:

> Outside it was getting dark. The street-light came on outside the window. The two men at the counter read the menu. From the other end of the counter Nick Adams watched them. He had been talking to George when they came in.

The possibilities for the omniscient point of view have not yet been fully enough realized. It was uniquely employed by Jules Romains as long ago as 1911 when his novella *The Death of a Nobody* appeared. He wanted to express the collective behavior and consciousness of social groups as they were affected by the death of a man who when he was alive was nobody and did nothing. See his introduction to the American edition, in which he describes his method; its implications for use by other writers are exciting but have so far been unrealized.

Here are some works in which the omniscient point of view functions especially well: Thackeray, *Vanity Fair*; Gogol, *Dead Souls*; Turgenev, *Fathers and Sons*; Trollope, *The Eustace Diamonds*; Balzac, *Eugénie Grandet*; George Eliot, *The Mill on the Floss*; Henry James, *The Bostonians*; E. M. Forster, *Howards End*; Virginia Woolf, *To the Lighthouse* and *Orlando*; D. H. Lawrence, "The Blind Man"; Thomas Wolfe, *Look Homeward, Angel*; John Hawkes, *The Cannibal*; William Gaddis, *The Recognitions*; Michel Tournier, *The Ogre* (Part II, etc.). Wayne C. Booth's *The Rhetoric of Fiction* provides a very readable explanation of the working of the omniscient point of view.

3 | If you have used the *first-person* point of view, have you realized all its potentials?

Traditionally, the author either narrated the story directly to the reader or allowed one of his characters to tell or write it. In a way, the first-person narrator has as much mobility and freedom and as much license to comment on the action as the omniscient narrator. The omniscient narrator's freedom limits him in some ways, but the first-person narrator is even more limited. The first-person narrator cannot get into the minds of other characters as the omniscient, godlike, all-knowing narrator can; first-person narration is limited to those things that the narrating character sees, hears, feels, knows himself or that have been reported to him by other witnesses. But the advantage of first-person narration is that it is dramatically immediate, as all quoted speech is, and thus has great authority. Here is the narrative voice of *Huckleberry Finn*:

> So somebody started on a run. I walked down the street a ways and stopped. In about five or ten minutes here comes Boggs again but not on his horse. He was a-reeling across the street towards me, bareheaded, with a friend on both sides of him a-holt of his arms and hurrying him along. He was quiet and looked uneasy and he warn't

hanging back any but was doing some of the hurrying himself. Somebody sings out:

"Boggs!"

I looked over there to see who said it, and it was that Colonel Sherburn. He was standing perfectly still in the street and had a pistol raised in his right hand—not aiming it but holding it out with the barrel tilted up towards the sky. The same second I see a young girl coming on the run, and two men with her. Boggs and the men turned round to see who called him, and when they see the pistol the men jumped to one side, and the pistol-barrel come down slow and steady to a level—both barrels cocked. Boggs throws up both of his hands and says, "O Lord, don't shoot!" Bang! goes the first shot and he staggers back, clawing at the air—bang! goes the second one and he tumbles backwards onto the ground, heavy and solid, and with his arms spread out. That young girl screamed out and comes rushing, and down she throws herself on her father, crying and saying, "Oh, he's killed him, he's killed him!" The crowd closed up around them and shouldered and jammed one another, with their necks stretched, trying to see, and people on the inside trying to shove them back and shouting, "Back, back! give him air, give him air!"

Colonel Sherburn he tossed his pistol onto the ground, and turned around on his heels and walked off.

Huck's "I was there, I was a witness" tone has an appeal that is characteristic of first-person narratives. By allowing one of his characters to narrate, the author surrenders part of his control over the elements of the story. He must achieve his own purposes, which may be very different from those of his character, through implication, irony, and other devices. For instance, suppose the author hates war, but the character telling the story loves war. How can the author convey his own attitude to the reader? The reader must remember that the first-person narrator is not the author.

The first-person narrator may be a major participant, a minor participant, or a witness to the story he tells; or he may simply retell a story he has heard. In effect, he is saying, "This happened to me," or "This happened mainly to someone else." He may tell the story to a clearly identified listener, or to an implied or to an ambiguous audience. Or he may write his story for a particular reader-character (as in a story told through letters) or for readers generally, as a kind of autobiography or memoir. The form of writing may be a report, a diary, a journal. In many first-person stories, whether the story is spoken or written is unspecified; we simply accept it as a literary convention. But each of these possibilities affects the story and thus the reader in different ways; they are not incidental, arbitrary elements; they are vital.

Here is an example of the *literary* first-person, written style, from William Faulkner's "That Evening Sun":

> Monday is no different from any other weekday in Jefferson now. The streets are paved now, and the telephone and electric companies are cutting down more and more of the shade trees—the water oaks, the maples and locusts and elms—to make room for iron poles bearing clusters of bloated and ghostly and bloodless grapes, and we have a city laundry which makes the rounds on Monday morning, gathering the bundles of clothes into bright-colored, specially made motor cars: the soiled wearing of a whole week now flees apparitionlike behind alert and irritable electric horns, with a long diminishing noise of rubber and asphalt like tearing silk, and even the Negro women who still take in white people's washing after the old custom, fetch and deliver it in automobiles.

The first-person narrator combines the subjective (how he feels about what he sees) with the objective (he wants to *show* the reader). He is both omniscient storyteller and subject of his story. Perception is an act of self-discovery for him. First-person narration is probably the most favored technique used today.

Some Questions to Ask When Revising First-Person Narrations

More possibilities for characterization, technique, and style arise out of the use of first-person narration than are usually discussed. As you revise, your answers to these questions may provide guides as to what to look for, what to change, what to add, what to cut. (Your reader does not necessarily need to be able to answer, or even raise, these questions.) Is the narrator *speaking* or *writing*?

If the narrator is speaking, *to whom* is he or she speaking? Himself/herself? How? Stream of consciousness? Revery? Interior monolog? To one or more listeners? Dramatic monolog (or duolog)? If the narrator is *writing*, *to whom* is he or she writing? Himself/herself? *How?* Diary? Journal? To others? How many others? Letter, confession, general publication?

If it is not clear whether the narrator is speaking or writing, we may rely on *literary convention*, that is, on the understanding between writer and reader that the writer need not, for certain effects, reveal whether the narrator is speaking or writing. It is literary convention to accept that.

When is the narrator speaking or writing? That is, what is the time distance between the events being narrated and the actual narration of those events?

Where is the narrator speaking or writing? That is, what is the spatial distance between the locale of events being narrated and the place in which the narrator is speaking or writing?

Why is the narrator speaking or writing to listeners or readers?

Who is the *surface focus* of the narrator's story? I, he, or she; they or we?

Who is the *submerged focus* (by implication) of the narrator's story? I, he, or she; they or we?

Is the narrator *reliable* or *unreliable*, and to what degree?

What is the *effect*, in general and specifically, line by line, *on style* of the answer to each of these questions in the story you are revising?

What is the *effect*, in general and specifically, line by line, *on the reader* of the revisions you make in answer to these questions?

Here are a variety of first-person voices: Defoe, *Moll Flanders*; Brontë, *Wuthering Heights*; Ford Madox Ford, *The Good Soldier*; Hemingway, *A Farewell to Arms*; James M. Cain, *The Postman Always Rings Twice*; Sherwood Anderson, "The Egg"; Ralph Ellison, *Invisible Man*; Ernest Gaines, "Just Like a Tree"; Jack Kerouac, *On the Road*. The narrator of some first-person novels achieves a kind of omniscience: Fitzgerald, *The Great Gatsby*; Henry Miller, *The Tropic of Cancer*; Ken Kesey, *One Flew over the Cuckoo's Nest*; Robert Penn Warren, *All the King's Men*. See Wayne C. Booth, *The Rhetoric of Fiction*, for an excellent explanation of the unreliable first-person narrator.

4 | *If you have used the third-person, central-intelligence point of view, have you realized all its potentials?*

In the third-person, central-intelligence point of view, the author filters the story through the perceptions of a character. The character is the center of consciousness. In both the first-person point-of-view technique and the third-person, central-intelligence point-of-view technique, the author removes himself from the story and works from inside the character outward. In central-intelligence narration, the story is presented in the third person, but all the elements of the story are filtered through the perceptions of a single character (the central intelligence), revealing his personality. The writer presents only what that character sees, hears, feels, thinks, knows. To use Henry James's phrase, the character "reflects" events; he is not a straight teller of events as the first-person narrator is. It is as if the author were paraphrasing in the third person what the character would say *if* he were telling the story in the first person. Usually, the author adjusts his style and vocabulary to the age, mentality, and social situation of the point-of-view character. Katherine Mansfield's "Miss Brill" is a near-perfect example:

Although it was so brilliantly fine—the blue sky powdered with gold and great spots of light like white wine splashed over the Jardins Publiques—Miss Brill was glad that she had decided on her fur. The air was motionless, but when you opened your mouth there was just a faint chill, like a chill from a glass of iced water before you sip, and now and again a leaf came drifting—from nowhere, from the sky. Miss Brill put up her hand and touched her fur. Dear little thing! It was nice to feel it again. She had taken it out of its box that afternoon, shaken out the moth-powder, given it a good brush, and rubbed the life back into the dim little eyes. "What has been happening to me?" said the sad little eyes. Oh, how sweet it was to see them snap at her again from the red eiderdown! . . . But the nose, which was of some black composition, wasn't at all firm. It must have had a knock, somehow. Never mind—a little dab of black sealing-wax when the time came—when it was absolutely necessary. . . . Little rogue! yes, she really felt like that about it. She felt a tingling in her hands and arms, but that came from walking, she supposed. And when she breathed, something light and sad—no, not sad, exactly—something gentle seemed to move in her bosom.

"In 'Miss Brill,' " Katherine Mansfield said, "I chose not only the length of every sentence, but even the sound of every sentence. I chose the rise and fall of every paragraph to fit her, and to fit her on that day, at that very moment."

Many writers favor the third-person, central-intelligence point of view. Its great advantage is that the reader consistently experiences everything through the character's own mind and emotions with the greatest intimacy and intensity. The limitation of this method is that it is a little weak dramatically, because we cannot see the character himself in action; he often remains physically passive, almost invisible.

The focus may be primarily upon the experiences of the point-of-view character or upon his responses to the experiences of a character more dramatic than himself. In important ways, the focus determines the reader's responses to the elements being developed in the story.

Just as readers sometimes mistakenly attribute to the author the attitudes of his first-person narrator, readers often forget that in third-person, central-intelligence narration, every perception is to be attributed to the point-of-view character. As in first-person narration, the immediate authority for everything in the story is the character (although the author is, of course, the ultimate authority).

Because nothing goes into the story that the point-of-view character has not experienced, the author is more likely to include only what is truly relevant. Because his character's perceptions may be limited, the writer must be very adroit in the use of such devices as implication, irony, and symbolism as ways of communicating to the reader more than the character himself can perceive.

You can do many things in the omniscient point of view that you cannot do through the third-person, central-intelligence point of view. The omniscient point of view was most appropriate and effective in times when the author might pretend to know all, to be the creator of the world he described, as Dickens could. Today's writers, feeling that to pretend to know all is an impertinence in a world so complex, specialize in select areas of human experience, and more often use the mind of a single character through which to reveal those selected areas to the reader.

The third-person, central-intelligence point of view is effectively illustrated in these novels: Henry James, *The Ambassadors*; Joyce, *A Portrait of the Artist as a Young Man*; Truman Capote, *Other Voices, Other Rooms*; Frederick Buechner, *A Long Day's Dying*; John Cheever, *Falconer* (with a few shifts for contrast); Wright Morris, *The Field of Vision* (alternate focus on five characters) and the sequel *Ceremony in Lone Tree*.

In the prefaces to his novels, collected in *The Art of Fiction*, Henry James discusses his own experiments in the third-person, central-intelligence point of view; his practice is described by Percy Lubbock in *The Craft of Fiction*. In *The House of Fiction* (the title is James's phrase), Caroline Gordon and Allen Tate describe all three point-of-view techniques.

See "The Day the Flowers Came," pp. 283–84.

5 | Have you used the device of *interior monolog* ineffectively?

Interior monolog is the silent speaking of a character, usually to himself as he is *doing* something; sometimes, still in his mind, he speaks to other characters.

The stream-of-consciousness and interior-monolog techniques provide the deepest, most intimate view of a character's feelings and thoughts. Stories employing these techniques exclusively are rare.

Interior monolog differs from revery or stream of consciousness in that the latter usually occurs while the character is in repose, most often in bed about to go to sleep, as in the classic instance, Molly Bloom's revery in the last twenty-five or so pages of Joyce's *Ulysses*. That novel offers illustrations of both interior monolog and stream of consciousness that will show the difference. Here is interior monolog, Mr. Bloom:

> Mr. Bloom entered and sat in the vacant place. He pulled the door to after him and slammed it tight till it shut tight. He passed an arm through the armstrap and looked seriously from the open carriage window at the lowered blinds of the avenue. One dragged aside: an old woman peeping. Nose whiteflattened against the pane. Thanking her stars she was passed over. Extraordinary the interest they take in a corpse. Glad to see us go we give them such trouble coming. Job seems to suit them. Huggermugger in corners. Slop about in slipperslappers for fear he'd wake. Then getting it ready. Laying it out. Molly and Mrs. Fleming making the bed. Pull it more to your side. Our windingsheet. Never know who will touch you dead. Wash and shampoo. I believe they clip the nails and the hair. Keep a bit in an envelope. Grow all the same after. Unclean job.

Narrative mingled with perception and conscious thought at various points, sometimes with ironic intent, is the process demonstrated above.

But in stream of consciousness or night revery the process is a mingling of conscious (silently talking to oneself) and unconscious thoughts, images, and feelings, without direct narrative or immediate perceptions. Here is stream of consciousness, Molly Bloom:

> and the wineshops half open at night and the castanets and the night we missed the boat at Algeciras the watchman going about serene with his lamp and O that awful deepdown torrent O and the sea the sea crimson sometimes like fire and the glorious sunsets and the figtrees in the Alameda gardens yes and all the queer little streets and pink and blue and yellow houses and the rosegardens and the jessamine and geraniums and cactuses and Gibraltar as a girl where I was a Flower of the mountain yes when I put the rose in my hair like the Andalusian girls used or shall I wear a red yes and how he kissed me under the Moorish wall and I thought well as well him as another and then I asked him with my eyes to ask again yes and then he asked me would I yes to say yes my mountain flower and first I put my arms around him yes and drew him down to me so he could feel my breasts all perfume yes and his heart was going like mad and yes i said yes I will Yes.

Joyce and Faulkner handled interior monolog and stream of consciousness so well—these devices stand out in literary history as experiments in form so successful—that few writers since William Styron have attempted to "do it again" (see Peyton Loftis's stream of consciousness in *Lie Down in Darkness* chapter 7). Evelyn Scott uses interior monolog on a massive scale in her long experimental Civil War novel *The Wave*. The two devices work best for carefully prepared short stretches in stories or novels. To use them as more distinct and separate entities calls attention to them and invites the question "Why"?

See Robert Humphrey, *Stream of Consciousness in the Modern Novel*.

6 | Have you used the device of *dramatic monolog* ineffectively?

Dramatic monolog is the long speech of a character in a dramatic situation: one or more listeners is tacitly assumed, implied, ambiguous, or clearly identified.

In "Haircut," Ring Lardner establishes the dramatic context:

I got another barber that comes over from Carterville and helps me out Saturdays, but the rest of the time I can get along all right alone. You can see for yourself that this ain't no New York City and besides that, the most of the boys works all day and don't have no leisure to drop in here and get themselves prettied up.

You're a newcomer, ain't you?

The specified setting (barber shop), the general setting (a small town), the relationship (barber and newcomer-customer), and something of the barber's educational background ("ain't no," "don't have no") are communicated directly or by implication to the reader right away, so that the writer can begin to demand of the reader that he catch the ironic implications upon which the story's effect depends. This device enables the reader to have the pleasure of filling in with his own imagination what the writer, given the unreliability of the narrator, must leave out; the reader is simultaneously the objective reader and the listener. In this story, we gather impressions of the barber as the newcomer in the chair gathers them. The dramatic monolog is usually a device for conveying dramatic irony; the barber assumes his listener looks at the situation as he does.

In Albert Camus's *The Fall*, the narrator is a very intelligent man trying to convince himself and his listener that his conduct and his ideas are right: "May I, *monsieur*, offer my services without running the risk of intruding?" he begins. Their relationship develops: "Really, *mon cher compatriote*, I am grateful to you for your curiosity." The implied listener even seeks out the narrator for more of his confession: "I'm embarrassed to be in bed when you arrive." We follow an implied listener and thus an *implied narrative*; one sign of the development of this implied narrative comes when the narrator says, concerning the effect of his own confession upon his listener, "I provoke you into judging yourself. . . . I shall listen, you may be sure, to your own confession with a great feeling of fraternity."

The possibilities of this device, or this form or genre, are rich. But here again, like interior monologs and stream of consciousness, this device calls attention to itself, because it marked a major development in the history of literature and it was so brilliantly handled by a few writers, and comparisons in handling and in quality are inevitable. But if you aren't willing to take risks, why write? asks every writer who attempts these devices anyway.

7 | What are the negative effects in *style* of the point-of-view technique you employed in your first draft?

This question assumes you have decided to change in revision the point of view you used in the first draft. Such a change will have positive and negative effects on character conflict, structure, theme. The focus in this entry is on style.

Point of view determines style. With a change in point of view comes major changes in style, as you can see in two versions of a scene in Barry Hannah's first novel, *Geronimo Rex*. The first version appeared in *Intro* as "The Crowd Punk Season Drew":

> Now, as a punk, he chose not to steal; he thought that would be begging. Sometimes, if he was waiting around the campus for any time at all, he would sneak up and efface the fender of one of the better cars parked in front of the administration building, Provine Hall. This he would do by crushing the heel of his boot against the car while no one was around. Buicks, Pontiacs, and Fords with eccentric horsepower and conveniences—he scarred them all. He sat on a fender until the campus depopulated, then ruined it with a flurry of his legs.

In this version, the omniscient point of view produces a rather formal, stilted style, despite the author's own slangy direct comments about his protagonist. Hannah *may* have decided the voice and its tone were not working in the omniscient, that it put the protagonist at too great a distance from both the author and the reader. He would retain some of that tone and style when he changed to the protagonist's first-person narration, but it is enhanced in the revision by dramatic immediacy, and a kind of frenzy, and a certain obnoxious aggressiveness that catches and holds the reader's attention. A possible factor in the success of the first-person voice in *Geronimo Rex* is that the narrator already thinks of himself as Geronimo, whereas in the short-story version, someone calls him Geronimo *after* the passage quoted above. Here is the scene in the novel:

> I was standing beside a skyblue Cadillac. You pretentious whale, you Cadillac, I thought.
> I jumped up on the hood of it. I did a shuffle on the hood. I felt my

boots sinking into the metal. "Ah!" I pounced up and down, weighted by the books. It amazed me that I was taking such effect on the body. I leaped on the roof and hurled myself up and pierced it with my heels coming down . . . again, again. I flung outward after the last blow and landed on the sidewalk, congratulating myself like an artist of the trampoline.

A comparison of the two versions of Henry James's first novel, *Watch and Ward*, would show the effect on his style of changing from omniscient to central intelligence.

In *Advertisements for Myself*, Norman Mailer talks about the effect on style of his first-person narrator in *The Deer Park*.

8 | Have you failed to imagine *other point-of-view techniques* and their possible effects on the reader?

Because the characters, the style, and all other elements are so vitally affected by the point of view you have used, test it by reimagining the story from all possible points of view.

To test the first-draft point of view on paper, identify the scene in your story that is giving you the most trouble. Try rewriting that scene from two other points of view. If the first draft is third-person, avoid simply transposing "she" to "I." Imagine the possibilities posed by each point of view; explore the possibility of using multiple point-of-view techniques. You may see clearly that technique is a mode of discovery; you may find the true emotive and thematic center of your story.

Taking all elements into consideration, what is lost and what is gained by changing the point of view? What happens to the story's elements and effects as you tell it from each of the other two points of view? How are conflict, characterization, and theme handled differently in the three different point-of-view techniques? What are some differences in techniques? In emotional effect?

Although the point of view of Faulkner's *Sanctuary* in the two major published versions is omniscient, he moves in and out of the third-person central intelligences of several characters. When he decided in the galley stage to revise the novel radically, it was a point-of-view restructuring that he performed, as we see in two versions of this well-known scene, in which Horace Benbow first sees Popeye, the impotent two-bit gangster.

When he rose, the surface of the water broken into a myriad glints by the dripping aftermath of his drinking, he saw among them the shattered reflections of the straw hat.

The man was standing beyond the spring, his hands in his coat pockets, a cigarette slanted from his pallid chin.

That scene appears on p. 21 of the recently published original text, but it appears on p. 1 of the novel as readers knew it for half a century. Now the point of view is reversed: it is Popeye who sees Benbow.

From beyond the screen of bushes which surrounded the spring, Popeye watched the man drinking. A faint path led from the road to the spring. Popeye watched the man—a tall, thin man, hatless, in worn gray flannel trousers and carrying a tweed coat over his arm— emerge from the path and kneel to drink from the spring.

Having opened with this scene, from Popeye's point of view, Faulkner restructured the novel, and created new relationships among the characters through whose perceptions he presented events: Gowan Stevens, Popeye, Temple Drake, and Horace Benbow (whose point of view had dominated the novel's galley version). If you read the first version and then the second, you will have two very different experiences—traceable to the differences in Faulkner's handling of point of view.

In revising *The Mysterious Stranger*, Mark Twain tested the possibilities of various point-of-view strategies; for him, explorations in point-of-view techniques were discovery ventures. In *Mark Twain, the "Mysterious Stranger" Manuscripts*, William Gibson publishes all versions except the one readers know and which is readily available.

Frank O'Connor's "First Confession" is one of his most admired stories because the first-person voice is the source of rare humor. O'Connor has said that in early drafts, the point of view was a heavily serious third person, and the story failed. Philip Roth had a problem in *Letting Go* similar to Frank O'Connor's. The third-person style was much too heavy and stilted, so he shifted to first person and achieved most of what he had failed to do with the third person (see Kuehl, *Creative Writing and Rewriting*, pp. 169–230). Although his characters often tell long stories within his novels and novellas, Thomas Wolfe turned his fiction over to first-person narrators only in a few instances, the most notable of which is the novella "Web of Earth." His imagination seemed closed to point-of-view possibilities, but among his manuscripts is a piece called "K 19" which is related to *Of Time and the River*; something about the third-person version didn't work for him, so he rewrote it in the first person.

You may want to look at the examples of point-of-view revision in a fuller context; for more complete details, see "Selected List of Revision Examples."

Stephen Hero is an early omniscient version of James Joyce's *A Portrait of the Artist as a Young Man*, a fine example of the third-person, central-intelligence point of view.

9 | Have you *ineffectively mingled* several points of view at once?

The assumption is that you deliberately mingled several points of view in your first draft, and so the question is, did that strategy work?

For the young F. Scott Fitzgerald it did not. In early drafts of his first novel, *This Side of Paradise*, he often mingled first-person, third-person, and omniscient points of view, probably unintentionally, because the manuscripts suggest that he did not really understand how the technique of point of view works. Nor did he understand the effect of point of view upon all other elements in a work of fiction: style, character, theme, etc. His problems are described by James L. W. West in *The Making of "This Side of Paradise,"* pp. 33–34, 38, 48–49.

For contrast, Graham Greene in *The Heart of the Matter* shifts a few times from the third-person central intelligence of Scobie, but in revision, he omitted an entire chapter because he thought it violated the focus on Scobie too radically; recently, in a new edition, he restored that chapter, having decided, after many years, that omitting it threw much of the novel out of kilter.

With particular effects in mind, writers do successfully mingle or juxtapose two or more point-of-view techniques. Here are some of the possibilities:

In *As I Lay Dying*, Faulkner has fifteen first-person narrators, shifting back and forth among them fifty-one times in only 250 pages, favoring Darl with seventeen and Vardaman with ten sections, allowing seven characters only one turn. Then William March came along in *Company K* with an entire company roster, from captain on down through the ranks, of 116 first-person narrators in only 182 pages.

Wright Morris experimented with mixed point-of-view techniques almost as often as Faulkner. Warren Howe narrates Part I, "Time Present," of *Cause for Wonder*, for about ninety pages; in "Time Past," the rest of the novel, two hundred pages, the point of view is third-person, central-intelligence, through Warren's perceptions.

Morris's *The Huge Season* opens with Chapter 1 of Peter Foley's long-in-progress (never-finished) autobiographical novel, *The Captivity*, told in his own first person; it is juxtaposed to "Foley," told in the third person through Foley's central intelligence. The book is composed of alternating "Captivity" and "Foley" chapters, a patterned juxtaposition of events of the twenties with events of the fifties. To demonstrate with a simple example what I mean by the effect of juxtaposition of points of view, here is the end of the last "Captivity" chapter, Foley's first-person voice, juxtaposed to the opening of the last "Foley" chapter, Foley's third-person, central-intelligence point of view.

> For five or ten seconds I thought nobody was there. Then I heard her inhale, gasp neatly, as if she had been holding her breath, and she said, "He's dead. He's dead, Peter." Then she hung up.

> FOLEY: 12

> In the men's room at Penn Station, Foley took the pistol from the Gimbel's carton, found a piece of paper clipped to the barrel with a rubber band. On it Lou Baker had scrawled:
> *See you at the next hearing.*
> *Foley's Chick*

The climax of the twenties experience, Lou Baker's telling Foley that their hero, Lawrence, has shot himself, is juxtaposed to the reunion when Lou Baker gives Foley the Colt revolver their friend Proctor accidentally fired at their reunion. The "hearing" refers to Senator McCarthy's House Un-American Activities Committee hearings. Foley's first-person narrative is juxtaposed to Foley's third-person, central-intelligence point of view, as a way of juxtaposing the past to the present, with the effect of dramatically illuminating both for the reader.

In *Man and Boy*, Morris alternates chapters from Ormsby's third-person, central-intelligence point of view with the point of view of Mother (as he calls his wife), often giving their very different views of the same scene.

In *Ceremony in Lone Tree* (companion novel to *The Field of Vision*), Wright Morris opens briefly with an omniscient view of the "scene," then alternates among ten characters' third-person, central-intelligence perceptions with an omniscient interlude midway.

Morris's point-of-view strategy is somewhat like Virginia Woolf's in *To the Lighthouse*. In Part I, called "The Window," we experience the perceptions of a variety of characters as they mingle at a summer house; an interlude, "Time Passes," is an extraordinary use of the omniscient point of view; in the third part, "The Lighthouse," Woolf returns to her strategy of Part I.

It was to realize the effects of a different juxtaposition of character points of view that Fitzgerald restructured *Tender Is the Night* some years after he published it. See Cowley in Bibliography.

Faulkner's *The Sound and the Fury* opens with the idiot Benjy Compson's first-person stream of consciousness, followed by Quentin's extremely intellectual, though sometimes regressively infantile, first-person thoughts and memories (even though he is already dead by suicide), followed by Jason's very immediate, slangy first-person monolog; the final part of the novel is presented through Faulkner's own omniscient point of view, favoring Dilsey, the black housekeeper for the Compsons. The first-person narratives of the three brothers and much of the omniscient narrative are dominated by their awareness of the sister, Caddy.

From his pervasive but restrained omniscient point of view, Faulkner shuttles back and forth among the fragments of five first-person narratives—with Colonel Sutpen's sustained first-person story as the centerpiece—in *Absalom, Absalom!* In several Faulkner novels and stories, Faulkner's Quentin Compson, a kind of alter ego, has a psychotic compulsion to tell stories.

Such a character for Joseph Conrad, whom Faulkner admired, was Marlow, a witness to the tellable experiences of other men; he tells all or parts of "Youth," "The Heart of Darkness," *Lord Jim*, and *Chance* (I like to think he is also the anonymous narrator of "The Secret Sharer"). A self-effacing "I" introduces Marlow in "Youth," then quotes him telling a long tale. Marlow gets the story of Lord Jim partly at an inquiry, partly from Jim, and partly from hearsay, a complex and instructive handling of point of view.

In the mingled use of point-of-view techniques, each of these writers strives for not one but many, often complex, effects. The device of juxtaposition (see Question 148), handled in various ways, enables them to achieve those effects.

10 | Have you not yet achieved the proper *distance* between yourself and your material?

The question of the author's distance arises on several levels, making the problem very complex. The problem begins with the source of ideas for fictions, discussed in the introduction (pp. 5–6). The spectrum of possibilities extends from the deeply subconscious origin of ideas to the extremely objective (an idea found in reading a textbook, for instance). The degree of distance on that level of origin usually bears little relation to the degree or kind of distance the reader senses that the author has in relation to the finished work.

As you interrogate your first draft, however, ask whether you have achieved the kind of distance that is needed to make the story effective. For instance, if the idea arose suddenly out of your subconscious, it just may be that to make it work you need great objectivity, and the reader needs to feel that objectivity in the work. On the other hand, and rather paradoxically, an idea gleaned from a casual reading of some technical work may justify the most lyrical subjectivity in your treatment of the idea.

Ask yourself, What is the depth or level of my involvement in this story? Does my emotional involvement show in every paragraph, and if so, is that good for *this* story's intended effect, or detrimental? Or am I an impartial, impersonal, detached, objective, invisible, disinterested narrator (I've listed most of the terms used in discussing this problem)? If so, is that objectivity working for or against all my intentions? A third general possibility is that you want a rhythmic alternation between modulations of subjectivity and objectivity. All the devices and techniques of fiction come into play, especially point of view and style, to enable you to achieve the degree and kind of distance you want for each story.

Distance in relation to what? To the characters, first of all, to the narrative generally, and to the reader. Do you want your reader to feel that you are intimate with your character? If so, it does not follow that the reader will share your intimacy; experiencing *your* intimacy, the reader may feel distant from the character. Paradoxically, it is often the effect that when the author is most distant (in his style, not in his personal feelings) from the main character (Flaubert from Madame Bovary), the reader is most intimate. "As to making known my own opinion about the characters I produce," said Flaubert, "no, no, a thousand times no!"

Do you comment thematically by intruding as the author to editorialize upon the narrative? Do you show partiality for one character over another, or are you neutral? Does your attitude come across in the *tone* conveyed by your style? There is no best answer to these questions except in terms of all your conscious intentions in each work. Revision poses the question of whether you should expand or lessen the distance between you and the character and/or you and the reader.

Again, the very techniques you have at your command enable you to discover an answer. For instance, if the point of view is third-person, central-intelligence, it follows logically that any word, phrase, or sentence that reveals your own attitudes, especially negative ones about the point-of-view character, should be cut, because the purpose of that point of view is to limit yourself entirely to the perceptions of that character. The style, then, must be appropriate to that character; where the style violates the character point of view, it may be cut, as being, for instance, too formal.

Here, as with most technical matters, it is impossible to deal with one technical question without considering it in relation to others. That is fortunate, because just as a problem in one area creates or worsens problems in others, each solution has beneficial ramifications.

In the serial version of *The Return of the Native*, Hardy failed to restrain himself, as omniscient narrator, from commenting positively or negatively on the situations, behavior, and attitudes of his characters. But for the book version, he made cuts and changes that set him at the appropriate distance from his characters—appropriateness being determined by his own intention to show that his characters live out their fate in an indifferent universe, an intention undermined by any show of personal feeling by the author. Eustacia sees Clym leave the Christmas party with Thomasin: "*How* the heat flew to Eustacia's head and cheeks *then*!" Hardy drew back: "The heat flew to Eustacia's head and cheeks."

Eustacia quarrels with Clym: "Her poor little hands quivered so violently as she held them to her chin to fasten her bonnet that she could not tie the strings." Hardy did not remove "poor" until a later edition of the book version. When he caught himself intruding with a long observation, Hardy cut it or attributed it, in shorter form, to another character or to people in general.

The cuts Willa Cather made in her famous story "Paul's Case" fifteen years after it appeared in *The Troll Garden* suggest that she felt that her style put her at too great a distance from Paul. See "Selected List."

As you read fiction, notice the degree to which the writer is involved, as an omniscient "I" or as a felt presence. Trollope, Thackeray, Fielding,

Eliot, and Forster offer varieties of omniscient involvement; Kerouac, Henry Miller, and Thomas Wolfe varieties of subjectivity; Joyce, Hemingway, and Flaubert varieties of objectivity.

11 | Do passages that reflect your own biases or judgments *intrude*?

This question is one aspect of the question of author distance, but it is such a common problem that it needs special attention. Consideration of point of view helps you to answer the question. If it is omniscient, you are free to intrude as often as you like to express your own biases toward characters ("We will tell the story of Lizzie Greystock from the beginning, but we will not dwell over it at great length, as we might do if we loved her") or to set humankind straight on philosophical matters ("There is no end to man's inhumanity to man!"). Such comments work in first person, but only if they are in character; if they are not, you have made your narrator a mouthpiece for your own ideas. Such passages are impossible in third-person, central-intelligence; if they are there in your first draft, you will want to cut them as violations of the point-of-view technique you have decided to use.

Revising *Watch and Ward*, Henry James realized that he had violated the central-intelligence point of view of Nora by intruding with his own judgments. Early version: "There he tossed, himself a living instance, if need were, of the furious irresponsibility of passion; loving in the teeth of reason, of hope, of justice almost, in blind obedience to a reckless personal need. Why, if *his* passion scorned counsel, was Nora's bound to take it?" James's revision places the reader back in Nora's point of view: "There was no discretion in his own love; why should there be in Nora's?"

Is your style appropriate to the point of view? Your answers to that question enable you to answer Question 11. Sometimes, your own biases and judgments come through in rhetorical maneuvers. ". . . but, dear me," wrote George Eliot in *Middlemarch*, "has it not by this time ceased to be remarkable—is it not rather the very thing we expect in men that they should have numerous strands of experience lying side by side and never compare them with each other?" The dubious occasion for this intrusion is Eliot's description of Lydgate's way of life. Once started, Eliot can't seem to stop; she continues for almost half a page, but keeps only what I have quoted, except for the phrase "the very thing."

If the point of view is omniscient, do you fail to distinguish clearly your perspective from that of your characters? Who, at any given moment, is the authority? This appears to be, but is not, a restatement of the question posed above. The writer does not allow his reader to become confused as to whose evaluation of events he is getting. For instance, in the omniscient point of view, he avoids jumping from one character's mind to another's without careful transition or without reorienting the reader. An example of clear and firm control is Evelyn Scott's *The Narrow House.*

When Dickens, Eliot, Thackeray, Stendhal, and Trollope, using the overall omniscient point of view, weave in and out of the minds of several characters within a novel, within a scene, sometimes within a single sentence, it is sometimes difficult for the reader to distinguish the author's perspective from that of a character. Rosamond's words "fell like a mortal chill on Lydgate's roused tenderness," wrote George Eliot in one version of *Middlemarch.* "It was a fatal sign that h—" Eliot stopped in midword, realizing she was being unclear as to whom it was "a fatal sign." It would not seem so to Lydgate himself; we are in his perception here, so Eliot cut that line. "He did not storm in indignation," she continued. The revisions of these and other omniscient authors show many instances where adjustments are made to make clear to the reader who the authority is. Authority confusion is not quite the same problem as author intrusion.

The careful reader will not accept the authority of the narrator too literally or too fully. Your knowing that will affect the way you revise. When you use the omniscient point of view, you are usually a reliable authority for what the reader is told. But human perception is limited and faulty; therefore, what the first-person narrator tells or writes or what the central-intelligence character experiences will be carefully evaluated by the reader. In such stories, the essence of your reader's experience lies in the differences between the way the reader perceives the story's elements and the way the point-of-view character perceives them. The reader has, in a sense, a certain omniscience.

In *The Rhetoric of Fiction* Wayne C. Booth discusses degrees of reliability among the various types of narrators.

12 | Are there *inconsistencies* in your use of point of view?

Strive to employ the point of view consistently and to make all elements consistent with the point of view as your major means of controlling the elements of your story.

It is unlikely that you will employ the first person inconsistently; if by chance you drift, in the first draft, from first person into third, you will see that immediately as a mistake. But maintaining consistency in the third-person, central-intelligence and in the omniscient point of view is a common problem throughout the revision process.

The reader does not want to have the experience of feeling that the point of view is arbitrarily handled, that the omniscient author simply happened to shift to a focus on this character, then that one, without fulfilling some expressive and meaningful pattern. Sometimes what may seem a violation of the author's own pattern may be deliberate, to achieve an effect that can be achieved no other way. For instance, James Joyce's "The Dead" is an excellent example of third-person, central-intelligence point of view (Gabriel Conroy's), but Joyce deliberately opens with an omniscient view of many people gathering, gradually focusing on Gabriel; at the end, he returns to omniscience for an even larger view than in the opening.

D. H. Lawrence provides another example of expressive inconsistency. The point of view in "Odour of Chrysanthemums" is omniscient, with a dominant focus on Elizabeth, wife of an alcoholic miner who is killed. In the scene in which his comrades bring his body home, the focus is very scattered, especially with the shift into the point of view of the men ("they"). But Lawrence's revisions do not drop the men to keep the focus on Elizabeth; rather they shift the focus *to* the men. He makes the inconsistency meaningful. The deliberateness of this odd solution to inconsistency in point of view is seen in Lawrence's further revisions for the version included in the collection *The Prussian Officer*. Lawrence's emphasis on the pronoun "they" has a mysterious quality, as if it includes not only the dead miner's comrades but his family as well, and so the community of the living as it responds to the dead. See Cushman in Bibliography.

The problem of inconsistency in point of view has a second dimension: What elements are inconsistent with the point of view? Is the style inconsistent? Suppose, for instance, your central intelligence is a young woman with a limited education who works in a towel factory in a small southern town. As you present everything through her perceptions, is your style too complex? If the point of view is first-person, do you allow your narrator to use a vocabulary she is not likely to have? Sometimes the way exposition or information is presented is inconsistent with the point of view. Do you attribute information, ideas, or emotions to a character that, given the point of view, she cannot know, think, or feel?

13 | Does the point of view you have used fail to express, in itself, some major aspect of the experience you are rendering?

The point of view you employ should express something in itself—it should not seem to the reader to have been arbitrarily chosen, or chosen as the easiest one for you to use. Your choice should be, in every way, so effective that the reader feels it is the only possible choice, the inevitable choice.

This question may help to put into clearer perspective other questions about point of view and to stress the overall importance of point of view.

In several major novels, for instance, the relationship between a kind of hero and characters who witness his behavior produces the point-of-view structure for the works. Fitzgerald's *The Great Gatsby* offers an example that is simple in structure but complex in its various ramifications: Nick Carroway tells the story of Gatsby; what makes Gatsby a hero is his effect on Nick's storytelling consciousness.

There is a similar hero-witness relationship in Robert Penn Warren's *All the King's Men*; Jack Burden, a reporter, feels a compulsion to tell the story of Governor Willie Stark, but it is Stark's effect on other people and on Jack that most commands our interest. Jack's first-person voice is that of a tough guy like Raymond Chandler's private eye Philip Marlowe. But Jack is also a historian obsessed with the past; when he is telling the reader about events in the historical past, his voice becomes very lyrical and philosophical. The tone of these two voices and their juxtaposition to each other throughout the book become the reader's major experience, not the narrative in itself about Willie Stark's rise and fall, interesting though it is.

Wright Morris combines first-person narrative with third-person central intelligence in *The Huge Season*. Chapters from Peter Foley's first-person autobiographical novel, about the relationship between a hero and his witnesses in the twenties, alternate with chapters presenting Peter Foley's thoughts and perceptions one day in the fifties as he goes to a reunion with surviving witnesses. The juxtaposition and contrast of the two point-of-view techniques express facets of this hero-witness relationship. I know of no instance in which a writer makes exclusive use of the third-person, central-intelligence point of view throughout a hero-witness novel; that point of view would not lend itself as readily, as effectively, to the expression of this hero-witness relationship as do the first-person and the omniscient. See the earlier example from *The Huge Season* in Question 9.

In *The Heart Is a Lonely Hunter*, Carson McCullers employs an overall omniscient point of view, but she alternates chapters that focus on the thoughts and feelings of the mute hero, Mr. Singer, with chapters that focus on his four witnesses. McCullers expresses in this omniscient-point-of-view strategy the paradox that these four very different people, each isolated in his own psyche, crave communication with others at the same time that they do not want a reciprocal relationship—that's why they are hostile to each other and why each tells his deepest feelings to a mute. The bitter irony, best expressed in this omniscient point of view, is that none of the four characters know what the author, the hero, and the reader know—that Mr. Singer doesn't understand a word any of them are saying. Thomas Hardy revised *The Return of the Native* to express, through his unique use of omniscience, a similar vision: each person, no matter how passionate his love for another person may be, is always and finally alone in an indifferent universe.

Both Virginia Woolf in *Mrs. Dalloway* and William Faulkner in *Absalom, Absalom!* express facets of a hero-witness relationship through the omniscient point of view, but they do it very differently.

Woolf uses the omniscient point of view to enable her to move rapidly in and out of several consciousnesses many times throughout the novel. Most of the witness characters either talk with or think about Mrs. Dalloway, the heroine, or they parallel in some way the reader's concern with her. The omniscient point of view expresses in itself the simultaneous separateness of the characters at a given moment and the way that fact relates them all to each other; though none know it, the reader does.

All these writers express through their various point-of-view strategies and through the thematic pattern of the hero-witness relationship the irony of an unconsciously shared community of vision. That concept is especially powerful in Faulkner's *Absalom, Absalom!* A great many of Faulkner's revisions were made in an effort to orchestrate, within an overall omniscient point of view, the first-person narratives of five characters, and most important, to make Quentin Compson's the most expressive. To express his concept that the telling of the story of Colonel Sutpen by various interacting voices creates a community of vision, Faulkner made all his narrators sound alike; he even assigned to them, in quotation marks but without stylistic changes, passages he had originally written in his own omniscient voice. In this case, all the witnesses share with each other their fixation on the hero. The effect is best observed at a point when most of the voices converge in a single passage. See Langford in Bibliography.

II STYLE

14 | Has your style evolved out of the *point of view* for this story?

Style is an author's choice of words (diction), arrangement of words in each sentence (syntax), and handling of sentences and paragraph units to achieve a specific effect.

Together, style and point of view are two of the most vital and dynamically related techniques. Variations on the writer's basic style are somewhat determined by the point of view the author decides to employ. Style evolves out of point of view, as discussed in Question 7.

In his introduction to the 1934 Modern Library edition of *The Great Gatsby*, Fitzgerald says he had "just re-read Conrad's preface to *The Nigger of the Narcissus*" when he approached the revision process. Conrad had said, "A work that aspires, however humbly, to the condition of art should carry its justification in every line." Art must aspire "to the magic suggestiveness of music. . . . it is only through an unremitting never discouraged care for the shape and ring of sentences . . . that the light of magic suggestiveness may be brought to play. . . ."

One aspect of style is the use of rhetorical devices (proven ways of stimulating the desired emotion, attitude, or idea in the reader)—imagery, symbolism, irony, understatement, and figurative language (the use of metaphors and similes, for instance). The writer, to achieve his effects, is very dependent upon such devices. His style, whether it is simple or complex, denotative or connotative, evolves through his use of them. Mark Schorer, novelist and critic, in "Fiction and the Analogical Matrix" (*The World We Imagine*) says, "Metaphorical language gives any style its special quality . . . expresses, defines, and evaluates theme . . . can be . . . the basis of structure," as "overthought" or "underthought."

"It reveals to us the character of any imaginative work." "Style *is* conception. . . . It is really style, and style primarily, that first conceives, then expresses, and finally tests" subject matter and theme.

In his 1957 introduction to the first legal American publication of Lawrence's *Lady Chatterley's Lover*, Mark Schorer notes that there is a "contrast in language between the two kinds of scene" that is "absolutely primary to the whole aesthetic purpose of the work." In Wragby Hall, "language is overintellectualized, abstract, polite, and cynical; in the wood, it is intuitive, concrete, coarse, and earthy." He suggests that "one might view the alterations in Lawrence's language" from *The First Lady Chatterley* to *John Thomas and Lady Jane* to *Lady Chatterley's Lover*, the three published versions, "as integral to his symbolic intentions."

Through the artfully arranged functions of style to achieve carefully prepared effects, you control the responses of your reader. "The writer learns to write," says Wright Morris in *About Fiction*, "the reader learns to read." "It seems the writer's intent is to involve the reader not merely in the reading, but in the writing. . . ." "What we choose to call 'style' is the presence in the fiction of the power to choose and mold its reader."

Many scholars of writers' revisions speak of changes in style as being of minor importance, even when dealing with a writer famous for style. The fixation is on meaning, not on the techniques writers use as they struggle through the revision process. As Wallace Hildick says in *Word for Word*, "James has been criticized for the triviality of many of the changes he made, for what some have considered to be mere stylistic tinkering. . . ." Henry James was appalled by Thomas Hardy's "verbose and redundant style." Edmund Gosse praised *Jude the Obscure* but said that "the genius of False Rhetoric" had placed a curse on Hardy. Hardy himself said, "The whole secret of a living style and the difference between it and a dead style, lies in not having too much style—being in fact a little careless, or rather seeming to be, here and there."

Samuel Butler, admired for the style of *The Way of All Flesh*, declared, "I should like it put on record that I never took the smallest pains with my style, have never thought about it, and do not know or want to know whether it is a style at all or whether it is not, as I believe and hope, just common, simple straight-forwardness." "—it should attract as little attention as possible." "Never consciously agonize." Butler's revisions contradict his declared preference for the unpolished style.

As the novel form matures, approaches art, its medium—language—becomes more self-conscious, controlled, *made*. James Joyce worked on one sentence in *Finnegans Wake* for fourteen years. See Hayman in

Bibliography. By contrast to some other scholars of revision, Ian Watt devotes nineteen pages to a stylistic analysis of only one paragraph, the first, of Henry James's *The Ambassadors* (Norton Critical Edition). One can clearly follow in James's revisions three phases in the development of his style, affectionately labeled: 1. James I; 2. James II; 3. James the old Pretender.

"In the beginning was the Word, and the Word was with God, and the Word was God. . . . And the Word was made flesh, and dwelt among us," according to the word of St. John. Word cannot easily be forced into flesh.

See "The Day the Flowers Came," pp. 283–84.

15 | Considering your overall conception, is your style inappropriately *simple* or *complex*?

A style may be simple or complex, or somewhere between the two, a midstyle.

"To write simply is as difficult," said W. Somerset Maugham, "as to be good." Economy, brevity, concreteness, clarity, and vividness are characteristics of the plain or simple style, as we see in this passage from the fishing scene at Burguete in Ernest Hemingway's *The Sun Also Rises* (Chapter 12):

> He was a good trout, and I banged his head against the timber so that he quivered out straight and then slipped him into my bag.
>
> While I had him on, several trout had jumped at the falls. As soon as I baited up and dropped in again I hooked another and brought him out the same way. I laid them out, side by side, all their heads pointing the same way, and looked at them. They were beautifully colored and firm and hard from the cold water. It was a hot day, so I split them all and shucked out the insides, gills and all, and tossed them over across the river. I took the trout ashore, washed them in the cold, smoothly heavy water above the dam, and then picked some ferns and packed them all in the bag, three trout on a layer of ferns, then another layer of ferns, then three more trout, and then covered them with ferns. They looked nice in the ferns, and now the bag was bulky, and I put it in the shade of the tree.

How the narrator, Jake Barnes, feels is in the feel of the style. Hemingway controls the style as Jake controls and focuses his feelings in the simple act of fishing. Each adjective and adverb is carefully chosen. Hemingway arranges denotative words in patterns of sound and thought that result in evocations. Far more, given the larger context of the novel, is implied about Jake here than is simply stated about the act of fishing and handling the catch. Hemingway revised to achieve the simplicity of his style. "Prose is architecture," said Hemingway, "not interior decorating, and the Baroque is over." Hemingway admired the simplicity of Jane Austen's style, but hers is a different kind of simplicity.

The complex, grand, or high style strives for memorable phrases, eloquence, rhythm, lyricism, now and then rhapsodic flights, as you can see in this passage from Chapter 14 of Thomas Wolfe's *Look Homeward, Angel*:

> The plum-tree, black and brittle, rocks stiffly in winter wind. Her million little twigs are frozen in spears of ice. But in the spring, lithe and heavy, she will bend under her great load of fruit and blossoms. She will grow young again. Red plums will ripen, will be shaken desperately upon the tiny stems. They will fall bursted on the loamy warm wet earth; when the wind blows in the orchard the air will be filled with dropping plums; the night will be filled with the sound of their dropping, and a great tree of birds will sing, burgeoning, blossoming richly, filling the air also with warm-throated plum-dropping bird-notes.
>
> The harsh hill-earth has moistly thawed and softened, rich soaking rain falls, flesh-bladed tender grass like soft hair growing sparsely streaks the land.

How the omniscient author himself feels is overtly expressed in the style; whatever is implied is incidental and perhaps accidental, because outward expression is Wolfe's intention. The proliferation of adjectives is intended to get the images and the emotion out there on the page, not to simplify and focus images and thereby imply emotion, as in the Hemingway passage. We attribute the author's rhapsodic feelings to his hero, Eugene Gant, only by association; we know he probably felt as the author does, but the focus is on the author's point of view and style.

Henry James's style also is complex but in very different ways and for very different reasons; its complexity derives from a more intellectual, analytical activity, which even so generates emotion of varying intensity. Examples of his style are given throughout this handbook.

The midstyle is, of course, a controlled use of simplicity and complexity and often relies on subtlety for its effects, as we see in this passage from near the end of Chapter 4 of James Joyce's *A Portrait of the Artist as a Young Man*:

> A girl stood before him in midstream, alone and still, gazing out to sea. She seemed like one whom magic had changed into the likeness of a strange and beautiful seabird. Her long slender bare legs were delicate as a crane's and pure save where an emerald trail of seaweed had fashioned itself as sign upon the flesh. Her thighs, fuller and softhued as ivory, were bared almost to the hips where the white fringes of her drawers were like featherings of soft white down. Her slateblue skirts were kilted boldly about her waist and dovetailed behind her. Her bosom was as a bird's soft and slight, slight and soft as the breast of some darkplumaged dove. But her long fair hair was girlish: and girlish, and touched with the wonder of mortal beauty, her face.
>
> She was alone and still, gazing out to sea; and when she felt his presence and the worship of his eyes her eyes turned to him in quiet sufferance to his gaze, without shame or wantonness.

Joyce's style here may seem as complex and lyrical as Wolfe's, but the key difference is that Joyce's style is far more controlled and the emotion more restrained, and so perhaps more powerful, coming out of a controlled context and having controlled ramifications throughout the rest of the novel.

Usually, the simple style works best for first-person narration, the complex for omniscient, and the midstyle for central intelligence. The passages above are examples of each. In the first-person story, stylistic questions revolve mainly around appropriateness and consistency, and the ways the author *manipulates*, in the benign sense of the term, his effects behind the style. It's important to be aware that the effect of the simple style may be complex, the effect of the complex style may be quite simple, while the effect of the midstyle may play over a spectrum of simplicity and complexity. Given the context of the novel, Jake Barnes's feelings are far more complex than Wolfe's (or Eugene Gant's) or Stephen Dedalus's.

The most obvious danger of the simple style is banality, of the complex style is overwriting or confusion, and of the midstyle is blandness. Sometimes style may be too simple, and you need to revise for greater complexity.

16 | Have you failed to *imagine* your style, line by line?

"But look," Evelyn Waugh once protested, in the middle of an interview, "I think that your questions are dealing too much with the creation of character and not enough with the technique of writing. I regard writing not as investigation of character, but as an exercise in the use of language, and with this I am obsessed." Few writers are willing to state so fervently their primary involvement with language. In the daily process of writing and rewriting, it is Waugh's imagination that works out his obsession.

The public romantic misconception of the workings of the imagination, shared by all too many writers, is that the imagination dreams up unrealistic characters and situations. As I suggest in the introduction, the imagination works in many other ways. Words and phrases don't just come to you in the rush and heat of the first draft—you imagine them. In the more deliberate, conscious process of revision, willfully imagine, line by line, other possibilities (see Introduction, pp. 8–9). "I've imagined a style for myself," said Flaubert.

17 | Does your style generally lack a sense of *immediacy*?

Word by word, your reader wants you to convey a feeling of immediacy, no matter what kind of experience he is having at any given moment. Michel Tournier's description of the act of riding a bicycle in *The Ogre* (pp. 315–16, first American edition) is just as immediate, word for word, as his later description of the ogre fleeing a burning castle with a child on his back. By immediacy, I don't just mean that the reader experiences the illusion in some general sense that what is on the page is really happening to him, I mean that the sense of immediacy in and of itself becomes the reality, becomes the power source of the illusion that the people are real and the events are happening now. In fiction, immediacy is in itself an experience. With every word, you are *doing* something to your reader, and whatever it is you are doing, the reader has a sense of immediacy—or he doesn't.

Even negative sensations—such as tedium—must be felt as happening immediately, now. Inert descriptions, dull exposition, dry factual accounts, passive verbs, etc. undercut, stifle, smother, retard that quality of immediacy. Fascinating characters involved in suspenseful, even melodramatic, action cannot in themselves convey a sense of immediacy if the style that presents those characters and that action lacks immediacy.

Most of the stylistic and other devices described in this handbook promote and stimulate that quality of immediacy writers strive for in revision.

"I would sooner die like a dog," said Flaubert, "than hurry my sentence by so much as a second before it is ripe ." When it's ripe, it's immediate.

18 | Does your style fail to work upon all the reader's senses?

Your reader expects to see, hear, touch, smell, taste. Bald statements do not necessarily stimulate the reader's senses. "Coughing, the tall man wearing a wool suit, reeking of garlic, ran into the flower shop." That sentence may or may not have stimulated one or more of your senses, despite my overt, rather strained effort to do so. A cluster of sensory experiences may not be as effective in a given context as focus on a single sense. "Fires on the dry mountain slopes surrounding the town had been smoldering for days." We can see that, but we can also smell it, even, or especially, without including such a phrase as "and I could smell the burning leaves throughout the village." No other sense is as difficult to stimulate in fiction as smell. But most senses are more sharply stimulated by implication than by direct attempts. "The man was so tall he had to stoop to enter the room" is less effective than "John entered the room, followed by a man who had to stoop."

Stimulation of the reader's senses is a major source of that sense of immediacy the writer works to achieve in revision.

"Fiction—if it at all aspires to be art—appeals to temperament . . ." said Joseph Conrad. "Such an appeal to be effective must be an impression conveyed through the senses; and, in fact, it cannot be made in any other way. . . ."

19 | Have you failed to make your style as clear, concrete, and simple as the various contexts demand?

The key phrase here is "as the various contexts demand." You are always creating contexts within which the reader experiences specific effects. There is usually a larger, general context, as suggested in the very title of the novel by James Agee's, *A Death in the Family*. Other contexts are created as the novel develops (little Rufus's fear of older boys in Agee's novel). The degree of clarity, concreteness, and simplicity in your style is determined by the kind of context in which a given sentence appears.

The general context for the following passage from Frank O'Connor's "Guests of the Nation" is that members of the Irish Republican Army have captured and made friends with two British soldiers; the immediate context is that they have suddenly been ordered to shoot their prisoners, and one of whom appeals to his captor friends over the duty-minded Donovan:

> "Ah, shut up, you, Donovan; you don't understand me, but these fellows do. They're my chums; they stand by me and I stand by them. We're not the capitalist fools you seem to think us."

Years after the story appeared in print as quoted above, O'Connor, on the occasion of the publication of a larger collection, drew on the context to make the lines simpler, clearer, more concrete:

> "Shut up, Donovan! You don't understand me, but these lads do. They're not the sort to make a pal and kill a pal. They're not the tools of any capitalist."

Those words cut deeper into the narrator's emotions and thus the reader's than the style of the earlier version.

"Any clearness I have in my own life is due," said Sherwood Anderson, "to my feeling for words."

See Question 22, on context.

20 | Is your style *literal* more often than it is *suggestive?*

It is the nature of fiction that sentences that suggest have more immediacy of impact than sentences that literally state. Your reader's expectation is that nonfiction will offer literal statements far more often than suggestive ones; your reader has turned to your fiction in the expectation of having predominantly suggestive experiences, line by line. It is your control of words that denote (literally state) and words that connote (suggest) that determines your reader's responses in the fictional environment you have conjured. One aspect of that control is your effort in revision to make denotative and connotative words play off each other to have the specific effects you intend on your reader. A style that is more often literal (a high incidence of denotative words) than suggestive (a low incidence of connotative words) will fail to stimulate the reader's senses, and will lack the qualities of subtlety and immediacy that the reader picks up your fiction to experience.

When Scobie says, "It's no good confessing if I don't intend to try," in Graham Greene's *The Heart of the Matter*, we take the statement as a literal expression by the character of what we feel is true of the character; but Greene realized that that literal wording did not reflect Scobie the way he had wanted it to, so several decades later, he revised for the definitive edition: "It's not much good confessing if I don't intend to try. . . ." Now the context set up in the novel and the context of that scene play suggestively and with deliberate ambiguity upon the connotative phrase "not much." Now the statement suggests an attitude he has about himself, perhaps that his confession does some good if "not much."

Try to create a rhythm by modulating from the literal to the suggestive. Play suggestive words off literal words.

See "The Day the Flowers Came," comment 21, p. 279.

21 | Do you *tell* your reader when to *show* would be more effective?

The advice Chekhov and other writers give, first and repeatedly to themselves, especially in revision, that derives from the nature of fiction in the most fundamental sense, is this: show don't tell. What about Albert Camus's *The Fall*, which is long on telling and very short on showing? The answer lies to some extent in a comparison of *The Fall* with Camus's *The Stranger*, which shows far more than it tells. What about talkative Henry James as compared with laconic Ernest Hemingway? We turn to genius for exceptions. But for the purpose of everyday struggle in the revision stages, the writer does well to listen to Chekhov, as a look at his stories, which demonstrate how he took his own advice, will show.

Telling, declaring, is the province of nonfiction; showing or rendering is the province of fiction. Telling is a passive experience; showing is active, immediate, involving the senses. Writing is hard. To tell is easy; to show is difficult. Much of the revision labor goes into converting passages that tell into passages that show. "Tell me a story" really means "Show me a story." And "show" doesn't just mean pictures, images in motion along a plot line. It involves stimulation of all the senses through subtlety and implication, a rhythmic modulation of the literal and the suggestive.

No fiction can or should be all showing and no telling. Dramatic scenes that vividly and memorably show do their work partly as a consequence of contrast with passages, usually shorter ones, that tell, that summarize other action, thoughts, scenes.

In the magazine version of "Babylon Revisited," Fitzgerald has Charlie *tell* the reader how he feels about Paris. In a taxi, Charlie crossed the Seine, and he "felt the sudden provincial quality of the left bank."

"I spoiled this city for myself," he thought. "I didn't realize it, but . . ."

First *show* Charlie and the reader what you want Charlie to tell himself and the reader, Fitzgerald seems to have said to himself, producing this:

. . . Charlie felt the sudden provincial quality of the Left Bank.

Charlie directed his taxi to the Avenue de L'Opéra, which was out of his way. But he wanted to see the blue hour spread over the magnificent facade, and imagine that the cab horns, playing endlessly the first few bars of *Le Plus que Lent*, were the trumpets of the Second Empire. They were closing the iron grill in front of Brentano's Bookstore, and people were already at dinner behind the trim little bourgeois hedge of Duval's. He had never eaten at a really cheap restaurant in Paris. Five-course dinner, four francs fifty, eighteen cents, wine included. For some odd reason he wished that he had.

As they rolled on to the Left Bank and he felt its sudden provincialism, he thought, "I spoiled this city for myself. I didn't realize it, but . . ."

In the first version, Charlie's thought, that he spoiled Paris for himself, is just a bit of information about Charlie; but in the second, after feeling the look of the city and Charlie's nostalgia for it, the reader is shocked, as Charlie himself must be, by the realization, and it sinks in. The showing supports not only the telling here but much of what Fitzgerald and Charlie, in thoughts and dialog, tell throughout the story, up to the last passage, which begins, "He would come back some day . . ."

22 | Do you neglect to prepare *contexts* that will enable you to use the device of implication?

Why and how you revise any given line depends upon the context you have created for it. There is an implied context that hovers outside a story (the South is the external context of any Faulkner story). There is the general context that has been developed at any point in a story (the threat of death by violence for Nancy in Faulkner's "That Evening Sun"). There is the immediate context for each line under scrutiny (Nancy is in her cabin telling the three Compson children a story to keep them with her because she expects her husband to come through the door any second and slit her throat). Faulkner heightens tension by starting a new section:

> Nancy looked at us. She quit talking. She looked at us. Jason's legs stuck straight out of his pants, because he was little. "I don't think that's a good story," he said. "I want to go home."

Except for one phrase, every word in this passage draws on the context and implies Nancy's ever-increasing fear and the narrator's, Quentin's, ever-increasing awareness of it; not one word refers directly to this fear and awareness. The effect in the version called "That Evening Sun Go Down," published in *The American Mercury* is undercut by the phrase "because he was little," a totally unnecessary bit of inert information. For a collection of his stories, Faulkner revised the sentence to focus the image so it could draw on the context for its effect and enhance the effect of the rest of the passage: "Jason's legs stuck straight out where he sat on Nancy's lap." Now the image contributes to the sense, conveyed by the context, that Nancy's own body is rigid with terrified expectation of a violent death. Jason's legs sticking straight out suggests, as contrast, his childlike innocence of what Nancy, on whose lap he sits reluctantly, feels.

Most of Faulkner's revisions focus on the last section, where he cuts every word that refers literally to what his carefully prepared context already so effectively implies. Direct references to what Nancy fears and to the ditch where her husband may lie waiting are cut.

Sometimes a line that doesn't work in one context will be more relevant in another.

Many writers look at a line that seems to need work in isolation from the immediate, the general, and the external context. If you look at each line, as Faulkner's revisions of this story suggest *he* did, in terms of these contexts, you will see opportunities that you will miss if you simply focus on each line in itself. Context generates implications whether you intend them or not, but being conscious of those implications enables you to revise to use the device of implication even more often and with more control. See the next question for a discussion of implication.

See "The Day the Flowers Came," p. 281. The full effect of Carolyn's speech at the end derives from implications triggered by the context developed throughout the story.

23 | Do you fail to use the device of *implication*?

Implication is the device of making a literal statement in a prepared context for the purpose of suggesting something else. This device involves the reader actively in the creative process; even when this involvement is unconscious, as is often the case, it has the desired effect. I exaggerate to make a point: never say what you mean. "What a writer is writing *about* is seldom the main point," says Thomas Mann; "it's what he's doing with his left hand that really matters." The experience is not described directly on the page, it is evoked in the reader's response through a "phantom circuit of the imagination" (James M. Cain's phrase).

Implication requires the reader's active, emotional, imaginative, and intellectual collaboration. Wright Morris says, "Underwriting is a species of underwater swimming. Is the pool empty? That is how it often looks," to the passive reader. "I want to use a minimum of words for a maximum effect." Several lines from *Man and Boy* indirectly describe that effect. A father strikes a match to read a telegram and discovers something else in the basement by the same light: "One match had done for both of them." One word of Morris's style often has that double effect. "The saying was plain enough, but Mother always managed to use it . . . in a very original way." And so Morris. "One good thought led to another." Morris's underwritten, indirect style bristles with implication—as does Mother's: "Mother made this observation from behind the cabinet. She had her best thoughts, seemed to do her best thinking, *behind* something."

Almost three decades ago, the summer my first novel appeared, I taught my first writers' workshop, at a small state college in the "dark and bloody ground" region of eastern Kentucky. Three other instructors and I met with all the students in an afternoon session to discuss the techniques used by the writers we were reading together. As an excellent example of description, I alluded to Chekhov's description of moonlight in a story we had read. Flipping through the pages, I tried to find the line or lines in which he so brilliantly described moonlight, creating a mood essential to the story. I couldn't find it. Each student and teacher remembered the moonlight and its effect and was sure he could find it; after thirty minutes, drenched in the reality of that moonlight as readers, we gave up, in amazed frustration, as teachers and students. The next afternoon, a mountain boy who wanted to become a great writer announced he had found, not the actual lines describing it, but the specific source of the moonlight. I can't quote it exactly because I forgot the story and the anthology, but not, for a moment, the image and the lesson. The student pointed out that the facts that it was night and that the hero is walking on the road had been established by Chekhov, so that when we come to the line "a piece of glass glinted in the road," moonlight, given the context, floods our consciousness—far more effectively than if Chekhov had literally described the moonlight.

The best example of implication I know is in Faulkner's novella "The Bear"; it also gives an impression of the way implication affects a reader. Sam Fathers is initiating young Isaac McCaslin in the rules, rituals, and mysteries of hunting bear. That's the general context; the immediate context is that all the boy's perceptions are now more focused on being alone and lost than upon tracking the bear.

> . . . he did next as Sam had coached and drilled him: made this next circle in the opposite direction and much larger, so that the pattern of the two of them would bisect this track somewhere, but crossing no trace nor mark anywhere of his feet or any feet, and now he was going faster though still not panicked, his heart beating a little more rapidly but strong and steady enough, and this time it was not even the tree because there was a down log beside it which he had never seen before and beyond the log a little swamp, a seepage of moisture somewhere between earth and water, and he did what Sam had coached and drilled him as the next and the last, seeing as he sat down on the log the crooked print, the warped indentation in the wet ground which while he looked at it continued to fill with water until it was level full and the water began to overflow and the sides of the print began to dissolve away.

Enhanced simultaneously by the external, the general, and the immediate context, the rhythm of this complex sentence simulates the beating of blood in the body of the boy as he walks, and even as he sits on the log, that walking, blood-beat rhythm continues. Without pause, Faulkner slips into the boy's perception of the print, which at that moment is perceived only subconsciously as a bear's print; watching the water rise in the print simulates the way a fact follows a perception—this is a bear print—and in the same instant, he *feels*, before he can think about it, the implication that the bear walked there just a moment before and so is very nearby. The timing, controlled by Faulkner's style, of the reader's own perceptions and realizations is just moments ahead of the boy's. The boy follows the prints, the wilderness coalesces in his own intense focus. "Then he saw the bear. It did not emerge, appear; it was just there . . ." This passage, on pages 208–209 of the Modern Library edition of *Go Down, Moses*, illustrates many other aspects of style.

Look next at the short version he revised to suit the editors and readers of *The Saturday Evening Post*.

He had not been going very fast for the last two or three hours. He went on faster now . . . he did what Sam Fathers had told him was the next thing and the last.

As he sat down on the log he saw the crooked print—the warped, tremendous, two-toed indentation which, even as he watched it, filled with water.

The intensity of the effect of implication in this version is diminished by the style, which is chopped up into a series of discrete sentences, which have information-bearing function more than the function of simulating the way perceptions work. It is as though Isaac gets the same information the reader does at the same moment; neither *gradually* perceive what water rising in the paw print implies, and the inserted, explicit phrase "two-toed" puts the emphasis on the literal fact of the bear print rather than the implied fact of the bear's having just walked there.

Do you undercut the effectiveness of implication by literally restating what you have implied? Do you imply, then undercut implication immediately with a literal statement; or does the literal statement come first, followed by implication; or do you imply poorly, then imply effectively in the next phrase or sentence?

Rewrite those lines in which you *tell* the reader how a character feels. Suppose that in telling a reader how a character feels you have given the reader three statements in logical order. The task of revision is to cut out one of those three statements and to reword the remaining two so that they imply how the character feels.

In the five versions of the opening of *Mrs. Dalloway*, Virginia Woolf sometimes strains to make a fullness of words on the page match the fullness of images in her imagination: "Blankness, indifference glances from plate glass windows, blankness and indifference. She refused me, he thought." Clarissa's refusal of Peter Walsh is so aptly suggested by "Blankness glances from pavement from plate glass windows" that "indifference" undercuts the effect, and the repetition of "blankness" *and* "indifference" destroys it. By cutting those words out, Woolf implies the quality of "refusal" even before Walsh thinks of it, and thus we experience it all the more intensely. (See Hildick, *Word for Word*, pp. 116-27, in Bibliography.)

Relying on implication can enable you to cut many minor elements that render your style stultifying. For instance, why ever say "she thought to herself"? To whom else *could* she think? It is absurd to state what is so clearly implied. "She could see the birds in the trees." *If* what? Did she or didn't she? She did. So "She saw the birds in the trees" says it.

To see writers revising to use implication, compare James Joyce's *Stephen Hero* with *A Portrait of the Artist as a Young Man*; Frank O'Connor's "Guests of the Nation" with the revised version; two versions of John Steinbeck's "The Chrysanthemums"; the basement scene in "The Ram in the Thicket" by Wright Morris with the *Man and Boy* version.

See "The Day the Flowers Came," comment 15, p. 274, comment 21, p. 279.

24 | Are your *verbs* passive, as opposed to active?

A passive verb tells what has already been done to the subject; it may diminish the energy of an action.

In "Miss Lonelyhearts on a Field Trip," an early short-story version of *Miss Lonelyhearts*, Nathanael West wrote:

> . . . the *glasses and bottles* with their exploding highlights sounded like a battery of little bells when they *were touched together* by the bartender.

The first-person male narrator, "Miss Lonelyhearts," wants the reader to experience the immediacy and energy of the action, but the passive construction provides the reader with a dull experience. "A novelist," said West, "can afford to be anything but dull."

The passage from the short story reappears, revised, in the novel:

The *glasses and bottles*, their high lights exploding, *rang* like a battery of little bells when the bartender *touched them together*.

An *active verb* tells what a subject does now; it is immediate, forceful. The effect of the action on the reader is immediate and vibrant. The active voice also lends immediacy to the third-person point of view that West uses in the novel version. The revision might have been even more effective had West started the sentence with "When the bartender touched them together . . ." Even in lyrical passages, passive verbs may be ineffective.

Long narrative passages that describe action but seem weak may benefit from the changing of all passive verbs to active ones.

See "The Day the Flowers Came," comments 6, 8, and 25, pp. 266, 268, and 282.

25 | Have you neglected to use *impingement* as a device for giving your style a sense of action?

Impingement occurs when you arrange the syntax so that one word or phrase acts upon another. The effect is almost kinetic, giving your style an active, dynamic quality, a sense of immediacy, as in this passage from the end of chapter 1 of Virginia Woolf's *Orlando*: "Faithless, mutable, fickle, he called her; devil, adulteress, deceiver; and the swirling waters took his words, and tossed at his feet a broken pot and a little straw."

The impingement occurs at the phrase "and tossed." The syntax leads the reader to feel that "the swirling waters took his words" climaxes the thought, but the parallel syntax of "and tossed" delivers a new and unexpected action. Woolf mirrors this effect very near the end of the novel, after several centuries, during which Orlando has metamorphosed into a woman. "But descending in the lift again—so insidious is the repetition of any scene—she was again sunk far beneath the present moment; and thought when the lift bumped on the ground, that she heard a pot broken against a river bank." That Woolf was consciously using this device of impingement, whether she had the term in mind or not, is indicated by the fact that she does not only repeat the action itself, with a variation, several centuries and 150 pages later, she repeats the impinge-ment syntax: ". . . and thought when the lift bumped on the ground, that she heard a pot broken against a river bank." The one action ("lift bumped on the ground") seems to cause, unexpectedly, "a pot" to break on the bank, a typical effect of impingement.

I have used this example from *Orlando* instead of one from the fiction of Wright Morris because it resonates so awesomely throughout Woolf's novel, but it was in the works of Morris that I first noticed the stylistic device of impingement. There are examples on almost every page of his many novels and stories, but here are a few from "The Ram in the Thicket" and its novel version *Man and Boy*. "When he heard Mother's feet on the stairs, Mr. Ormsby cracked her soft-boiled eggs and spooned them carefully into her heated cup." The kinetic impingement of her "feet on the stairs" seems to crack the eggs. This is an example of one object impinging upon another. It reappears unchanged in the novel, except for "her heated cup," which Morris changed to "the heated cup," probably to avoid any ironic, satirical effect, the context being that Mother dominates her meek husband, Mr. Ormsby. The story is overtly satirical; the novel is subtly satirical, but transcends satire in its overall intention.

The element of surprise, or reversal of expectation, in the impingement device lends an air of momentousness to the end of a chapter. Seeing some pigeons, Mother calls out their Latin names, as is her habit, but Mrs. Sutcliffe's cigarette smoke obscures them; Mother waves to them anyway. "When she could see again the pigeons were gone, but a tall policeman near the safety zone, seeing her wave her orchid, took off his hat and waved in return." Mother's speech and behavior sets many things in motion and impingement enhances her effect.

When impingement is only syntactical, the effect is still to sustain a sense of movement within the style itself, a sense of ongoingness. "He turned slowly on the bed, careful to keep the springs quiet, and as he lowered his feet he scooped his socks from the floor." "As he lowered" impinges upon "he scooped." To see the effect of impingement by its absence, make three sentences out of Morris's one. For the novel, Morris changes "scooped" to "reached for," again because he had developed an attitude of greater respect toward Ormsby and "scooped" strikes a slightly comic note that diminishes him.

See "The Day the Flowers Came," comment 6, pp. 266–67.

26 | Do you neglect to provide *contrast* to your general style?

Your general style may be simple like Hemingway's, complex like Henry James's, or a midstyle like James Joyce's (see Question 15), but one feature that makes it effective is *contrast*. There are strategic moments when a little complexity of phrasing contrasts with the general simplicity, for instance. Just when his simple, short sentences threaten to become monotonous, Hemingway, for a specific effect, drifts into long, complex sentences. Just when Henry James's long, complex sentences threaten to weary a reader, James shifts, with good reasons, into a series of short sentences.

In dialog you attempt to be true to the way people really talk; in narrative descriptive passages, you may be more careful, more unique, although too great a contrast may jar. The substandard English that characters often speak in dialog offers the relief of contrast to the general style, as when Dickens's own style as omniscient narrator contrasts with the dialect style of his characters.

27 | Have you failed to use *repetition* as a device for emphasis?

Unnecessary, awkward, or ineffective deliberate repetition is one of the blemishes in style you will work hard in revision to delete. In a draft of *The Way of All Flesh*, Samuel Butler wrote, ". . . and now that Mrs. Theobald had taken to good ways she might bring him more grandsons, which might be desirable." He cut the second "might" and substituted "would be desirable." That's the kind of repetition you will most often seek out and cut out.

But controlled repetition for emphasis is an essential element of style. Gertrude Stein, Hemingway, Wright Morris, Joseph Heller, Günter Grass, and Kurt Vonnegut cultivated a higher incidence of repetition of words and phrases than most writers, but repetition serves every writer to emphasize an image, a character's speech patterns, the narrator's tone or attitude, and so on.

D.H. Lawrence deliberately repeated the rather trite phrase "he wanted her" in a key passage in *The Rainbow*.

The kiss lasted, there among the moonlight till he wanted her. He wanted her exceedingly. They stood there enfolded, hanging in the balance. It was pain to him that he wanted her. It was a new thing to him. He had never wanted her, he had never wanted any woman before. His wanting her seemed to separate them. It hurt him.

Feeling the monotony of the repetition, Lawrence started over.

The kiss lasted, there among the moonlight. He kissed her again and she kissed him. And again they were kissing together. Till something happened in him, he was strange. He wanted her. He wanted her exceedingly. She was something new. They stood there folded, suspended in the night. And his whole being quivered with surprise, as from a blow. He wanted her, and he wanted to tell her so. But the shock was too great to him. He had never realized before.

The repetition starts to go wrong in the next two lines, which he later cut: "She had a face, she had hands and feet and soft dresses, but one could not want her. Yet now he did want her." Then Lawrence got back the rhythm of the repetition:

He trembled with initiation and unusedness, he did not know what to do. He held her gently, gently, much more gently. And he was glad, and breathless, and almost in tears. But he knew he wanted her. . . .

To decide that repetition would be effective and then to do it is not enough. It must work.

In *Catch-22*, Joseph Heller used in narration the technique of repetition that distinguished the dialog of screwball comedy movies of the 1930s. Here is an example from the early short-story version, "Catch-18":

None of the nurses who knew Yossarian liked Yossarian. One of the reasons Nurse Duckett didn't like Yossarian was that she knew he didn't care whether she liked him or not.

This is a typical example of the technique of stylistic repetition— almost a formula mechanically applied at times—that Heller uses throughout the novel, but it does not work here, so he cut it and only "None of the nurses liked Yossarian" appears.

Repetition as a device for handling larger elements is discussed in Question 128.

28 | Is your style lacking in the elements of *reversal and surprise?*

Examine your sentences to find those that may lend themselves to the use of the stylistic device of reversal and surprise. Suppose that in a previous sentence you have led the reader to expect a certain continuation, a further development of an action, image, or observation; in the next sentence, reverse that expectation and surprise the reader. Sometimes the syntax of a single sentence sets up an expectation that you may reverse in the latter part of the sentence. This sort of effect now and then provides the reader with delight and with the anticipation that you will do it again further along. Henry James, Wright Morris, and G. K. Chesterton are masters in the use of this device.

A good example is Morris's revision of a sentence in the story version of "The Ram in the Thicket":

Seated on the attic stairs she trimmed her toenails with a pearl handled knife that Mr. Ormsby had been missing for several years.

Here is the *Man and Boy* version:

Seated on the steps she trimmed her toenails with Mr. Ormsby's pearl-handled knife, the one he had been missing, along with the chain, for several years.

The image is so clear and what Mrs. Ormbsy is doing is so odd and specific, the reader feels the main business of the sentence is done, so that the last part of the sentence reverses our expectation and its idea surprises us, and when we grasp the implication—that she has secretively kept the knife, knowing he misses it, and that he also liked the chain that goes with it—the last part proves to be more arresting than the first.

29 | Are your sentences monotonous in structure for lack of such rhetorical devices as *parallelism?*

When you coordinate and repeat the syntax of three or more phrases in a complex sentence, or series of short sentences or sentence fragments, the reader is swept along, sometimes rather breathlessly, to a climax, and a dramatic emphasis is placed upon the emotion, the image, or the idea you are expressing. Experiencing your use of the device is in itself pleasurable for the reader.

Eudora Welty, "From the Unknown":

> And anyways, I seen him fall. I was the one.
> So I reach me down my guitar off the nail. Cause I've got me a guitar, what I've always kept, and I'll never drop that, and I set in my cheer, with nobody home but me, and I start to play, and sing a-Down.

In the revision, the repetition of the word "never"—which characterizes the narrator's negative attitude toward blacks—is not enough; Welty wants it to ride on the rhythm of his speech.

The "Where Is the Voice Coming From?" version:

> Anyways, I seen him fall. I was evermore the one.
> So I reach me down my old guitar off the nail on the wall. 'Cause I've got my guitar, what I've held onto from way back when, and I never dropped that, never lost or forgot it, never hocked it but to get it again, never give it away, and I set in my chair, with nobody home but me, and I start to play, and sing a-Down. . . .

30 | Have you used *parenthetical phrasing* ineptly?

Used without a conscious effect in mind, but simply for sentence variety—mechanically—a parenthetical phrase is often a chore to read. Controlled for effect, the parenthetical phrase may involve the reader in the development of the sentence and, by delaying the completion of the sense, make the reader feel more intensely the purpose of the sentence.

In the first published version of "Guests of the Nation," Frank O'Connor wrote:

> At dusk the big Englishman Belcher would shift his long legs out of the ashes and ask, "Well, chums, what about it?" and Noble or me would say, "As you please, chum" (for we had picked up some of their curious expressions), and the little Englishman 'Awkins would light the lamp and produce cards. Sometimes Jeremiah Donovan would come up of an evening and supervise the play, and grow excited over 'Awkins cards (which he always played badly), and shout at him as if he was one of our own. . . .

Parenthesis should be used sparingly in most fiction, especially when a first-person narrator is, as he is here, speaking in modified vernacular. O'Connor overused parentheses throughout both versions, but apparently here in the first paragraph where he was settling into the first-person voice he felt two parenthetical items were one too many, so he cut the second. Parentheses lend an aura of formality that undercuts the effect of informality in first-person narration. This passage is from the first published version of Henry James's *The Portrait of a Lady*:

Gilbert Osmond came to see Madame Merle, who presented him to the young lady seated almost out of sight at the other end of the room. Isabel, on this occasion, took little share in the conversation; she scarcely even smiled when the others turned to her appealingly; but sat there as an impartial auditor of their brilliant discourse. Mrs. Touchett was not present, and these two had it their own way.

The style in this passage is effective enough, but it is not distinguished by the recognizable Jamesian touch, nor by his characteristic use of the parenthetical delay. In his revision for the New York edition years later, he adds a few choice words, a distinctive metaphor, and the parenthetical delay in the last line that makes all the difference:

Gilbert Osmond came to see Madame Merle, who presented him to the young lady lurking on the other side of the room. Isabel took on this occasion little part in the talk; she scarcely even smiled when the others turned to her invitingly; she sat there as if she had been at the play and had paid even a large sum for her place. Mrs. Touchett was not present, and these two had it, for the effect of brilliancy, all their own way.

Interpolation differs from parenthetical delay, mechanically in the use of dashes, which are more obvious and forceful, but also in presenting a sudden intrusion upon consciousness of a contrasting memory. Wright Morris's "The Ram in the Thicket":

With his pants on, but carrying his shirt—for he might get it soiled preparing breakfast—he left the bathroom and tiptoed down the stairs.

Morris uses dashes mechanically simply to interject another facet of the same idea; in revision, for the novel version, *Man and Boy*, he introduces a contrasting idea:

With his socks on, but carrying his shoes—"The hour I love," Mother had said, "is the hour before rising"—Mr. Ormsby left the bathroom and tip-toed down the stairs.

Morris meshes thought and action. Mr. Ormsby's memory of Mother's statement is Morris's use of the device of interpolation, which demonstrates an aspect of consciousness as he expresses, through contrast, Mother's relaxed use of this hour, while Ormsby himself is very uptight.

31 | Do you fail to use the *question* device where it might be effective?

More than any other writer, Wright Morris uses the rhetorical question —appropriately because his central-intelligence characters are very meditative, and question posing and answering keeps their thought processes lively with intellectual vigor. The three versions of the ending of *One Day*, published in Kuehl's *Creative Writing and Rewriting*, show a high incidence of the use of questions and how Morris revised to control their effects.

. . . some time later the throbbing of the jukebox could not be felt in the springs of Cowie's bed. . . . From the hall at his back, leading to the stairs, she came to stand framed in the doorway. To see her he had to twist around his head. He was able to do that, having no idea what he would see. Her hair was down. She wore only a cloak of light? The faintly luminous ointment was not on her face. She spoke his name, then came forward to take his head in her arms, his face pressed close between her breasts. With both hands she gripped his hair as if to lift his head from his shoulders, tipped it upward, and placed her lips on his mouth. And Cowie? Is it necessary to say? Isn't this the point, precisely, where the good clean books and the movies ended, where Rin Tin Tin rubbed noses with Lassie, if not much else? Precisely, but that was not for Cowie.

The questions in that second version did not work. Notice his more effective use of questions in the published version:

Was it in Cowie's head, or the floor, that the jukebox continued to throb? A faint buzzing persisted in his ears. So he had no idea, none, how long she had been standing in the hallway, or what it was that led him to turn his head. The doorway framed her. Was she clad in more than her hair? To Cowie's eye she wore only a cloak of light. He said nothing, dry-mouthed he sat there with his head twisted on his shoulders. She spoke his name, then came forward to take his head in her hands. With both hands she gripped his hair as if to lift his head from his shoulders, tipped it upward, and placed her lips on his mouth. And Cowie? Did he resist her? Or was this not the point where resistance ended? Of what was he conscious? Of the odour of the ointment.

Had Katherine Anne Porter failed to employ frequently the interrogative device in her classic story "Flowering Judas," the effect of staticness that threatens that story at every turn would have taken hold: "Still she sits quietly, she does not run. Where could she go?" The rhetorical question is one of several devices Porter employed to enliven an inherently static presentation of images of Laura's predicament (emotional, intellectual, spiritual paralysis).

32 | Have you created ineffective *phrases* that may be refined into key phrases?

"A well-made phrase," said Zola, "is a good action." In his book about the writing of *Doctor Faustus, The Genesis of a Novel,* Thomas Mann describes such a "good action": "Only now, in the rewriting of the passage, did I hit upon the phrases 'transcendence of despair,' the 'miracle that passes belief,' and that poetic cadence, quoted in almost every discussion of the book, about the 'voice of mourning' changing its meaning and abiding as a 'light in the night.' "

Most often a dead phrase needs burial, not resurrection; or just enough change to make it work in one place only. But one source of inspiration is the empty phrase that your imagination turns into something fine and charged with electricity. When you encounter an ineffective phrase try to imagine ways to transform it into a key phrase in the story; then repeat it in prepared contexts.

In an early draft of *The Great Gatsby*, Nick tells Gatsby he can't repeat the past. Gatsby's response:

"I've got to," he announced with conviction, "that's what I've got to do—live the past over again."

Fitzgerald reimagined that phrase to create one of the most memorable, thematically evocative lines in the novel:

"Can't repeat the past?" he cried incredulously. "Why of course you can!"

Thomas Hardy, *Tess of the D'Urbervilles*:

And then these children of the open air, whom even alcohol could scarce injure permanently, betook themselves to the field-path; and as they went there moved onward with them, around the shadow of each one's head, an opalized circle of glory, formed by the moon's rays, upon the glistering sheet of dew.

"An opalized circle of glory" is a typical example of sloppy first-draft phrasing. "A circle of opalized light" is the kind of modest improvement typically produced in the revision process.

Try to identify and cut superfluous phrases. In "Odour of Chrysanthemums," D. H. Lawrence wrote:

Then she went out, locking the door behind her.
Something scuffed down the yard as she went out, and she started. . .

The "started" effect is undercut by the superfluous phrase "as she went out."

Ineffective phrases are often pseudopoetic ones: "mountains towering high," "sighing winds," "softly pervades," "seething humanity," "snow-capped peaks," "cannot fathom," "heavy-laden," "swaying in the breeze," "radiant smile," "opalescent," "proffered," "silhouette," "furled," "mute," "enmeshed," "sere and yellow leaf," "linger," "chaste moonlight," "tracery of branches," "fierce beauty," "sadly yearn," "silvery laugh," etc. These are only a few listed by poet John Frederick Nims in *Western Wind*. Such lists appear frequently in books and articles because people who really care for words are eager to call attention to those that are lifeless. Let's call the use of such phrases the "fierce beauty" fallacy.

33 | Is your style overloaded with inappropriately formal phrases?

Fiction is seldom compatible with formal phrasing. Generally avoid: "however," "moreover," "as a matter of fact," "in fact," "it would seem," "as it were," "ergo," "nevertheless," "thus," "therefore."

Even so, in *Man and Boy*, as in much of his fiction, Wright Morris uses formal phrases for a mildly humorous effect and to create a little distance between himself and his characters, who may, in fact, use such phrases themselves *in character*. When Mr. Ormsby wakes from nightmares, he shakes the bed: "As his first thought was always for Mother, he would turn on the bed to reassure her, but, strange to relate, the commotion never woke her up." Mr. Ormsby is the kind of man who would say or even think a formal phrase like "strange to relate."

The phrase Morris uses most often is "that is": "He could leave it, that is, but he could never get over it." Other examples of formal phrasing: "*As* he had nothing else to do he prepared the vegetables, and dressed the meat, *as* Mother had never shown much of a flair for meat." "Therefore when Annie Mae smiled . . . Roy had to turn away"; "but if the truth were known"; "As a matter of fact, Mr. Ward didn't look just right." Some readers of Morris find the tone of such formal phrasing dull and tiring to read.

Frank O'Connor worked to achieve the informal style of his first-person narrator in "Guests of the Nation," but the following formal phrases appeared in the first published version:

> Anyway, he took little 'Awkins by the arm and dragged him on, but it was impossible to make him understand that we were in earnest. From which you will perceive how difficult it was for me, as I kept feeling my Smith and Wesson. . . .

He cut the second sentence for a later edition. He cut the word "perceive" when it appeared again in the same paragraph. Several pages later, the narrator says:

> It is the first time I have heard him laugh, and it sends a shiver down my spine, coming as it does so inappropriately upon the tragic death of his old friend.

The tone of the last clause is too stiff and formal. O'Connor cut it.

34 | Have you failed to make each *sentence* (or sentence fragment) a carefully crafted unit?

Through the wide doorway between two of the painting galleries, Emma saw Alfred Eisenburg standing before "The Three Miracles of Zenobius," his lean, equine face ashen and sorrowing, his gaunt frame looking undernourished, and dressed in a way that showed he was poorer this year than he had been last.

Jean Stafford's first sentence of "Children Are Bored on Sunday" is an intricate machine designed to do the work of a chapter in a novel: totally involve the reader, not with plot complications, but with rhetorical intricacies.

"The sentence is a single cry," says Herbert Read. "It is a unit of expression, and its various qualities—length, rhythm and structure—are determined by a right sense of this unity."

"I discovered," says James Dickey, "that the simple declarative sentence, under certain circumstances and in certain contexts, had exactly the qualities I wanted my lines of poetry to have."

Insistence in most English classes that one avoid at all costs the sentence fragment has inhibited fiction writers to some extent. Sentence fragments give a sense of natural psychological processes in narratives that use the third-person, central-intelligence point of view. Used for conscious effect, they lend emphasis to an image or a point. They contribute to rhythm in style.

It is important to reimagine the sequence of sentences, as Eudora Welty did in revising "Where Is the Voice Coming From?" In the "From the Unknown" version, she wrote:

> "They'll never find him," a man trying to sell me roasted peanuts tells me to my face.
> You can't win.

Welty changed the sequence of sentences for emphasis.

> You can't win.
> "They'll never find him," the old man trying to sell roasted peanuts tells me to my face.

Look for opportunities for compressing several sentences, where appropriate, into one. Here is one of many examples from two published versions of George Moore's *Esther Waters*:

The young gentlemen were home for their summer holidays. She was going up to her room, and had stepped aside to let Master Harry pass her on the stairs. But he stood staring at her with a strange smile on his face.

That sluggish passage moves smoothly in the revision:

The young gentlemen had come home for their summer holidays, and one day as she stepped aside to let Master Harry pass her on the stairs, he did not go by, but stood looking at her with a strange smile on his face.

35 | Do you neglect to play short sentences and long sentences off each other and vary the length of paragraphs to achieve *rhythm*?

Rhythm is the alternation of stressed and unstressed phrases and long and short units of expression, from sentences to paragraphs, and the alternation of varying kinds of narrative elements, to achieve variety and combat monotony. The overall effect is what D. H. Lawrence called "the living rhythm of the whole work." Try to alternate long sentences with short ones to achieve a flow, a tempo. Sometimes it may be best to turn several short sentences into a longer one by combining them. Sometimes it is best to compress one long sentence into a short one to concentrate the effect.

In an early version of George Eliot's *Middlemarch*, this passage moved clumsily:

What she cared for, liked, what she spontaneously cared for seemed to be always excluded from her life, for what was only granted by her husband and not—

Here she noticed that the awkward cadence had led her to a syntactical dead end, so she revised:

The thing that she liked, that she spontaneously cared to have seemed to be always excluded from her life, for if it was only granted and not shared by her husband it might as well have been denied.

Conscious attention to paragraphing is one means of controlling your reader's responses. Rhythm "is born, not with the words," says Herbert Read, "but with the thought, and with whatever confluence of instincts and emotions the thought is accompanied. As the thought takes shape in the mind, it takes *a* shape. It has always been recognized that clear thinking precedes good writing. There is about good writing a visual actuality. It exactly reproduces what we should metaphorically call the contour of our thought. The metaphor is for once exact: thought has a contour or shape. The paragraph is the perception of this contour or shape" (*English Prose Style*, p. 61). In his novel *The Green Child*, Read practices what he preaches here.

For a clear study of paragraphing in revision, compare the first published version of Frank O'Connor's "Guests of the Nation" with the version he revised for the 1956 Vintage collection. For instance, the first paragraph was too long for a first-person vernacular narrative. O'Connor made numerous new paragraph divisions.

To study the art of short paragraphing, see Ernest Hemingway's *The Sun Also Rises*. For varied paragraph lengths, see F. Scott Fitzgerald's *The Great Gatsby*. To consider the effectiveness of very long paragraphs, see Henry James's *The Wings of the Dove*, James Joyce's *Ulysses*, and Faulkner's *Absalom, Absalom!*

Rhythm is impeded when the mechanics of paragraphing are faulty. In revising the published version of *The Portrait of a Lady*, Henry James frequently joined dialog with narration to make it clearer who is speaking. In revising the magazine version of "Babylon Revisited," F. Scott Fitzgerald broke one paragraph into two to achieve clarity for the same purpose.

[Alix] smiled faintly. "Remember the night of George Hardt's bachelor dinner here? . . . By the way what's become of Claude Fessenden?"

In the version reprinted in *Taps at Reveille*, Fitzgerald wrote:

Alix smiled.
"Remember the night of George Hardt's bachelor dinner here?" said Charlie. "By the way, what's become of Claude Fessenden?"

Now it is clear that it is not Alix who asks, "Remember the night . . . ?" The rhythmic handling of larger units may be seen in Fitzgerald's alternation of interior with exterior scenes in *The Great Gatsby*.

36 | Is your style burdened with *empty words and phrases?*

The "burden" is on you, unless such phrases survive the revision process; they then become the reader's burden. The urgent quality of immediacy is affected by wooden, limp, passive words and phrases.

The style of Victorian poetry had become so sloppily turgid, while fiction, in the hands of Flaubert, Turgenev, and Henry James, had become so rhetorically controlled and thus more effective in doing what poetry had once done best that Ezra Pound demanded that "poetry should be at least as well written as prose." W. H. Auden later said, "Of the many definitions of poetry, the simplest is still the best: 'memorable speech.' "

We may feel such a style at work in Fitzgerald's *The Great Gatsby*.

> There was, *after all*, something gorgeous about him, some heightened sensitivity to *things* as if he were related to one of those intricate machines that register earthquakes ten thousand miles away. This sensitivity had nothing to do with that flabby *unethical* impressionability which is dignified under the name of the "creative temperament"—*I have always felt the same disgust toward the artist that I do for that other necessary evil, the garbage man*—it was an extraordinary *aliveness to life, an alert vitality* such as I have never found in any *human* person and which it is not likely I shall ever find again.

Nick got off some key words and phrases in this very early passage ("gorgeous," "heightened sensitivity," "extraordinary"), but empty or dull words and phrases and the one digression impede the flow and dilute the effect. I have underlined what Fitzgerald cut, and in the revision below I have underlined the new words and phrases which are repeated, with variations, throughout the rest of the novel:

> *If personality is an unbroken series of successful gestures, then* there was something gorgeous about him, some heightened sensitivity to *the promises of life*, as if he were related to one of those intricate machines that register earthquakes ten thousand miles away. This responsiveness had nothing to do with that flabby impressionability which is dignified under the name of "the creative temperament"—it was an extraordinary *gift for hope, a romantic readiness* such as I

have never found in any other person and which it is not likely I shall ever find again.

In *Middlemarch*, George Eliot first wrote: "It was not until late that evening Rosamond said to her husband . . ." By cutting "It was not until" Eliot unburdened the line of empty words. Only half a page later she caught herself using the exact same words and cut them before she could get further into the sentence. Such phrases make the line sluggish. In another place, she starts to use the phrase "to have a name by which to address," then quickly compresses: "to know names."

Is your style plagued by *diminutives*? When you use diminutives ("little," "petite," "miniature," "small," "slight," "tiny," "minute," "speck") you affect your reader's attitude toward the subject; the critical mind in revision finds them repugnant.

In "Odour of Chrysanthemums," D. H. Lawrence went too far with near-sentimental descriptions of the children of the dead miner; he cut out much of their activities, but he targeted diminutives in his style: "little flannelette shirt sleeves," "little parted lips," and "small wan flowers."

A controlled use of "little" for ironic effect is another matter, as we see in James Joyce's "A Little Cloud." Little Chandler "emerged from under the feudal arch of the King's Inn, a neat modest figure and walked swiftly down Henrietta Street. The golden sunset was waning and the air had grown sharp. A horde of grimy children populated the street." Joyce combines literal diminutives (the title and Chandler's nickname) with implied diminutives (the contrast between "feudal arch" and the "neat modest figure" of Little Chandler). In the next sentence, "waning" contrasts with "sharp," sustaining the *impression*, by contrast, of littleness. "Children" suggests littleness, but by contrast with the solitary Little Chandler, who is, ironically, an adult, they seem, by contrast, large because they are a "horde."

37 | Do *clichés* dull your style?

A cliché is an expression that once had the force of orginality and freshness but has become trite and stale through overuse. In most instances, clichés should be stricken. Avoid clichés unless you are using them in a special way.

As he gets into a humorous anecdote about a bottle of water from the Jordan River, Samuel Butler in *The Way of all Flesh* begins to deal out the stock, trite, cliché phrases that often go with the anticipation of such a passage:

> Mr. Pontifex took the bottle into his own hands and held it up to the light after carefully examining the seal. He then smiled with evident satisfaction, and retreated slowly with his prize.

Possibly the tone struck him as too arch; a simple style was best for getting to the key moment. He struck most of the last line, and substituted: "He smiled and left the bin with the bottle in his hands."

Some writers (and some readers) do not react against clichés as strongly as others. But since language is the medium he works in, the writer tries to be as original as he can without calling too much attention to his style. Some writers deliberately use clichés to give an aura of everyday reality to the world they are creating. Other writers imagine a special context for a cliché that resurrects its original vitality, but with a new meaning or emotional power.

No other writer provides as many examples for study of the transformation of clichés as Wright Morris in his many novels. In *The Deep Sleep*, he prepares a context for the transformation of a cliché spoken by Mrs. Porter, the widow of a judge. Through the third-person points of view of four other characters, and her own as well, the reader has gotten the impression that Mrs. Porter is a cold, unfeeling woman, methodically preparing for her husband's funeral. At the end of the day, near the end of the novel, she stands alone on the back porch; she has been calling the names of the stars and taking one of her paper towels from the line where she had let it dry all day. The moment is perceived from her daughter Katherine's point of view:

> "I'm going to miss your father," her mother said, and Katherine turned, her hand on the stair rail, as if another person, not her mother, had spoken. A voice, perhaps, from one of the letters she never mailed. Katherine wanted to speak, but now that this voice had spoken to her, broken the long silence, she could hardly believe what she heard (302).

In the death-in-the-family situation, no expression is more superficially cliché than "I'm going to miss" the deceased. But in the context Morris prepares, it becomes one of the most moving clichés in all of Morris and one of the most moving lines in contemporary literature.

Wright Morris has also written a good deal *about* the negative and positive effect of the cliché: "Every cliché once had its moment of truth. At the moment of conception it was a new and wonderful thing." "Clichés, bless them, both destroy life and make it possible." See Morris's, "Made in U.S.A." in Bibliography.

Clichés are especially alluring to photographers of all kinds, who too seldom transform them. Wright Morris has been a master photographer almost as long as he has been a writer. In the process of experimenting with phototext techniques, Morris discovered, experienced, the difference between "exposure" and "revelation." For him, the farmer's life exemplifies the sanctity of privacy. On his uncle's farm in Nebraska in the early forties, he photographed a bed, which clearly showed a human shape in the sagging mattress and springs, a chamber pot squatting under it beside the farmer's shoes. One may imagine Morris in his darkroom, watching the image rise toward him out of the solution in the pan. The sight of the chamber pot, a folksy, Norman Rockwell cliché invasion of privacy, exposure of character, makes Morris cringe, there in the dark, with shame. "In the honest guise of telling the facts," Morris wrote, "this photograph ended up lying, since in such a context the larger statement . . . the revelation could not be heard above the shout." Shock, even comic shock, "is the technique of invasion, and it marks a signal failure of art," the purpose of which is to reveal.

He rejected that photograph. He kept a shot of another bed without a pot. Its details harmonized with the conception, a portrait not of a cliché habit but of a way of life, an eloquent expression of the atmosphere and the meaning of privacy. The effect of this experience on Morris may be seen in the photograph itself on p. 134 of *The Home Place* and read in the accompanying fictional passage on pp. 132 and 135.

38 | Does your style lack a *play on words?*

"Lack" is relevant only if your story would benefit from such play. Wright Morris's predisposition to play on words, sometimes to the point of tiresomeness, but usually to the reader's delight, is evident in everything he writes. "The Ram in the Thicket":

Although he had been through this a thousand times it seemed he was never ready for it, never knew when it would happen, never felt anything but nearly sick.

Man and Boy version:

> Although he had been through this a thousand times—into it, that is, he had never been through it—he was never ready for it, somehow it always took him by surprise. And after all these times it never left him anything but sick.

Is your style barren of *puns* and *epigrams*? Usually, you do well to shun puns and epigrams because the writer's love of language and the opportunities language provides for games and horseplay often lead you astray, but it is certainly true that fictive language by its nature is playful. A particular story or section of a novel may then benefit from the use of puns or epigrams.

In Joyce's *A Portrait of the Artist as a Young Man*, Stephen Dedalus and other characters, and the author himself, indulge in quite a number of epigrammatic statements, but in the early version, *Stephen Hero*, there are a few too many. Joyce cut this one: "It seems to me you do not care what banality a man expresses so long as he expresses it in Irish."

These are among the novels more heavily laden with epigrams: Joris-Karl Huysmans, *Against the Grain*; Oscar Wilde, *The Picture of Dorian Gray*; Walter Pater, *Marius the Epicurean*; George Gissing, *The Private Papers of Henry Ryecroft*; most of the fiction of John Cheever and John Updike.

39 | Is your *syntax* awkward or contorted?

Syntax is the arrangement of words, phrases, clauses—the structure of the sentence. Sounds deadly dull, but not to Flaubert, who said that "a phrase is an adventure."

Samuel Butler, no avowed stylist but clearly a practicing one, may have regarded the idea of syntax as dull, but duller to him apparently was contortion in his sentence structure:

> Here, indeed, this freak of fortune was felt to be all the more cruel on account of the impossibility of resenting it openly; but this was nothing to the delighted grandfather.

What was nothing? Butler recast the first clause of the sentence: "But the delighted grandfather cared nothing about this." What was "this"?

Butler cut "about this" and finished with "for what the John Pontifexes might feel or not feel" (*The Way of All Flesh*).

George Eliot often worked her syntax into awkward twists and turns.

> "What can *I* do, Tertius?" said Rosamond, turning her eyes on him again. That little speech of four words, like so many others in all languages, is capable by varied inflexions of voices of expressing all states of mind from helpless dimness to exhaustive argumentation. . . .

Eliot felt the contortion occur at "inflexions of voices" and she heard all those "of" phrases; she revised to get "is capable by varied vocal inflexions of expressing," thus eliminating the contortion and one of the "of" phrases (*Middlemarch*).

40 | Have you used *adjectives* and *adverbs* indiscriminately?

Some people think one Thomas Wolfe was one too many. What they have in mind is such adjective-laden passages as this one:

> At night, great trains will pass us in the timeless spell of an unsleeping hypnosis, and endless, and unfathomable stupefaction. Then suddenly in the unwaking never sleeping century of the night, the sensual limbs of carnal whited nakedness that stir with drowsy silken warmth in the green secrecies of Lower Seven, the slow swelling and lonely and swarmhaunted land—and suddenly, suddenly, silence and thick hardening lust of dark exultant joy, the dreamlike passage of Virginia!
> —Then in the watches of the night a pause, the sudden silence of up-welling night, and unseen faces, voices, laughter, and farewells upon a lonely little night-time station—the lost and lonely voices of Americans:—

Other people lament the fact that there was only one Thomas Wolfe and argue, as Faulkner did, that the distinctive effect of his adjective-and-adverb-laden prose is one of the achievements of American literature.

What can depend upon a mere choice of adjective? Usually, enough, but not a great deal. But when Nick summed up his own character at the end of Chapter 3 of *The Great Gatsby* by saying, "I am one of the few decent people that I have ever known," he risked losing quite a few readers; Fitzgerald changed "decent" to "honest" and the line became somewhat charming and finally ambiguous (he is and he isn't), perhaps ironic.

Consider this line from a draft of *The Great Gatsby*:

> Gatsby believed in the green light, the orgastic future that year by year recedes before us.

Much of the novel depends upon the adjective "orgastic," which appears at the end of the book. " 'Orgastic' is the adjective for 'orgasm,' " Fitzgerald explained to his editor, Maxwell Perkins, "and it expresses exactly the intended ecstasy." Gatsby's dream and Daisy, the ideal embodiment of that dream, are inseparable. The orgastic consummation did not take place for him, or for Nick and other Americans. So for Fitzgerald this adjective, in the spirit of de Maupassant and Stendhal, is vital. The only problem is that you will not find it in most editions of the novel, beginning with the first, because Perkins insisted it was dirty and prevailed over Fitzgerald; the word substituted is "orgiastic," the adjective for "orgy," and so at the end the entire novel is thrown out of kilter. But now you know.

The standard advice, and it's good advice, is to go easy on the adjectives and the adverbs because in most cases two adjectives for one noun compete with each other for the reader's fullest response and both tend to lose; adverbs modifying verbs tend also to dilute the impact of the verb: " 'Die!' he shouted insanely." The word "die," with its exclamation point, is already too much, "shouted" is implied, and "insanely" overwhelms all three words before it. The effort collapses under its competing components.

"Whatever you want to say, there is only one word to express it," said de Maupassant, "one verb to set it in motion and only one adjective to describe it." Stendhal would have agreed. "Often I ponder a quarter of an hour," he said, "whether to place an adjective before or after its noun."

41 | Do you use too many vague *pronouns*?

When pronouns are made to signify too many persons, places, and things, the effect is to disorient the reader. "He" who? "It" what? First drafts are usually overpopulated with pronouns because the writer is rushing ahead and even vague pronouns are a convenient reference to what he has in mind; they make do until later. The problem for the reader arises when later never comes, when the writer neglects to assign to as many pronouns as he can a more specific name. Often the writer himself doesn't remember what the pronoun refers to. A sloppy use of "this," for instance, when the reference is unclear, causes a lapse in your reader's attention and interest.

In the 1887 edition of *Daisy Miller*, Henry James's repeated use of "it" was clear enough but stultifying:

> Winterbourne walked to the middle of the arena, to take a more general glance, intending thereafter to make a hasty retreat. The great cross in the centre was covered with shadow; it was only as he drew near it that he made it out distinctly.

For the definitive edition, James eliminated two of the "its": "The great cross in the centre was almost obscured; only as he drew near did he make it out distinctly."

Virginia Woolf uses "it" effectively as a pronoun reference in "Kew Gardens" as a way of focusing the reader's attention upon the atmosphere she has cumulatively evoked: the ecological interaction of human mind and flesh with nature.

> "Isn't it worth sixpence?" [a girl asks her boyfriend.]
> "What's 'it' —what do you mean by 'it'?"
> "O anything—I mean—you know what I mean."

He does, actually, but the reader knows even more intensely.

"Revision word by word and sentence does follow, for me," says Paul Horgan, "not once, but many times, each for a different value." One time, perhaps, for pronoun values only.

42 | Do you use too many mechanical conjunctions or connectives?

Conjunctions *and* connective phrases are very important *when* succinctly *and* carefully used, *but* too many, awkwardly employed, lend an aura of the mechanical to your style, making it sound too formal, *as if* phrases were hooked together like boxcars rather than having a natural flow. I have stressed the conjunctions and connectives in the preceding sentence. Others are: "or," "so," "nor," "yet," "for," "after," "because," "if," "since," "till," "where," "while," "as," "although," "unless," "until," "also," "finally," "however."

Hemingway's mastery of "and" is seen in the opening paragraph of "In Another Country" and the very similar opening of *A Farewell to Arms*. The manuscripts for that novel show Hemingway, in the famous passage describing Frederic Henry's near death, for instance, controlling his use of "and":

I felt myself slide back as though my soul was sliding down a long tight wire through space and the wind and then it slid suddenly and stopped and I breathed and I was back.

He edited that that line to read: "The me that was gone out slid down that wire through nothing and the wind and then it jerked and stopped and I was back." Still too many "ands," ineffectively positioned. The final version reads:

Then I floated, and instead of going on I felt myself slide back. I breathed and I was back.

A recent addition to the "what every writer must read" (and reread) list is philosopher-novelist William Gass's essay "And," in which he finds enough brilliant things to say about the use of "and" in fiction (with astonishing examples) to fill twenty-six pages. When he delivered the piece as a lecture to a gathering of writers, he had their rapt attention. For Gass, words, style, are the power source of fiction. "And" is an instructive "for instance."

The anonymity of *and*, its very invisibility, recommends the word to the student of language, for when we really look at it, study it, listen to it, *and* no longer appears to be *and* at all . . . the unwatched word is meaningless . . . it falls on the page as it pleases . . . the watched word has many meanings, some of them profound; it has a wide range of functions, some of them essential; it has many lessons to teach us about language, some of them surprising; and it has metaphysical significance of an even salutary sort. . . . A single example from Gertrude Stein's "Melanctha" should be sufficient to show our small word's true and larger nature.

> "She tended Rose, and she was patient, submissive, soothing, and untiring, while the sullen, childish, cowardly, black Rosie grumbled and fussed and howled and made herself to be an abomination and like a simple beast."

Gass analyzes in detail the several aspects of each of the six different uses of "and" in that sentence. And of course he quotes from a Hemingway story, "After the Storm," and gives it the same scrutiny.

43 | Do you dull your style in your frequency and use of *prepositions*?

"Of" and "with" are, by far, the two prepositions that contribute most to dullness and to an aura of the mechanical.

> Lydgate startled and jarred, looked up in silence for a moment with the air of a man who has been disturbed in his sleep. Then with the recovery of an unpleasant consciousness, he asked, "How do you know?"

George Eliot wants the reader of *Middlemarch* to experience "startled and jarred," but her use of "in silence" and more especially of the two "with" phrases dulls impact. She senses that and revises:

> Lydgate startled and jarred, looked up in silence for a moment like any man who has been disturbed in his sleep. Then flushing with an unpleasant consciousness, he asked, "How do you know?"

She cut the first "with"; the second one is less dull because of the rhythm of the phrasing. In many instances "with" can be avoided. " 'I'm very unhappy,' she said, with tears in her eyes." Simply omit the "with."

A companion piece to the article by William Gass on "and," cited in Question 42, is "The Ontology of the Sentence, or How to Make a World of Words," in *The World Within the Word*, pp. 308-38, in which he examines the word "of," discussing fourteen different uses that create ambiguity.

Wright Morris uses prepositions, especially "up" and "down" and "in" and "out," in such a way that they provide emphasis and contribute a sense of motion to his style: "Turning *up* the water, she sat *down* on the stool." "The rays that had soaked *into* him were now sweating *out*." "The fog is *in*. The lights are *out*." "She was cold *down* where it would take some time to thaw her *out*."

44 | Have you committed *grammatical errors*?

Most writers pick up a sense of proper grammar in the practice of writing and out of a natural love of the way good writing feels and sounds, but that same love of sound and rhythm may distract you from the presence in your story of unfortunate grammatical errors. A predisposition to regard concern for grammar as tedious or uncreative may make you inattentive to possible problems, so you may need to see the consequences of a few horrors to convince you that neglect of grammar can do harm.

"Naked, he carried her into the bedroom." Sounds fine, except that it is she who is naked, not he. "She kept gumdrops while ironing in the sugar bowl." If she irons in the sugar bowl, she needs something stronger than gum drops. Dangling modifiers plague the best writers; searching for variety in sentence structure, they often like the sound but fail to notice the senselessness. The thrill in discovering lines such as these in revision is in knowing that you have, in advance, disarmed hostile reviewers. If you fail to catch them, your second chance may not come until all your works are reissued in red morocco leather bindings.

. . . we sat down side by side in a wicker settee and taking her face in her hands, as if feeling its lovely shape, Daisy's eyes moved gradually out into the darkness.

Fitzgerald knew, of course, that Daisy's eyes did not take her face in their hands. He revised:

Daisy took her face in her hands as if feeling its lovely shape, and her eyes moved gradually out into the velvet dusk.

If you were one of those who unburdened yourself of your grammar handbook only moments after taking your final freshman-English exam,

you cannot do better than to repair the damage with William Strunk and
E. B. White's *The Elements of Style*, seventy pages of lucid, witty prose
and examples.

45 | Are the *verb tenses* inconsistent?

Inconsistent verb tenses are inconsistent with the purpose of the verb,
which is to propel the reader forward. Encounters with inconsistent verb
tenses delay the reader as long as it takes him to do your work for you.
Irritated, he stumbles onward, hoping it won't happen again. It usually
does.

Now and then, you may find that a *controlled* shift in the verb tense is
effective, as when Katherine Anne Porter used it in "Flowering Judas":

> He goes away. Laura knows his mood has changed, she will not see
> him any more for a while. . . . Now she is free, and she thinks, I must
> run while there is time. But she does not go.

Having deliberately used the present tense (very unusual in those days)
as one way to counteract the static quality of her predominate method (a
series of tableaux vivants showing Laura's daily activities and her typical
relationships), and to express a sense of Laura's captivity in an inactive
present tense (no living sense of a past, no prospects for a future), Porter
suddenly shifts at the end into the past tense to convey a sense of death in
life:

> The tolling of the midnight bell is a signal, but what does it mean?
> . . . Laura cried No! and at the sound of her own voice, she awoke
> trembling, and was afraid to sleep again.

"A change of tense," says Wallace Hildick, "can produce a heightening
of tension."

Inconsistency is appropriate in stories told by a narrator in the oral
tradition, as Frank O'Connor's "Guests of the Nation" seems to be.
Gerard, the narrator of Jorge Semprun's *The Long Voyage*, shifts from
past to present tense as he senses opportunities for emphasis; the shift
also has thematic relevance in this story about a survivor of a Nazi
death camp: all time is one in the consciousness that evaluates and shapes
its own raw material, as Gerard's does. A major example of effective use

of the device of shifting back and forth from present to past tense, somewhat ambiguously, but on purpose, is Albert Camus's *The Stranger*:

> Mother died today. Or, maybe yesterday. I can't be sure. . . . The funeral will bring it home to me, put an official seal on it, so to speak. . . . I took the two o'clock bus.

In much of recent fiction, use of present tense has become fashionable, as in some of the stories of Raymond Carver.

46 | Does your use of *punctuation* fail to serve a conscious and controlled effect?

The assumption here is that you have consciously tried and failed to achieve some sort of effect with an unconventional use of punctuation or by refraining from using it in the way readers normally expect its usage. For an extreme example of what I mean, I naturally turn to Gertrude Stein, who was preoccupied with the possibilities:

> As a wife has a cow a love story.
> As a love story, as a wife has a cow, a love story.
> Not and now, now and not, not and now, by and by not and now, as not, as soon as not not and now, now as soon now now as soon, now as soon as soon as now. Just as soon just now just now just as soon just as soon as now. Just as soon as now.

Stein has obviously given some thought to where she will and where she will not use commas and periods. She imagines possibilities and tries them out, and what we have here is, as a Stein work, inevitable. This is and is not a special case, because all cases in fiction are special. Here is Stein on punctuation: "So now to come to the real question—of punctuation, periods, commas, colons, semi-colons and capitals and small letters. I have had a long and complicated life with all these."

Faulkner often experimented with punctuation and typography. One of the things he did in *The Sound and the Fury* was to devise a new punctuation scheme for dialog in relation to the speaker. " 'Now, just listen at you,' Luster said" was the way he did it in manuscript, but " 'Now, just listen to you.' Luster said" is the way he consistently did it in the Benjy section, with no comma after "you," as the convention requires. In *Absalom, Absalom!* he used a very intricate system of punctuation, not always consistent, but the manuscript shows that he deliberately made changes to fine-tune the effect he wanted.

Sloppy punctuation can lead, like grammatical errors, to some horrendous distortions of meaning at most and to unintentional ambiguity at least. You don't want to work long and hard on a passage to create an important effect and then wreck the whole thing with a misplaced comma.

In "A Note on the Text" for the Riverside edition of *The House of the Seven Gables* the consequences of Hawthorne's sloppiness in punctuating are described, with examples, one of which is: "A powerful, excitement had given him energy and vivacity."

Some strict rules of punctuation must be violated in fiction. "He loved her. He wanted to leave her. He hated her. He wanted to live with her forever." That's correct, as opposed to a series of comma splices, but in context and for a reason, and if the device is used now and then in the story so that it doesn't seem arbitrary, a more effective punctuation might be: "He loved her, he wanted to leave her, he hated her, he wanted to live with her forever." For one thing, the tone and feel is totally different with the comma splices, and that counts for more than correct punctuation.

Commas may sometimes be more effective than conjunctions. In "The Ram in the Thicket," Morris writes:

He added half a cup, then measured three heaping tablespoons of coffee into the bottom of the double boiler, buttoned his pants.

He revised that sentence for the novel version, *Man and Boy*, but for reasons other than punctuation:

As the water had boiled down considerably he added half a cup, wiped the steam from the face of the stove clock.

In both versions the last comma enables Morris to sustain a sense of ongoing action, which "and buttoned" or "and wiped" would have impeded.

Conrad spent three days reworking the tense and the punctuation of the last paragraph of *Heart of Darkness*. He probably had that kind of dedication while writing his first novel, *Almayer's Folly*, but he first wrote each of the following sentences without commas; imagine the effect of each of them without their commas: "Shortly after, the murmur of many voices reached him across the water." "And as he drank, his teeth chattered against the glass." "When she attempted to speak, her first words were lost in a stifled sob." "Here is where you can land, white men." Macmillan's copy editor put the commas in. You can expect most copy editors to come behind you, undoing all your special effects with punctuation, but you can also hope they will be vigilant where you have not been.

"Give me the right word," said Joseph Conrad, "and the right accent and I will move the world." Conrad was the kind of writer for whom that effect might well hang upon the placement of a comma. Every morning Conrad's wife locked him in his study (at his request, of course). One day, when she released him for lunch, she asked, "Joseph, what did you accomplish this morning?" He said, exultantly, "I put in a comma." After lunch, she locked him in again. When she released him for dinner, she asked, expectantly, "And what did you achieve this afternoon, Joseph?" He said, with a sense of accomplishment, "I took the comma out."

Semicolons in fiction lend it an aura of the stiff and formal. But not always. Some writers underpunctuate, some overpunctuate, some even overuse dashes. You can, of course, do whatever you want, as long as you know what you want to do, and as long as you actually succeed in doing it.

One way to achieve a sense of informality is to increase contractions, especially in the first-person, but also in the third-person, central-intelligence point of view. "I did not go to bed immediately." Depending upon the context, it sounds more natural to say, "I didn't go to bed immediately." If the author himself says, "He did not go to bed immediately," the "did not" carries more force than it is intended to. Henry James, as a pervasive general rule in revising his works for the New York editions, increased contractions.

47 | Have you used a singular where a *plural* would be more effective?

An example from the end of *The Great Gatsby* may persuade you that the question is not trivial:

> So we beat on, a boat against the current, borne back ceaselessly into the past.

That was probably not a lapse. Fitzgerald may have had in mind the image of "we" as being like a single boat. That metaphor is appropriate in the sense that Nick, Gatsby, Daisy, Tom, and Jordan were representatives of their generation. But Nick has learned that each person, especially himself, moves on alone. Fitzgerald revised:

> So we beat on, boats against the current, borne back ceaselessly into the past.

48 | Does your style lack economy?

The answers to all these questions of style depend upon the context for each sentence you are considering. Generally, less, given the context, is more. Hemingway was exceedingly conscious of the function of economy, as the second version of this paragraph from *A Farewell to Arms* shows:

> There was a whistling that changed to an in rushing scream of air and then a flash and crash outside in the brick yard. Then a bump and a sustained incoming shriek of air that exploded with a roar, the crash of high explosive tearing steel apart on contact and vomiting earth and brick.

> A big shell came in and burst outside in the brick yard. Another burst and in the noise you could hear the smaller noise of brick and dirt raining down.

For demonstrations of economy, compression, and compactness, see most of Hemingway's stories, especially "The Killers" and "A Clean, Well-Lighted Place"; James M. Cain's *The Postman Always Rings Twice*; Albert Camus's *The Stranger*; and the stories of Raymond Carver. Compare Joyce's *Stephen Hero* with *A Portrait of the Artist as a Young Man*. Compare the two versions of Eudora Welty's "Where Is the Voice Coming From?" in John Kuehl's *Creative Writing and Rewriting*.

49 | Have you drifted too early into *lyrical* passages?

If you write the first draft in a lyrical mood, you may rush at the first opportunity to express it, as Fitzgerald did at the end of the first chapter of *The Great Gatsby*. Nick, in character, begins that chapter with the staid and sober line (which put me off reading the rest for twenty years) "In my younger and more vulnerable years my father gave me some advice that I have been turning over in my mind ever since." It was probably the author himself who got carried away at the end of that first chapter, because the truly magnificent, lyrical passages that now end the book itself came much too early in the early draft. Fitzgerald retains a more restrained lyrical passage; the rest of the novel seems to flow toward a recapturing of those two passages that Fitzgerald moved to the end.

James Joyce delays the overtly lyrical strain in "The Dead" until the last paragraph. For comparison, see the last paragraph of "The Day the Flowers Came," p. 282. Thomas Wolfe is notorious for his frequent lunges into lyricism, but it is too seldom noted that even in his first novel, a Byronic irony and satire alternate with the lyricism. A comparison of *Look Homeward, Angel* with his last novel, *You Can't Go Home Again*, reveals Wolfe's maturing tendency to restrain the lyricism and to achieve a controlled balance between the lyrical and the satirical.

"We are in fact rotten with lyricism," said Zola; "we believe, quite wrongly, that the grand style is the product of some sublime terror always on the verge of pitching over into frenzy; the grand style is achieved through logic and clarity."

50 | Are parts of your story overwritten?

"Anything that is written to please the author is worthless," said Blaise Pascal. Is your story bloated with purple patches? A purple patch is a pseudopoetic, hyperlyrical passage that calls attention to itself by inflating a situation, as in a description of the protagonist waking up in the morning full of angst, or walking down a city street, assaulted by dehumanizing technology and insensitive crowds, or in a description of the sky, or in a digressive philosophical statement.

By example, Great Writers may teach us a great many things. In the following verbose and redundant version of the opening of his fourteenth novel, *The Rescue*, Conrad teaches us that writers do not learn to write, they teach themselves to write each story, one at a time:

> There is no peace like the peace of narrow seas. The great ocean knows not the perfect rest, the unruffled glitter, the smooth repose of seas held in close bondage by the unyielding grasp of enclosing lands.

The narrow sea, captive, sleeps profoundly; forgetting the freedom of great winds that sweep round the globe; and wakes up now and then only to short-lived furious and foaming rages; to quick gales that stirring up its most intimate depths, are followed by long periods of exhausted respose; a repose which would resemble death itself, were it not for the tender murmur exhaled—like a faint and subtle perfume—from the lacelike tracery of foam fringing the reefs the shallows, the low, dark coasts of scented and mysterious islands.

Conrad goes on laboriously to describe the look of the sea when the sun rises, when it sets, when night comes; when the ocean is in repose, when it's raging, and what lurks under the surface. But he taught himself how to write *The Rescue*, as the opening page of the published version will show. Never mind that it's not one of his best novels.

"If a writer of prose knows enough about what he is writing about," said Ernest Hemingway, "he may omit things that he knows and the reader, if the writer is writing truly enough, will have a feeling of those things as strongly as though the writer had stated them. The dignity of movement of an iceberg is due to only one-eighth of it being above water." "All good writing," said Fitzgerald, "is swimming under water and holding your breath." (Compare this with Wright Morris's comment quoted in Question 23.)

Does your style lack subtlety? Blatancy will enable your reader to move from sentence to sentence, but the dominant experience will be one of blatancy. Subtlety engages your reader's own faculties—emotions, imagination, intellect. Readers who must participate through subtlety and other devices have a deeper, more intense, more lasting experience. Subtlety is not the province only of the sophisticated, refined, or snobbish reader. A subtle phrase or sentence may in actuality stimulate a violent response.

Do unintentional hyperboles obtrude?

Intentional hyperbole is exaggeration for effect; unintentional hyperbole is rhetoric in excess of the occasion. The unintentional hyperbole often stands in for the imagination when the writer must describe mental anguish or physical violence. An extreme mental state in the character may produce ineffective hyperboles in the style. As Gore Vidal opens *The City and the Pillar*, the hero, Jim Willard, is getting drunk; the reader doesn't know that he has just murdered his childhood friend, but Vidal is full of that knowledge and thus of rhetoric.

At last he came to a decision. He would have to desert the booth. He would have to talk to the man behind the bar. It was a long way to go but he was ready to make the journey.

Jim's emotional state is extreme and the style is extreme, but the diction ("decision," "desert," "long way," "journey") is excessive for the specific act being described.

Revising the novel twenty years later, Vidal tries to undo some of these excesses:

At last he came to a decision. He would leave the booth and go talk to the man behind the bar. It was a long voyage but he was ready for it.

The revision makes clear Vidal's intention to use hyperbole, sustained over twenty years, but he also knows he has gone too far. He rearranges the syntax and drops "desert," but the misguided hyperbole of the journey persists, although his reason for changing it is good; Willard was a merchant seaman, so "voyage" fits better than "journey," but nothing has changed to make the hyperbole fit the occasion—the simple act of going from booth to bar. The effect, then, of the exaggeration is that it seems ludicrous, like the hackneyed line "She was so weary it took an eternity to get out of bed."

Are some passages philosophically *pretentious*, given their contexts? There is a natural tendency in the first draft to get it all down, and the easiest way to do that is to *tell*, because to show requires the bringing to bear of the full force of the craft of writing, which takes more time and conscious effort than is possible in the writing of the first draft as most writers do it. Thematic intentions tend to get overtly expressed in long philosophical passages, especially when the point of view is omniscient or first-person; sometimes such passages intrude as violations of the third-person, central-intelligence point of view. In the first draft, the writer is often the principal reader for such passages because he is trying to explain to himself the meaning of it all. The task of revision is to find ways to embody those images in character behavior, in images, etc. The term "philosophically pretentious" applies only when the philosophical passage fails to be profound. Thomas Mann recorded in his diary: "Difficulty with the chapter," concerning *Doctor Faustus*, a philosophical novel. "Must keep back certain cherished items that would overload the book."

Is your style *pseudoliterary*? The literary-tone fallacy plagues the beginning writer, but most writers continue to commit it. The writer writes what he hopes will become literature. How does literature *sound*? Victorian, unfortunately. Is your style turgid with formal Victorian syntax? D. H. Lawrence wrote "lamentation and self-communication"; "lament and self-pity" is how that got changed for the publication of "Odour of Chrysanthemums." The young writer who rebels against public-school exposure to literature often, ironically, turns, when he begins, to the models most available, which, because he has read very little fiction, are those he hates most in the Victorian mode. To get the "literary tone," the writer resorts to stock phrases, formal phrases, trite observations, overloading his style with abstractions and generalizations. It never occurs to him that clichés, always obsequiously handy in the wings of one's half-conscious first-draft writing state, may be transformed in the stylistic imagination.

A less important but irritating type of misplaced emphasis is the tedious reproduction of trivia, or the lighting-a-cigarette fallacy. The hero's most trivial action is described as though stars were altered in their courses. The reader regards that kind of cause and effect as purely literary. See Question 173.

Is your style *pseudo-original*? The term applies when style conveys an aura of originality—as if the writer seems convinced it is, when it is only faintly reminiscent of someone else's originality, Gertrude Stein's, Samuel Beckett's, Joyce's, Faulkner's. The reader is embarrassed and irritated.

"One never tires of anything that is well written," said Flaubert. "Style is life: Indeed it is the life-blood of thought! . . . I shall try to show why aesthetic criticism has remained so far behind historical and scientific criticism: it *had no foundation*. The knowledge everyone lacked was *analysis of style*, the understanding of how a phrase is constructed and articulated."

"I have come into my strength," said W. B. Yeats, "and words obey my call."

51 | Are parts of your story *underwritten* in the negative sense?

I do not mean here those parts of the narrative that may cry out for further development, but those sentences or passages that are too skimpy or slapdash as a natural consequence of first-draft writing.

Even late in the revision process, George Meredith saw that an all-important comment on his hero at the end of *The Tragic Comedians* was underwritten:

> [Comparison of Alvan] amid the multitudinously simple of the world, stamped him a Tragic Comedian. The characters of the hosts of men are of the simple order of the comic. . . .

The tip-off may have been the capitalization of the key term of the novel, "Tragic Comedian"—one of the many devices writers unconsciously use to convince themselves they have written what they have felt, imagined, and thought. Meredith did not settle for that:

> [something] amid the multitudinously simple of the world, stamped him a tragic comedian: that is, a grand pretender, a self-deceiver, one of the lividly ludicrous, whom we cannot laugh at, but must contemplate, to distinguish where their character strikes the note of discord with life; for otherwise, in the reflection of their history, life will seem a thing demoniacally inclined by fits to antic and dive into gulfs. The characters of the hosts of men are of the simple order of the comic. . . .

"That is" is almost a declaration to himself that Meredith is developing a passage that is underwritten.

Even in the galley stage, Faulkner saw moments, in *Sanctuary*, that needed further development, especially given his greatly revised conception of the work; but this passage in almost any context seems underwritten:

> Lee was in our room. He came to the door and looked at me and I said "Yes. What. What is it." About noon the car came and he sent word for the sheriff.

Faulkner shifts from first person to third person:

> The blind man was sitting on the front porch, in the sun. When she entered the hall, she was walking fast. She was not aware of the child's thin weight. She found Goodwin in their bedroom. He was in the act of putting on a frayed tie; looking at him, she saw that he had just shaved. "Yes," she said. "What is it? What is it?"

The further development continues for another page or so.

52 | Do you overindulge in *abstract* statements?

A dominant tendency in the first draft is to overindulge in abstractions and generalizations. This frame of mind produces a barrage of passive verbs. For example, the opening pages often consist almost entirely of statements about the protagonist's habitual behavior, introducing each with a dull "he would": "He would take the subway to work and then he would call Melissa." Very little happens in the immediate present. The phrase "he would" appears repeatedly throughout the first 150 pages of Herbert Gold's four-hundred-page novel *Salt*, creating a deadening effect. By contrast, when Gold uses concrete language, he uses it so well, he only increases irritation with the dull generalizations. A controlled use of generalization, a major characteristic of nonfiction style, may function well in fiction.

But in the first draft, writers often delude themselves into feeling that an impressive-sounding abstraction expresses thought and emotion forcefully.

Abstractions or generalizations leave a reader cold, and he drops out of the story momentarily. Abstract phrases convey a quality of timelessness; concrete phrases stimulate a sense of the here and now.

General words, such as "beautiful," "terrific," "enormous," "sad," "mysterious," "life," "death," "love," "hate," almost never have the effect intended.

One of the most thoroughly revised passages in Hemingway's *A Farewell to Arms* is one which we may take as a credo for the underwritten style:

I was always embarrassed by the words sacred, glorious, and sacrifice, and the expression in vain. We had heard them, sometimes standing in the rain almost out of earshot, so that only the shouted words came through, and read them, on proclamations that were slapped up by billposters over other proclamations, now for a long time, and I had seen nothing sacred, and the things that were called glorious had no glory and the sacrifices were like the stockyards at Chicago if nothing was done with the meat except to bury it. There were many words that you could not stand to hear and finally only the names of places had dignity. Certain numbers were the same way and certain dates and these with the names of places were all you could say and have them mean anything. Abstract words such as glory, honor, courage, or hallow were obscene beside the concrete names of villages, the numbers of roads, the names of rivers, the numbers of regiments and the dates.

Compare with early version: see Reynolds in Bibliography.

It is good to be able to draw upon a masterpiece for examples of what not to do. Here are several examples of abstractions or generalizations that became concrete images in Henry James's *The Portrait of a Lady*: "Their multifarious colloquies" became "their plunge . . . into the deeps of talk." Henrietta "was very well dressed" became "she rustled, she shimmered." The Countess "entered the room with a great deal of expression" became the Countess "entered the room with a flutter through the air." Madame Merle "referred everything to Isabel" became Madame Merle "appealed to her as if she had been on the stage, but she could ignore any learnt cue without spoiling the scene." Here is a longer passage:

> It pleased Isabel to believe that he had the qualities of a famous captain, and she answered that, if it would help him on, she shouldn't object to a war—a speech which ranked among the three or four most encouraging ones he had elicited from her, and of which the value was not diminished by her subsequent regret at having said anything so heartless, inasmuch as she never communicated this regret to him.

Those who cannot read Henry James without squirming in agony have such passages in mind when they refrain, but they give him enough credit for his ability to embody abstractions in vivid images, as when he rewrote that passage:

> It pleased Isabel to believe that he might have ridden, on a plunging steed, the whirlwind of a great war—a war like the Civil strife that had over-darkened her conscious childhood and his ripening youth.

Here concrete and general words enhance each other.

The first several pages of the first draft of Virginia Woolf's *Mrs. Dalloway* are much too general, especially since there is no context to enhance them with implications. See Hildick, *Word for Word*.

Generalizations are not, of course, to be excluded altogether; the problem is one of degree. A consistent and effective use of abstract words and phrases may be seen in the fiction of Saul Bellow, especially in *Mr.*

Sammler's Planet. Anaïs Nin describes a different and more positive type of abstraction in *The Novel of the Future* (pp. 24-43).

"Go in fear of abstractions," said Ezra Pound to the Imagist poets.

Do you fail to embody all, or most, of your abstractions and generalizations, especially about character and meaning, in vivid images? "Never present ideas," said André Gide, "except in terms of temperaments and characters."

See "The Day the Flowers Came," comment 23, p. 280, comment 23, p. 281.

53 | Is the *tone* of your style inappropriate?

Tone is the pervasive sense of the writer's attitude toward his characters and their dilemmas and/or his readers. Ask yourself: Have I imagined the appropriate tone for the kind of experience I am trying to create?

One of the achievements of Samuel Butler's *The Way of All Flesh* is control of tone, and that is an achievement of revision. The narrator describes "the sense of importance which was given us by our having been intimate with someone who had been interesting enough to die." The tone went wrong in the last four words. "Who had actually died" struck the right note in the context, and for Butler's attitude. In another place, another death: "Before the next sunset the poor old man was gone." The sentimental tone is un-Butler-like. "Before the next sunset he was gone" sustains the Butler tone.

The tone of a writer's narrating voice is revealed in the writer's attitude toward his raw material or his subject. The pervasive tone of a work may be tragic, comic, ironic, skeptical, pessimistic, compassionate, sentimental, formal, informal, and so on. The author's distance in relation to his story affects his tone. By becoming too chummy with the reader, the writer commits the cute-tone fallacy, characteristic at one end of the literary spectrum of many women's magazine stories and at the other of "little" or underground magazine fiction. Somehow in the first draft writers often drift into a tone that is too precious, or too sarcastic or pseudosatirical, disrupting the overall tone.

Is the tone of your story consistent, is it fitting, controlled, is there a unity of tone, or do you deliberately set up two contrasting tones, as Robert Penn Warren does in *All the King's Men*? Jack Burden's tough-guy tone contrasts with his lyrical tone. Listen to the tone of *A Catcher in the Rye*, sustained throughout. Listen to the very different tone of *Moll*

Flanders's voice. Compare the tone of John Hawkes's "The Nearest Cemetery" with the novel version *Second Skin* (see Kuehl, *Creative Writing and Rewriting*, pp. 265-87).

Frank O'Connor's "First Confession" is a classic example of the humorous story with serious implications; the tone is certainly humorous. But O'Connor says the first two major versions were heavily serious in tone and effect. While he was writing *The Charterhouse of Parma*, "in order to acquire the correct tone," said Stendhal, "I occasionally read a few pages of the Code Civil. . . ." "Everything," said Sherwood Anderson, "is in the tone."

See "The Day the Flowers Came," p. 284.

54 | Is your style overloaded with *archaic* or *Latinate* words?

The overuse of Latinate words is not a major problem for writers today, but Thomas Hardy was typical of his time in his deliberate use of such words. However, in *The Return of the Native*, and a few others of his novels, he had a clear purpose—to create an aura of classical tragedy. Even so, as he revised to insert Latinate words, he also revised to cut them out when they seemed mechanical, pretentious, not part of the vocabulary he wanted for this novel. To avoid arbitrary use of Latinate words, Hardy changed "apex" to "spot," "irradiated" to "lit up," "oblivious" to "forgetful," "attire" to "dress," "evinced" to "shown." To make deliberate use of Latinate words, he changed "life" to "vitality," "went down" to "descended," "without" to "devoid," "richness" to "fertility," "thoughtful" to "meditative."

55 | Does your *diction* seem unconsidered?

Diction is the deliberate choice of words for a clear purpose.

The impact of the well-chosen word is suggested in *The Great Gatsby* by one of the novel's characters. Daisy describes Tom as "hulking."

"I hate that word hulking," objected Tom crossly.
"Hulking," insisted Daisy.

For Henry James each word was like a painter's daub of color on the large canvas. His uses of such key words as "romantic" and "vulgar" were often inserted into the later version of *The Portrait of a Lady*: "it entertained her to say nothing" became "it was more romantic"; "the public at large" became "a vulgar world."

Virginia Woolf struggles intricately with diction in the manuscript of *Mrs. Dalloway*: "And then," thought Clarissa Dalloway, "what a morning—fresh as if issued to children on a beach."

"What an ecstasy!" Not the best words. "What a miracle!" "Ecstasy" was better; she reinstated it. Still, it didn't look or sound right. "What a lark!" That was it. Somehow "lark" suggested "plunge," and she added, "What a plunge!" and that word was so right, she very soon used it again, and that suggested the word "wave" for the next passage. See Hildirk, *Word for Word*.

Because George Moore was a stylist he sometimes tried too hard to imagine a fresh way of saying such things as "He had been to a lawyer" in *Esther Waters*. What he came up with for the first edition was "He was applying himself to solution." For the revised edition, "He had been to a lawyer" sounded much more to the simple point.

"The difference between the right word and the nearly right word," said Mark Twain, "is the same as that between lightning and the lightning bug." That's one reason why William Gass said, "There are no events but words in fiction."

III CHARACTERS

56 | Do your characters evolve out of *point of view* and *style*?

Characterization is the creation of imaginary people through descriptions of physical appearance, actions, speech, thoughts, or what other characters say or think about them. "Character is action," said F. Scott Fitzgerald in *The Crack-up*. "Characters without action are lame," said Hugo von Hofmannsthal, "action without characters blind."

In the midst of one of the most painful revisions on record—working from page proofs of *The Deer Park* when the publication of the book was in doubt—Norman Mailer discovered in the sweat of the task that "the most powerful leverage in fiction comes from point of view," and that he had to admit "at last" that "the style was wrong, that it had been wrong from the time I started, that I had been strangling the life of my novel in a poetic prose which was too selfconsciously attractive and formal, . . . false to the life of my narrator who was the voice of my novel . . . a style which came out of nothing so much as my determination to prove I could muster a fine style." If he kept his style, he would have to change his narrator to fit it; if he wanted to recover the characters he had originally imagined, he would have to change "the style from the inside of each sentence," to search the galleys, "sentence by sentence, word for word."

The aim of his thorough revision was to make the characters evolve out of point of view and style. "Before, the story of Eitel had been told by O'Shaugnessy of the weak voice; now by a confident young man," and "giving O'Shaugnessy courage gave passion to the others."

Mailer seems to delight in sounding out for his readers the differences between the two versions in style, in voice, with simple examples, beginning with the opening:

> In the cactus wastes of Southern California, a distance of two hundred miles from the capital of cinema, is the town of Desert D'Or. There I went from the Air Force to look for a good time.

He changed "wastes" to "wild," but more important, he added, "as I choose to call it," after Desert D'Or; and most important for tone, he added this short fragment after "good time": "Some time ago." He says, "I did that with intent, to slow my readers from the start," to "poke" "the reader with its backed-up rhythm." To "and she gave me a sisterly kiss," he added, "Older sister." "Just two words, but I felt as if I had revealed some divine law of nature," bringing "an illumination and *division* to the cliché of the sisterly kiss." Mailer offers other examples of changes in his narrator's voice; for instance, "at least I was able to penetrate into the mysterious and magical belly of a movie star" becomes "I was led to discover the mysterious brain of a movie star."

As a novel about sexuality, told in what Mailer had thought was a style imbued with sexual energy, *The Deer Park* had offended his original publisher, who dropped it in page proofs; ironically, Mailer found himself changing some of the phrases to which the publisher had objected, not on moral but on aesthetic grounds. "Fount of power" for female genitalia became "thumb of power."

In "The Last Draft of *The Deer Park*" in *Advertisements for Myself*, Mailer offers a comparison between the first three pages of the page proofs and the published versions, five pages in the middle, and part of a later page.

Even so, the stylistic changes did not make a style most critics could praise. Some thought the style was terrible, a "blistering" criticism. "Having reshaped my words with an intensity of feeling I had not known before," wrote Mailer, "I could not understand why others were not overcome with my sense of life, of sex, and of sadness."

D.H. Lawrence's story of Lady Chatterley offers a rare opportunity to study, in three accessible, published versions, the ways a writer has reconceived one of his major characters—the gamekeeper, called Parkin in *The First Lady Chatterley* and in *John Thomas and Lady Jane* and Mellors in *Lady Chatterley's Lover*. For a summary of what to look for, see Mark Schorer's introduction to the Modern Library edition, *Lady Chatterley's Lover*, pp. xxviii-xxix.

57 | Does your *protagonist* fail to grow, experience changes in attitude or fortune?

The protagonist is the main character; the reader is usually for him. The antagonist is the character in conflict with the protagonist; the reader is usually opposed to him.

The reader is not content simply to watch the conflict develop and climax and be resolved; the conflict must have some effect upon the character with whom we emphathize. The growth of the character may be more apparent to the reader than to the character, with the implication that the character will realize that the growth has occurred later on, or that the character will simply act in the future out of that growth. The reader enjoys having a sense of that kind of future consequence.

Change in fortune usually occurs in stories that move primarily along plot lines, rather than psychological development. Changes in the protagonist's attitude are usually the result of a psychological process in which the character is his or her own antagonist. In early drafts, writers are not always certain where they want the emphasis—on change in attitude or fortune. The reader who says, "A fairly interesting story, but so what, what's the point?" probably feels that no growth or change has occurred for the protagonist. Why is that an important consideration—a major consideration in most instances? There is some enjoyment in imagining characters in stasis, in a static situation, but that is not enough; the enjoyment readers expect to have comes from imagining characters involved in some process of change that they can follow and care about.

In "The Chrysanthemums," John Steinbeck shows a woman experiencing a change in attitude. Two different versions of this famous story appear in various anthologies and in *The Long Valley*, a collection of related stories; each version is ambiguous about the nature of Eliza's change in attitude, but the fact that Steinbeck revised key passages after the story was published suggests that he was eager to clarify Eliza's character. In *Harper's*:

> Eliza's voice grew husky. She broke in on him: "I've never lived as you do, but I know what you mean. When the night is dark—the stars are sharp-pointed, and there's quiet. Why, you rise up and up!"
> Kneeling there, her hand went out toward his legs in the greasy black trousers. Her hesitant fingers almost touched the cloth. Then her hand dropped to the ground.

In *The Long Valley:*

> Elisa's voice grew husky. She broke in on him, "I've never lived as you do, but I know what you mean. When the night is dark—why, the stars are sharp-pointed, and there's quiet. Why, you rise up and up! Every pointed star gets driven into your body. It's like that. Hot and sharp and—lovely."
> Kneeling there, her hand went out toward his legs in the greasy black trousers. Her hesistant fingers almost touched the cloth. Then her hand dropped to the ground. She crouched low like a fawning dog.

Notice the lines added to each of the two paragraphs. Eliza gives the wandering tinker the chrysanthemums he has admired. When she is driving into town with her husband and sees the flowers dumped in the road (he had kept the pot to sell), the reader's interpretation of how she feels and of the kind of change that this event will cause depends upon the version he has read and the response to this key passage in that version. The lines Steinbeck added to each of the two paragraphs may seem sexual to some readers, but not necessarily to all. In any case, he is striving here to delineate growth and change in his protagonist.

58 | Does the *protagonist* fail to affect other characters?

The structure of the first major version of William Faulkner's *Sanctuary* derives from his focus on the point of view of Horace Benbow, a character who reacts to character relationships and events out of an almost psychotic need rather than initiating events or affecting other characters in dramatic ways. When Faulkner decided, in the galley stage, to restructure the novel more along dramatic-action lines than out of a rather closed psychological process, focus shifted to Popeye and Temple Drake, the two characters who most affect others. Attention to Horace had inflated Faulkner's third novel, *Flags in the Dust*; he cut most of the Horace material from that novel for the same reason. The short version was published as *Sartoris.*

F. Scott Fitzgerald's response to the complaint of his editor, Maxwell Perkins, that the character Jay Gatsby was too vague was that he had worried about the problem himself. His solution was rather unusual but crucial for his intentions in this particular novel. "His vagueness I can repair by *making more pointed*—this doesn't sound good but wait and see. It'll make him clear." Later, he wrote, "I had him for awhile, then lost him, and now I know I have him again." The most crucial changes cluster in Chapter 6, in which Gatsby's mythic image contrasts with his factual past. A comparison of the published facsimile of the manuscript with the published version of *The Great Gatsby* will illustrate this observation, as I can't do here without a great deal more space.

But this unusual, very conscious reversal process—delineation of a character by softening rather than sharpening focus—applies to Daisy as well and can be shown here. Fitzgerald wanted her to exist for the reader as well as for Gatsby as a kind of mythic, ideal beauty, one whose effect on Gatsby was finally negative:

> "Listen, Nick," she broke out suddenly, "did you ever hear what I said when my child was born?"
> "No, Daisy."
> "Well, she was less than an hour old and Tom was God knows where. I woke up out of the ether with an utterly abandoned feeling as if I'd been raped by a company of soldiers and left out in a field to die."

The simile that ends the last line gives a too realistic picture of Daisy if we are to be convinced by her effect on Gatsby (and on Nick), especially coming from Daisy herself, and this early in the novel. Fitzgerald revised it.

> Well, she was less than an hour old and Tom was God knows where. I woke up out of the ether with an utterly abandoned feeling . . . I said: "I hope she'll be a fool—that's the best thing a girl can be in this world, a beautiful little fool."

59 | Are any characters not *explored* fully enough?

Exploration of the possibilities of each character, major or minor, is a willful act of the imagination. Bring the technical function of your imagination into play by imagining what happens to your conception of a character's potential when you consider the possible point-of-view strategies. A character who is insufficiently created in the omniscient point of view may become far more complex when imagined in third-person, central-intelligence; if you decide that the omniscient remains the most expressive point of view, you may bring the now more complex character back into that perspective.

For instance, if you look at revisions Thomas Hardy made in *The Return of the Native*, you will see him trying to get the reddleman in focus in three distinctly different approaches. Hardy may have found it difficult to shift his imagination from the omniscient mode to a more subjective one. But at some point, he must have gotten into the reddleman's mind and imagined *his* perception of the other characters and events, and in that act, he created a more complex character. If so, he only *explored* the reddleman in the third-person, central-intelligence mode; he retained the overall omniscient mode for the entire novel, focusing now and then on the reddleman as a character, not just as a mysterious image moving elusively over the landscape.

Minor characters are, of course, most likely to be neglected in the first draft. Most of our energy goes into trying to develop major characters. But even major characters are often undeveloped in the first writing. At the other extreme, very minor characters sometimes have the potential to play more important roles. In writing his novella *The Pistol*, James Jones discovered that his imagination had not sufficiently explored the character O'Brien. His protagonist, Mast, has gotten hold of a pistol, something rare for men of his rank. "On the way down to the beaches he received only one comment on the pistol. A guy in the same truck but from another squad, a huge heavy-bearded black Irishman of twenty-two named O'Brien, asked him enviously where did he get the pistol?" From that mere mention in the draft, Jones developed O'Brien into the second-most-important character in the novella. In the published version, immediately after O'Brien asks Mast where he got the pistol, he offers to buy it. In that passage, Jones describes O'Brien and brings him alive in dialog. Passages of narrative summary develop his character further:

Mast could not help feeling rather smugly sorry for O'Brien, somewhat the same feeling a man who knows he has salvation experiences for one who knows he has not; but Mast did not know what he could be expected to do. There was only one pistol. And through fate, or luck, and a series of strangely unforeseeable happenings, it had been given to him, not O'Brien.

Quite plainly O'Brien talked about it. About this free-floating, unrecorded pistol loose at Makapoo in Mast's hands. Out of his hunger for it, plus his lack of success in getting hold of it, O'Brien had talked about it to somebody, if not everybody.

*   *   *

The offers to buy it ranged in price from twenty dollars to sixty dollars, none as high as the seventy dollars O'Brien had offered him under the stress of that first day.

You can see that Jones is exploring the possibilities of a character who began as a mere mention. O'Brien becomes a major character, more interesting in some ways than Mast.

To watch a writer make his character more complex, see James Jones's revision of *The Pistol* and Kay Boyle's revisions of "The Ballet of Central Park." To see a writer get to know his character more deeply over several revisions, see Wright Morris's *One Day*. The Jones, Boyle, and Morris revisions are in Kuehl's *Creative Writing and Rewriting*. To follow at length a writer's development in greater depth of an entire cast of characters, see Paterson, *The Making of "The Return of the Native,"* pp. 9, 17, 48, 59, 66, 75, 80, 102, 107.

60 | Are any *minor characters* overdeveloped?

The overdeveloped minor character is one of the several types of first-draft digressions that writers identify in the more objective mood of the revision process. The omniscient and the first-person points of view allow such a digression more than the third-person, central-intelligence point of view, because when you limit your narrative to the responses of a single character, the characters to whom he responds are much more likely to be relevant.

In *Stephen Hero*, Emma Clery, the girl Stephen is attracted to, appears often (pp. 46, 65, 152, 158, 187, 192, 196-99, 203, 215, 233); the scenes are realistic, with fairly long stretches of dialog. A few murky passages in *Stephen Hero* anticipate the carefully controlled few images devoted to her as an idealized figure (only her initials are given, E.C.) in *A Portrait of the Artist as a Young Man*. Here's *Stephen Hero*:

One rainy night when the streets were too bad for walking she took the Rathmines tram at the Pillar and as she held down her hand to him from the step, thanking him for his kindness and wishing him good-night, that episode of their childhood seemed to magnetize the minds of both at the same instant. The change of circumstances had reversed their positions, giving her the upper hand. He took her hand caressingly, caressing one after another the three lines on the back of her kid glove and numbering her knuckles, caressing also his own past towards which this inconsistent hater of inheritances was always lenient. They smiled at each other; and again in the center of her amiableness he discerned a point of illwill. . . .

The context for this episode is so murky and ill-defined, it is not clear whether Stephen is remembering it or whether it is happening in the present, when he and Emma are older. Joyce's allusion to "that episode of their childhood" contributes to the ambiguity. For *A Portrait*, Joyce carefully prepares a context for the episode and deliberately juxtaposes it to Stephen's memory of an overtly sexy girl, Eileen, thus by contrast emphasizing for the reader Stephen's idealization of Emma:

They seemed to listen, he on the upper step and she on the lower. She came up to his step many times and went down to hers again between their phrases and once or twice stood close beside him for some moments on the upper step, forgetting to go down, and then went down. His heart danced upon her movements. . . . Yet a voice within him spoke above the noise of his dancing heart, asking him would he take her gift to which he had only to stretch out his hand.

Stephen does not. In the *Portrait* version he is always more introspective, passive, "seemingly a tranquil watcher of the scene before him." Ten years later, he recalls that image of Emma on the tram:

They stood on the steps of the tram, he on the upper, she on the lower. She came up to his step many times between their phrases and went down again and once or twice remained beside him forgetting to go down and then went down. Let be! Let be!

The last words of the *Stephen Hero* version—"in the center of her amiableness he discerned a point of illwill"—are indicative of the realistic complexity of their relationship in that version. In *Portrait* also her attitude toward him is ambiguous but it is implied through the very few lines devoted to her in that version.

Confined in *Portrait* to recurrent images, Emma is only alluded to in another device—Stephen's diary in the novel's final pages. The problem with Emma in *Stephen Hero* is that her important function got lost because Joyce delineated her in the same detailed, realistic manner in which he created all other characters. Her fewer, more vivid appearances in *Portrait* have a more powerful effect.

For another example, see the 1972 Bobbs-Merrill edition of Thomas Hardy's *Jude the Obscure*, pp. xxxiiix-xxvi.

61 | Are the *relationships* among the characters unclear?

Unless you have a clear, controlled purpose to the contrary, make certain all the relationships of your characters are as clear on the page and for the reader as they are in your imagination. That is, of course, elementary, but if relationships remain unclear the consequences can be harmful, even disastrous. By "controlled purpose to the contrary," I mean that the vagueness or mysteriousness of a key relationship may be one of the effects you want—all the more reason not to distract readers with unintentional confusion of relationships.

You may want to explore possibilities that are latent in your draft. For instance, a brother-sister relationship may be less interesting for your purpose than an aunt-nephew. Reimagine your charcters and their relationships as many different ways as possible. One result of such an effort may be that you do not change, but are able to clarify, the relationships you have already set up.

An excellent example of the overall impact of changing and clarifying character relationships is seen in a comparison of Thomas Hardy's early manuscript of *The Return of the Native* with the published version. For instance, the reddleman goes from very clear relationships with local characters to being a man of mysterious origins. The boy Johnny was originally not the son of Susan Nunsuch. The heroine, Eustacia Vye, originally lived with her father instead of her grandfather. Thomasin Yoebright was originally the sister of the hero, Clym. The shifting of relationships forced a massive reorganization, the cutting and adding of all types of passages, including narrative.

In several of his revisions of "Idiots First," Bernard Malamud clarifies the nature of Mendel's and Ginzburg's relationship and thus of their conflict. See Kuehl's *Creative Writing and Rewriting*.

62 | Do you need to clarify the underlying *motives* of your characters?

Motivation is the cause, inducement, stimulus to act—conscious or unconscious—of a character's behavior. Unless you have a reason, at any given point, not to, make clear the motives that make a character *move*. One way to clarify motivations is through distinct behavior now and then (Mary, motivated by disdain for Brenda, ignores a simple question from Brenda, or cuts a conversation short); another way is to use dialog as a means of clarifying motives ("Brenda, some questions contain their own answers," said Mary; disdain is implied in the speech).

In the second draft of *The Pistol*, James Jones explains Mast's motivation for struggling to keep his pistol and offers motivations for the efforts of others to buy or steal it:

> It was interesting to speculate upon just why everyone was so desirous of possessing this particular pistol. . . . Perhaps . . . he had not yet, at nineteen, acquired the equipment with which to speculate deeply enough to find the real reason. All he knew was that everyone wanted it, wanted it badly, and that he was having a hard time keeping it. . . . The sense of personal safety that it gave him, the awareness that here at last was one object which he could actually depend on, the almost positive knowledge that it would one day actually save him, all of these comforted him as he lay rolled up in his two blankets and one shelterhalf with the rocky ground jabbing him in the flanks or as he toiled backbreakingly all day long at the never-ending job of putting up barbed wire. The world was going to hell in a basket, but if he could only hold on to the pistol, remain in possession of that extra margin of safety its beautiful blued-steel pregnant weight offered him, he could be saved, could come through it.
>
> Obviously, a lot of other people seemed to feel the same way.

In having Mast ponder his own motives and speculate on those of the other men around him, Jones prepares a motivation for the behavior of O'Brien and an explanation of the conflict between O'Brien and Mast:

It was interesting to speculate upon just why everyone was so desirous of possessing this particular pistol. . . . Everybody had always wanted pistols of course, but this was somehow becoming a different thing, he felt. . . .

Certainly, a lot of it had to do with the fact that it was free, unattached. . . .

* * *

All Mast knew was the feeling that the pistol gave him. And that was that it comforted him. As he lay rolled up in his two blankets and one shelterhalf at night with the rock ground jabbing him in the ribs or flanks and the wind buffeting his head and ears, or he worked with his arms numb to the shoulder all day long at the never-ending job of putting up recalcitrant barbed wire, it comforted him. Thy rod and thy staff. Perhaps he had no staff—unless you could call his rifle that—but he had a "rod." And it would be his salvation. One day it would save him. The sense of personal defensive safety that it gave him was tremendous. . . . The world was rocketing to hell in a bucket, but if he could only hold onto his pistol, remain in possession of the promise of salvation its beautiful blue-steel bullet-charged weight offered him, he could be saved.

The two versions say essentially the same things; what is different is the ways Jones expresses those things. One way to make your characters' motivations clear is to intrude in the omniscient voice of the author, saying, in effect, "Now here is why my character feels and acts as does." Jones takes that approach in the first version, even referring to Mast as an immature nineteen-year-old in language that is very stiff and formal. Throughout this version, Jones's style calls attention to the fact that he is informing the reader of Mast's motives. But in the second version, we see him trying to suggest that Mast himself is sorting out his motives; and such more specific images as "beautiful blue-steel bullet-charged weight" (instead of "beautiful blue-steel pregnant weight") help to eliminate the abstract language. The style and tone of the first version is typical of motivation explanations in early drafts; the reader feels as if the author, usually so close to his protagonist, is saying to the reader, "Let's you and me leave the room and have a private chat about our friend here."

The three published versions of D. H. Lawrence's story of Lady

Chatterley provide an excellent opportunity to study how a writer deals with motivation; in each version the motivations of the gamekeeper and Lady Chatterley are different (See "Selected List").

63 | Do you present characters too much through description and commentary?

For literary and cultural reasons too complicated to discuss here, the practice of describing characters' physiques and personalities all in a large chunk upon their first appearance in a novel became standard early and has not yet become less frequent enough. Omniscient narrators are, of course, more prone to indulge in this stultifying practice. James M. Cain, a master of first-person narration in such novels as *The Postman Always Rings Twice*, defied this convention: "I care almost nothing for what my characters look like." His readers did not miss "aquiline noses" and "bee-stung lips." But when he shifted to omniscience for *Mildred Pierce*, the obligatory description and commentary made its demand on him. Mildred Pierce, he told us, "was a small woman," with "a pair of rather voluptuous legs," etc. He still doesn't care. Few writers really do; they just assume their readers do. They don't.

If the reader must see what a character looks like, select one or two distinctive features of speech, gesture, or action (the components of more lengthy descriptions seem interchangeable and routine) and repeat them, with variation, throughout the story. If the purpose of fiction is to create an illusion of actuality through the predominant use of the technique of showing rather than telling, does the reader ever really need *your* commentary on a character? Usually, when the writer stops his narrative dead in its tracks to *tell* us about a character, he eventually *shows* as well (or has already shown). If what he tells can be found only in the commentary, he has failed. Blocks of character description and commentary fall into the category of mere information, a form of plodding journalism.

Nick's role as a "guide" in *The Great Gatsby* was so important that Fitzgerald inserted this passage very early in Chapter 1:

It was lonely for a day or so until one morning some man, more recently arrived than I, stopped me on the road.

"How do you get to West Egg village?" he asked helplessly.

I told him. And as I walked on I was lonely no longer. I was a guide, a pathfinder, an original settler. He had casually conferred on me the freedom of the neighborhood.

This is a rather general and symbolic image of a character but one that Fitzgerald proceeds to illustrate in many major and minor ways throughout the novel.

64 | Do you make a *claim* for a character that you cannot demonstrate?

"Helen was the wittiest woman who ever lived." If you say that in your own omniscient voice or through a first-person narrator, or even allow a character to say it in dialog, you are obliged to put into Helen's mouth witticisms that Oscar Wilde would have envied. If you can do that, the reader will be very happy. If not, the reader will resent your undemonstrated claim.

In the first chapter of *Vanity Fair*, Thackeray committed the claims fallacy by calling Amelia "one of the best and dearest creatures that ever lived," but he revised to read "a dear little creature."

Even in the "Catch-18" short-story version of *Catch-22*, Joseph Heller opens with a claim that the reader's experience never comes close to proving out:

It was love at first sight.
The first time Yossarian saw the Chaplain he fell madly in love with him.

65 | Do you need to change the *functions* of certain characters?

If you discover that a character is in your first draft simply because you liked writing about that character and that his or her function is, or seems to be, a mere pretext for working that character into the story, you need to find a more clearly useful function or eliminate the character. Henry James often talks in his prefaces for the revised editions of his novels of the various functions of his characters and how, from conception to finished work, their functions often changed. A character's function has to do with his contribution to the development of the plot or to the development of the protagonist's inner conflict; he must be interesting in and of himself, while serving that function, but he must never seem to be in the story simply to serve a function. Ask, as you revise, what the function is of each of your characters. How does each, for instance, serve to develop the conflict between protagonist and antagonist? Or, if the story is one of inner conflict, as opposed to outer, how does each draw out some facet of the protagonist's mental or spiritual problem? You may find that two characters perform the same function: as confidante to the heroine, for instance. The question then is whether you *need* two characters to serve that function. Perhaps you do, but usually one such person is enough.

Maybe Glenda's function is to serve as a contrast to Carol, the heroine. But perhaps you can imagine Emily as serving that function much better, so you might cut Glenda out or use her in some other way, and develop Emily further. Some characters serve as parallels to the protagonist. Mona is in the story because she has traits that are like Carol's; her function is to give us a clearer sense of Carol herself. George's function is to offer Carol an alternative to Bill, the man whom she loves but who is very bad for her. Fred is a lot like Bill, and so his faults suggest to the reader that Bill is not right for Carol either. The nexus of functions can get to be quite complex; you need to have the characters' functions clearly in focus.

For reasons too complex to go into here, Thomas Hardy had a great deal of trouble getting Diggory Venn, the reddleman, in focus in *The Return of the Native*. As a crude farmer, his function was to serve as a suitor to Thomasin Yeobright in competition with Clem, the hero. But Hardy was attracted to his possibilities as a reddleman, a mysterious figure always stained red whose function is to move elusively between the natural life of the heath and the supernatural world with which Eustacia Vye, the heroine, has some ambiguous connection. Hardy still needed him to function as Thomasin's suitor; he continued as a reddleman, but as one who had once been a respectable dairyman, thus making him more credible as a suitor to Miss Yeobright. Hardy gave him other functions that figured in the lives of each of the major characters. He had the potential for being one of the most interesting and singular characters in Hardy's fiction, but Hardy's frequent shifting of background and function in various versions left him only tantalizingly close to being that sort of memorable character. Hardy never did present Diggory Venn, the mysteriously appearing and disappearing and reappearing reddleman, clearly. See John Paterson, *The Making of "The Return of the Native."*

66 | Do you need to *combine* two or more characters into one?

This is less of a Dr. Frankenstein operation than the question makes it seem. An overpopulated story or novel will often prove to have extraneous scenes written solely to bring unnecessary or redundant characters into play; by combining two or more (sometimes as many as four) characters, you may also discover that the scenes you wrote for them serve no other purpose and may now be deleted, helping your overall cutting effort, especially in manuscripts that are too long. An exciting prospect is that the new character, composed of several, becomes far more complex and interesting than the others were separately. If the process sounds appallingly mechanical, it is also true that such characters may strike you as *more* real than any of the characters who had seemed so real to you before.

Combining characters may serve the overall conception of the story more effectively than their use separately. Fitzgerald discovered in writing his first novel, *This Side of Paradise*, that an episode in *The Romantic Egotist* version in which Amory watches a group of college students having a good time was too diffuse—no one character attracted Amory's attention more than another. To focus the scene and Amory's responses to it, Fitzgerald gave the traits, speeches, and behavior of several boys to one, and to give that one more presence, he created a distinctive sidekick for him. Now what Amory watches is very focused and his responses are more intense and pointed. But Fitzgerald also, in another line of development, merged two girls into one, creating the Isabelle of the novel, a far more interesting character than the two were separately. It is interesting to note that the two characters were based on one real person; that person resembles the new Isabelle very little.

In revision, you may, like John Hawkes, want to derive two characters from one. The Princess in "The Nearest Cemetery" becomes two major women, Miranda and Cassandra, in the novel version, *Second Skin*.

You are more likely, of course, to cut one or more characters out than you are to combine two or more. In *Stephen Hero*, Stephen's brother, Maurice, is quite interesting; he keeps a diary of his conversations with Stephen. But Joyce cut him out of *A Portrait of the Artist as a Young Man*, even though both versions are autobiographical. We know that Joyce's brother, Stanislaus, was important to him; the complexities of their relationship in life may well have proved distracting from the conception of the fiction. On the true-to-life principle, Joyce seems to have put everything into *Stephen Hero*; having a brother, he put him in. But for Joyce the artist, having or not having a brother was irrelevant. Did the brother fit into the conception of the novel? Apparently not.

67 | Do you depend too much upon *stereotypes?*

A stereotype, a character or situation that has been overused in life or in fiction in story after story, is cut to a pattern or conforms to a formula that seldom varies. The shootout between the sheriff and the outlaw in front of a western saloon is a stereotypical situation involving stereotyped characters. A stereotypical character is like a cliché expression.

Thomas Hardy had dealt with stereotypes in his early novels, but in the process of revising *The Return of the Native*, he placed similar stereotypes in a context of events and style that enables them to transcend to a mythical level.

Joseph Heller's early thinking about *Catch-22* seems drawn toward a satirical handling of ethnic and other stereotypes in a stereotypical war story. Even before he explored the first chapter in the short story "Catch-18" (also called "Catch-14"), Heller wrote a sketch, "A Perfect Plot":

Now they had just about everything to make a perfect plot for a best-selling war novel. They had a fairy, they had a slav named Florik from the slums, an Irishman, a thinker with a Ph.D., a cynic who believed in nothing, a husband whose wife had sent him a Dear John letter, a clean-cut young lad who was doomed to die. They had everything there but the sensitive Jew, and that was enough to turn them against the whole race. They had a Jew but there was just nothing they could do with him. He was healthy, handsome, rugged, and strong. . . .

One of *Catch-22*'s achievements is that it uses stereotypes, stock situations, and clichés only in ways that force readers to question them.

68 | Are you *inconsistent* in the presentation of your characters?

This is one of the classic problems, one that writers find difficult to understand. Having observed in life that many people, even people whose lives are excruciatingly routine, behave inconsistently and that this very inconsistency is one of the inspirations to becoming a writer, so that you can show them in action, the writer is frustrated when reviewers and readers tell him that a flaw in his work is that he is inconsistent in the presentation of his characters. Art imitates life, life imitates art, but not in ways that are for the writer's convenience. The charge of inconsistency usually applies to the range of devices and techniques the writer uses for presenting characters and to their overall effect, not to traits of personality or character behavior. Through technique, the writer can make any inconsistency in a character's behavior convincing.

Paradoxically, Stephen Dedalus has more behavior traits in *Stephen Hero* than in *A Portrait of the Artist as a Young Man*, but he is far more complex and interesting in the later version than in the first. The *Stephen Hero* version:

> —'Scuse me, sir, said Temple to Stephen across the intervening bodies, do you believe in Jesus . . . I don't believe in Jesus, he added.
> Stephen laughed loudly at the tone of this statement and he continued when Temple began to shamble through a kind of apology:
> —'Course I don't know . . . if you believe in Jesus. I believe in Man. . . .

Scornful laughter is not inconsistent with the Stephen of this version, who is also at times a silent observer. But Joyce's conception of him changed; his portrait is of an artist who is more often than not "a tranquil watcher of the scene before him." External events stimulate a drama of internal events. Stephen's loud laughter here would be disruptive of that process. In *Portrait*, Stephen makes no external response to Temple:

> He turned again to Stephen and said in a whisper: —Do you believe in Jesus? I believe in man. Of course, I don't know if you believe in man. I admire you, sir. I admire the mind of man independent of all religion. Is that your opinion about the mind of Jesus?

69 | Have you taken enough care in the selection of *names* for your characters?

This is another of those seemingly trivial matters, but most manuscripts accessible to us show a good deal of preoccupation with names and name changes. The names of characters are as important as titles and, of course, often *are* titles: Moll Flanders, Madame Bovary, David Copperfield, Huckleberry Finn, Herzog, Gatsby, Daisy Miller, Mrs. Dalloway, Anna Karenina, Don Quixote, Werther, Steppenwolf, Sister Carrie, Tom Jones, Lord Jim, Emma, Rebecca. Do we like Holden Caulfield's name only because *A Catcher in the Rye* deeply affected us, or because it was well chosen and contributed to the novel's effect? Would David Canfield have worked just as well? It has been argued that both Horace Benbow and Quentin Compson are shadows of Faulkner himself, but these two very different-looking and different-sounding names have two quite different effects on the reader in the contexts of *Sanctuary* and *The Sound and the Fury*. The first two words of *The Sun Also Rises* are "Robert Cohn"; could the name Jake Barnes have served just as well, with the name of the first-person narrator proving to be Robert Cohn? That Hemingway gave some thought to his choice of names is suggested by the fact that "Robert Cohn" is set out at the beginning as a contrast to "Jake Barnes." The name you give one character must be considered in relation to the names of your other characters. Could Twain have switched to good effect the names of Tom Sawyer and Huckleberry Finn around?

One of the simplest considerations is this: Do some of the names of your characters sound too similar (Sarah and Susan, Tindall and Tidings), causing confusion in the mind of the reader?

Fitzgerald enjoyed, but with good reason, giving his characters names that were puns. In *Tender Is the Night*, Albert McKisco sounds like "gasoline or butter," Fitzgerald said; Tommy Barban, the barbarian; Campion, who was campy; and, of course, Dick Diver, who dived from high to a low place in life. See the guest list for Gatsby's party, at the opening of Chapter 4, names Nick Carroway obviously enjoyed making up to make a satirical point.

In *Tess of the D'Urbervilles*, Tess was originally called Sue. Rose Mary was better (*Rose Mary of the D'Urbervilles*?), but Tess had the right ring.

You may want to reconsider the use of real people's names, as Eudora Welty did in "Where Is the Voice Coming From?" The narrator assassin refers to Ross Barnett, governor of Mississippi when Medgar Evers, black civil-rights leader, was shot:

I might even sneak old Ross in to be my lawyer, if ever should come a little trouble. How about that, Ross? I sure as hell voted for you.

Here's Welty's revision:

> Even the President so far, he can't walk in my house without being invited, like he's my daddy, just to say whoa. Not yet!

70 | Does your story need one or more *new* characters?

In the writing of the first draft, it often happens that new characters, not dreamed of earlier, intrude, sometimes with negative but usually with positive effects. Let's say you have imagined your protagonist so well, she has become so real, that she, quite on her own, out of some inner necessity, requires the presence of another character. "Barbara felt she would lose her mind if she didn't hear a human voice. She called up Frank." Who's Frank? you ask yourself. Barbara knows but you don't. Frank comes alive as you flounder through the dialog. You like Frank. You want to know more about him. You write to get to know him. Suddenly Frank has become more interesting, more functional, with more potential than Mark, who dominates every paragraph of your outline. A new character is born in the first draft.

Imagine new characters, what they might do to the story you're revising. New characters are usually minor, though they may make a great difference. If you have a nagging feeling as you revise that something is missing, it may be a character. Characters already in the story, and their relationships, will suggest possibilities to your imagination. If the story is based on your life or the lives of people you know, your imagination becomes subordinate to reality and you are less able to imagine new characters. But stories that derive from your imagination are always full of possibilities.

Sometimes a new character migrates from a different fictional realm and proves to become a major character. In her first plan for *Middlemarch*, Eliot made no mention of Dorothea Brooke, a major character. Two years into the writing of the novel, she got sidetracked by another project called "Miss Brooke." She decided to fuse it with *Middlemarch*. Critics take sides on the question of whether the novel is too diffuse as a result. Imagine the novel without Dorothea.

71 | Have you given readers the *wrong impression* about any of your characters?

"The main reason for rewriting," said Saul Bellow, "is not to achieve a smooth surface, but to discover the inner truth of your characters." In the early revisions of *Tender Is the Night*, Fitzgerald had discovered the inner truth of Dick Diver, but technical miscalculations gave his readers a distorted or unfocused impression of that truth. The first published version presents Doctor Diver already in decline, mostly from the unreliable third-person point of view of a seventeen-year-old girl who is infatuated with him. One hundred and fifty pages into the novel, Fitzgerald gives us a massive flashback to the idealistic beginning of Dick's career too late for the effect of tragedy he wanted. When he decided to restructure the novel several years later for a new edition, his intention was to give the reader, at last, the proper impression of Dick Diver. Malcolm Cowley brought out that version in 1953, with an excellent introduction describing Fitzgerald's rationale.

Graham Greene was haunted for two decades by the ways in which readers and critics had gotten the wrong impression of Henry Scobie (and of himself by association, given suspicions of autobiographical parallels). See the discussion of the third-person, central-intelligence point of view in Question 4. The success of *The Heart of the Matter* made the pain of misinterpretation all the greater. Greene became famous as a Catholic writer; he received confessions in the mail.

The novel gave Greene trouble from the start. "In 1946 I felt myself at a loss. How had I in the past found the progression from one scene to another? How confine the narrative to one point of view, or at most two? A dozen such technical questions tormented me as they had never done before the war when the solution had always come easily." At that time, as Wilson stood on a balcony watching Scobie, Greene was undecided whether to give the novel over to Wilson and let it become a murder mystery, what he called an "entertainment," or to write a serious novel about "the disastrous effect on human beings of pity as distinct from compassion." Finally, he left Wilson on the balcony and went down into the street to follow Scobie.

Disturbed by reader misinterpretation, Greene reevaluated the novel. "The scales to me seem too heavily weighted, the plot overloaded, the religious scruples of Scobie too extreme. . . . The character of Scobie was intended to show that pity can be the expression of an almost monstrous pride. But I found the effect on the reader was quite different.

To them Scobie was exonerated, Scobie was a good man, he was hunted to his doom by the harshness of his wife.'' Greene assumed, it seems, that his reader would consider the source of everything about Scobie, that Scobie and his wife were seen through Scobie's unreliable third-person central intelligence. Too few readers know how to read character through technique; the problem gets worse when the writer violates his own point-of-view strategy. In *The Portable Graham Greene* (1973), Greene explained:

> Here was a technical fault rather than a psychological one. Louise Scobie is mainly seen through the eyes of Scobie, and we have no chance of revising our opinion of her. Helen, the girl whom Scobie loves, gains an unfair advantage. In the original draft of the novel a scene was played between Mrs. Scobie and Wilson on their evening walk along the abandoned railway track below Hill Station . . . . This put Mrs. Scobie's character in a more favourable light, but the scene had to be represented through the eyes of Wilson. This scene—so I thought when I was preparing the novel for publication—broke Scobie's point of view prematurely; the drive of the narrative appeared to slacken. By eliminating it I thought I had gained intensity and impetus, but I had sacrificed tone. I have reinserted the passage, so that this edition for the first time presents the novel as I first wrote it, apart from minor revisions, perhaps more numerous than in any other novel in this [collected edition]. See pp. 74-79, of the 1978 Penguin edition.

Was Greene right when he took the chapter out, or when he put it back in? That is, did he solve the problem of giving readers the wrong impression of Scobie? If not, could he have solved it by using some other technique or combination of techniques?

In revising ''Catch-18,'' the short story which parallels the opening pages of the novel *Catch-22*, Joseph Heller changed a number of lines that had given the reader the wrong perception of the protagonist, Yossarian, and that had detracted from the development of the character who made the novel famous.

After he had finished the manuscript of *The House of Seven Gables*, Hawthorne went back through to change his ''Old Maid'' references to Hepzibah Pyncheon to various appellations that expressed the respect he had gained for her in the act of creating her from chapter to chapter. This is a major revision, because the term ''Old Maid'' turned her into a comic stereotype, putting Hawthorne and his readers at a distance from an increasingly sympathetic character.

IV NARRATIVE

72 | Is the *plot* inadequately developed?

Loosely speaking, a narrative is composed of a series of events. Plot is the arrangement of narrative events to demonstrate the development of an action involving characters. To deal with this aspect of revision, describe for your own use the plot of your story. Any delineation of the plot should trace the development of the story's meanings simultaneously with its storyline, for plot is an action that illustrates a basic idea. It is the simultaneous ordering of *all* the elements, including conflict, incidents, episodes, theme, etc., not just characters in action, in such a way as to produce a unified effect. "There must be combustion," said Elizabeth Bowen in "Notes on Writing a Novel." "Plot depends for its movement on internal combustion."

If you're satisfied the plot fits the description given above reasonably well, the next question is: Have you developed the plot adequately? Even if you decided that you have, should you change or alter the situation that sets the plot in motion? Perhaps it lacks the combustive power Elizabeth Bowen refers to. To test that possibility, look for indications of its effect throughout the story. Does it figure in the climax?

My desire is to supply for every question raised in this handbook an example of revison to demonstrate how published writers employ the various techniques in the revision process, but for two reasons, I cannot do that in every case: (1) my research may have failed to turn up a workable example; (2) even if I have an example in hand, the entry may deal, as this one does, and as several others in this narrative section do, with such large technical elements that the space required to show it would be excessive. In such instances I sometimes offer a hypothetical example, such as the following:

A severe accident occurs at a nuclear power plant, situated close to a major penitentiary and a small town, both of which share the only escape route, a narrow winding road that moves *toward* the plant before it reaches the main highway. Escaped convicts and townspeople clash in their efforts to flee to a safe distance. The accident figures in the climax as the cause of the chain of events, but the accident itself does not figure directly in the conflict between convicts and citizens. The plot is adequately developed thematically—we are all prisoners of nuclear power— but not dramatically. The accident that starts the plot moving is not directly functioning in the climax. Why nuclear power? The larger theme is that we are all prisoners of our own limitations. The situation or event then that sets this story off need not be a remote nuclear accident. One possibility is a flood: the prison and the town are surrounded on three sides by a great river; the flood threatens to cut off the fourth side, where the road leads to safety. Both inciting situations serve the thematic and dramatic intention: to show how human limitations make all humans prisoner, from convicts in prison to citizens of a small town, who are supposedly free.

Twain's manuscripts for *Tom Sawyer* show a struggle with the problem of plot, of relating earlier events to some sort of climax. He had planned at one point to carry Tom's adventures further: "the Battle of Life in many lands." For a novel that already seems too episodic, such a move would have made plot coherence almost impossible. Twain not only dropped that plan, he revised to give phases of the story as we know it a series of climaxes to diminish our sense that the plot is inadequately developed.

If you can identify important character or narrative issues that are raised but not pursued, your plot is probably inadequately developed. Perhaps extraneous episodes distract you from the main line of development. Perhaps you are too preoccupied with character development to pay enough attention to other elements in the story. Perhaps you devote too much space to a character who does not further the plot—not just the action, but plot in the fullest sense, as described above.

"As regards plots I find real life no help at all," said Ivy Compton-Burnett. "Real life seems to have no plots. And as I think a plot desirable and almost necessary, I have this extra grudge against life." George Eliot complained about "the vulgar coercion of conventional plot."

For a description of Eudora Welty's changes in the plot of *Losing Battles*, with a focus on Part 6, see Marrs in the Bibliography.

73 | Have you inadvertently created *stock situations?*

Stock situations are most often found in commercial fiction that is written to a formula, involving stock characters. In serious fiction, they may serve by providing contrast to enhance the effect of more imaginative or complex situations. I use the adverb "inadvertently" on the assumption that very few people become writers with the fervent desire to deal in surplus goods. A stock situation is like a cliché expression or a stereo-typed character—too familiar, too predictable, too often used, its possi-bilities exhausted. On a critical reader, they have a deadening effect.

A policeman discovers his partner is dealing cocaine—that's a stock situation, probably involving stereotypes. A young woman is pregnant by one man but wants to marry another. The imagination goes blank. The reader goes to sleep—or to another story. On the other hand, given the limited range of possible situations for stories, the phrase "stock situa-tion" arises when the author has failed to transform an overused situation through style, imagination, and technique. "Stock" is a good word; it suggests a warehouse stuffed with mass-produced, surplus items, like the cheese the federal government stockpiles and periodically doles out to the poor. With the worst commercial fiction, you have to take what's in stock; in a sense, that's true of serious fiction, too: one more story about an adolescent's rite of passage, or about the middle-aged woman who sits and only thinks about the fact that it's too late to strike out on her own to live a new and different life, is too many, even if it's well done.

Fiction is sometimes the art of breathing life into a dead horse—somebody can make literary history with the stock situations I have mentioned—but generally stock situations are to be avoided; trust your imagination to be able to avoid them.

74 | Are there flaws in the *structure?*

A story may be broken up into three major phases of structural develop-ment: the beginning, the middle, and the end. For instance, a conflict is introduced in the beginning, goes through a series of complications in the middle, and reaches a climax or denouement in the end. Previous to the climax, several minor climaxes may occur. An anticlimax is a weak or disappointing climax. Peter Benchley's *Jaws* has a clearly delineated structure: beginning, middle, and end (an obvious climax). Compare it with Virginia Woolf's *To the Lighthouse*, which seems rather episodic and vaguely structured, and ask yourself how the structure of each affects you.

Structure is often mistaken for plot. Plot, as I have suggested, is the simultaneous development of many elements, while structure is more strictly speaking the sequential organization of narrative events; it is the skeleton of form. You can easily outline structure; it's difficult to outline plot; it's impossible to outline form, an organic phenomenon. Paradoxically, it is conceivable that you can totally restructure a story's action and retain the essence of its original plot, plot being understood, again, as more than story.

The published notebooks of writers—Eliot, Dickens, Zola, Dostoyevsky—include several structure outlines. Whether or not you outline your story or novel before you write the first draft, it is often an even better idea—especially if you now wish you *had* started with an outline—to outline the now written story as a guide to revision. Once you have outlined what is actually on paper, you may discover that there are flaws in the structure—gaps, repetitions, nonsensical twists and turns, an obvious lack of symmetry—and you will have demonstrated the reason why I suggest something so mechanical as an outline.

If the existence of a structural outline (almost like the listing of action shots in a movie scenario) on your desk freezes your imagination, you will not thank me. But I am assuming that it will *free* your imagination. If you discover problems with the structure, reimagine it as many different ways as possible. You may end up simply fixing the structure you have or you may totally restructure the story (as Faulkner and Fitzgerald did with *Sanctuary* and *Tender Is the Night*).

Some stories have a double plot structure: Robert Penn Warren's *All the King's Men*; Tolstoy's *Anna Karenina*. Some good examples of turning points in structure are: Ernest Hemingway, *The Sun Also Rises* (Chapter 16); Twain, *Huckleberry Finn* (Chapter 16).

Some readers complained that James's *The Portrait of a Lady* did not really end. No ending, as his brother William said of *The Tragic Muse*, "rather a losing of the story in the sand"—just what James developed his method to produce. Having stopped writing it, he wrote in his notebook: "With strong handling it seems to me that it may all be very true, very powerful, very touching. The obvious criticism of course will be that it is not finished—that it has not seen the heroine to the end of her situation—that I have left her *en l'air*. This is both true and false. The *whole* of anything is never told; you can only take what groups together. What I have done has that unity—it groups together. It is complete in itself—and the rest may be taken up or not, later." Imagine a living character or group of characters, then "invent and select" complications true to those characters. Turgenev encouraged James in that approach.

James's psychologist brother William expressed the effect: "to give an impression like that we often get of people in life: Their orbits come out of space and lay themselves for a short time along side of ours, and then off they whirl again into the unknown, leaving us with little more than an impression of their reality and a feeling of baffled curiosity as to the mystery of the beginning and the end of their being." A difficult method, but one that has "a deep justification in nature." James himself said: "Really, universally, relations stop nowhere, and the exquisite problem of the artist is eternally but to draw, by a geometry of his own, the circle within which they shall happily *appear* to do so."

The most radical restructuring of a novel that you can actually examine, and rather easily and dramatically, is that performed by Faulkner on *Sanctuary* in the galley stage. Both versions are now published.

Fitzgerald changed *Tender Is the Night* from a flashback structure to chronological. See *Three Novels of F. Scott Fitzgerald*, edited by Malcolm Cowley, p. vi, for his outline of the rearrangement.

Stephen Hero's structure is mechanical, slapdash ("The second year of Stephen's University life opened early in October") as opposed to the highly controlled structure of *A Portrait of the Artist as a Young Man*.

Malamud's "Idiots First" is an example of spatial structure: the reader moves with the characters from one place to another. His revisions rearranged the sequence of those places.

To see how changes in a key chapter may affect the structure and form of a novel, compare the English with the American edition of Virginia Woolf's first novel, *The Voyage Out*. See also Wright Morris's revisions of Chapter 7 of *One Day* in Kuehl, *Creative Writing and Rewriting*. See Aristotle's *The Poetics*.

See "The Day the Flowers Came," pp. 278–84.

75 | Have you presented the *narrative line* too mechanically?

You will know it if you have. The narrative line will have an aura of the assembly line about it, or the effect of watching boxcars hurtle past you at a railroad crossing: introduction of the conflict—inciting moment—

development of the conflict—rising action—climax—falling action—resolution of the conflict. You start with the romance-of-trains attitude and end bleary-eyed. Your outline—even if you haven't actually written one—will stick out like the bleached bones of a dead horse on the prairie.

Hemingway's *A Farewell to Arms* would seem to escape the classic structural formula sketched above, but a close look at the structure reveals that he not only followed it, he repeated the structure five times over. He followed a narrative line too mechanically in the sense that he repeated it *within* each of the novel's five major events: Frederic is wounded; Catherine gets pregnant; Frederic is almost executed; Frederic and Catherine escape; Catherine dies. Discussion of other elements in this novel would show that Hemingway's achievement transcends this underlying repetition of narrative sequences.

The structure of "Duel," Richard Matheson's famous story of a duel between the driver of a car and the driver of a truck, is powerful partly because there *is* a certain mechanical precision and sequence to the events, but that quality functions beneath the surface and hovers over it only as a possible metaphor in the reader's mind.

See also "The Day the Flowers Came," p. 283.

76 | Have you made *chapter* divisions too mechanically?

Paradoxically, a chapter must be both complete in itself in some ways and a particular contribution to a whole.

Wright Morris realized that the first version of the love scene between Harold Cowie and Concepcion, in Matamoros, Mexico, in *One Day* was flawed.

"The climax proved to be crucial—a highly unorthodox Latin romance. This had to be resolved within the scene itself (one version) and in terms of the demands of the novel (the final version). . . . I was helped rather than hindered by the development of the story. This persuaded me to recast the love scene, and I feel that the scene itself profits." See Wright Morris's endings of a chapter of *One Day* in Kuehl's *Creative Writing and Rewriting* and Morris's essay on the writing of *One Day* in Thomas McCormack's *Afterwords*.

Try to bring your chapters to a close in such a way that the reader feels the satisfaction of an ending even as you leave some opening for the next development.

In one version of *The Way of All Flesh*, Samuel Butler ends a chapter this way:

"Talk of his successful son," snorted my father, whom I had fairly roused, "he is not fit to black his father's boots. He has his thousands of pounds a year, while his father had perhaps three thousand shillings a year towards the end of his life; he *is* a successful man; but his father, hobbling about Paleham Street in his grey worsted stocking, broad brimmed hat and brown swallow tailed coat was worth a hundred of George Pontifexes, for all his carriages and horses and the airs he gives himself."

This paragraph neither ends nor leaves an opening. So Butler added: "But yet," he added, "George Pontifex is no fool either." And this brings us to the second generation of the Pontifex family with whom we need concern ourselves.

The starting and stopping of chapters give the reader a sense of discontinuity and continuity simultaneously. Even as we experience the stop of a chapter we retain a sense of continuity and know the novel goes on. Philip Stevick has written a useful book on this subject, *The Chapter in Fiction*.

The making of chapters is not a mechanical act. Chapter divisions undergo frequent revision. Consider the effects of altering the order of your chapters; of combining two or more; of making more frequent chapter breaks.

Some writers play off this convention, beginning with Sterne's satirical playing with chapters in *Tristram Shandy*. Evelyn Waugh parodies chaptering. Philip Wylie in *Finnley Wren* made a chapter of a few words. In *Ulysses*, Joyce experimented, showed the many uses of chapters. The gestalt-making tendency of readers inclines them to need a limit. *Mrs. Dalloway* seems to have no chapters, but other devices perform the same function. Most fictional works of art have a rhythm that chapter division merely calls attention to.

When Fitzgerald restructured *Tender Is the Night*, several years after it was published, he imagined the effects of placing the present Chapter 1 of Book II where it is now or of ending Book I with it. He restructured so that he could place the emphasis on Dick Diver, rather than begin with a focus on Rosemary. He would introduce Rosemary in Book II. But if he did that in the first chapter of Book II, too much focus would again be placed on Rosemary. So he decided to ease the reader into Rosemary's perspective by starting Book II with a continued focus on Dick and Nicole, letting Nicole ask at the end of the chapter, "Rosemary who?" He decided then to use that chapter not to end Book I but as a transition into Book II. The second chapter brings Rosemary in gradually; Fitzgerald's style keeps her at a distance. *Three Novels by F. Scott Fitzgerald*, edited by Malcolm Cowley, includes Fitzgerald's restructured version of *Tender Is the Night*.

One of the dangers of the first person lies in the garrulousness of the narrator. When he first starts talking, who knows what he will say? At the end of Chapter 1 of *The Great Gatsby*, Fitzgerald realized, Nick Carroway had said too much too soon. He had not only ended Chapter 1, he had ended the novel. The last words certainly sounded that note of no-more-to-be-said: ". . . and beyond that the dark fields of the republic rolling on under the night." When Fitzgerald shifted that passage to the end of the novel, its rhetoric unleashed in Nick another paragraph that made all the difference, that made the last three paragraphs of the novel one of the high points in modern American fiction. The omniscient voice also sometimes gets ahead of itself on a roll of rhetoric.

You may be considering whether to give names to the chapters of your novel. One way to test that possibility is to ask yourself what effect names for chapters in four or five of your favorite novels would have had on you. The general practice these days is not to name chapters or even parts unless your purpose is to enhance the effect of a comic or satirical novel (Walker Percy's *Love in the Ruins, The Adventures of a Bad Catholic at a Time Near the End of the World*, "In a pine grove on the southwest cusp of the interstate cloverleaf, 5 p.m./July 4") or an extremely lyrical novel.

When he revised his lyrical novel *A Place on Earth* twenty years later, Wendell Berry, a poet, decided to enhance the 317-page book with about seventy-eight chapter titles.

77 | Is the *conflict* clearly posed?

A conflict is a struggle between opposing forces. A character may have an external conflict with another character, with a group, or with nature or society in general, or he may have an internal conflict between opposing feelings or attitudes. Conflict is sometimes considered to be only the struggle between the hero (protagonist) and the villain (antagonist), but the main character is often his own antagonist. A story usually contains minor conflicts, also. Conflict, tension, and suspense are sometimes confused as being very much the same. See the discussion of suspense in Question 131 and that of tension in Question 167.

"Is the conflict clearly posed?" is a question you ask only, of course, if you have set out to pose and develop the elements of a strong conflict.

If the conflict is external, this question will arise in the minds of very few readers; but if you have not clearly posed the conflict, the reader will almost certainly spend more time than you can afford vaguely wondering what is wrong with this story. If the conflict is internal, your ideal reader will willingly suspend his insistence on a clearly posed conflict from beginning to end, but at the end may ask, "What was *that* all about?" You may feel, or you may consciously decide, that clearly to pose the conflict will detract from other, possibly subtle, values you want the story to have. You can do that effectively. You *must* do that effectively or lose even the most ideal reader of your work.

Must every story have a conflict, external or internal? No. But the fact that most, by far, *do* is worth your attention.

Even in such impressionistic stories as Katherine Mansfield's "Miss Brill," the conflict is clearly posed: Miss Brill has a clear concept of the world and of her role in it; this lack of an internal conflict throws her into conflict with the external world, which has a conception of her that is in total conflict with her own. Many readers of "Miss Brill" finish it with a sense that nothing really has happened, but it is as completely structured and plotted as any detective story.

Consider the question of conflict in *A Farewell to Arms* (see Question 75, narrative line). There are five separate dramatic narratives, each with its own conflict, but none of them is clearly posed. Take the first one: Frederic is wounded. His external conflict is with the enemy, but that is so general as to be unclear in plot terms. In the final narrative, Catherine's death, Frederic's conflict is with death, another vague generality, and this time it isn't even his own death. What gives overall urgency to all five conflicts is Frederic Henry's various internal conflicts (to make or not to make a separate peace, for instance). The external conflicts give play to the internal ones. What remains insufficiently focused in this very good novel (though not as good, I think, as *The Sun Also Rises*) is the synchronicity between the internal and the external conflicts.

78 | Are your *key scenes* weak?

Make your most important narrative points through scenes. Most stories don't require a multiplicity of fully rendered scenes. Some full scenes in your first draft may work more effectively as half scenes (narrative, with very selective portions in dialog) or as pure narrative passages.

A scene in fiction is like an image in a poem, especially an image that serves as an *objective correlative* (see Question 142).

Like an image, a scene is presentational and immediate, not speculative and remote. A scene is dramatic narration, showing, rendering, as opposed to narrative summary, which tells *about*. Combine scene with summary.

Here are some effective key scenes: Huckleberry Finn dressed as a girl, discovered by the woman in the shanty; Scarlett's visit to Rhett in jail in *Gone with the Wind*; Maxim telling his new wife why he killed Rebecca; Rodolphe trying to seduce Madame Bovary as they pretend to watch the agricultural show from a window; the meeting of Heathcliff with Catherine when he returns after many years in *Wuthering Heights*; the reunion of Gatsby and Daisy in Nick's house.

What's the difference between an episode and a scene? "Episode" is a likable word, standing for an "incident," complete in itself, in a narrative. But the often-used pejorative word "episodic" ("his novel is too episodic") deprives us of a confident use of the term. Still, it is sometimes used interchangeably with "scene." If we use it in that sense we are talking about a part of the narrative that may or may not seem complete in itself, but that must *be* open-ended, that is, must carry the reader forward to another part in which something already underway is continued. It is perhaps better to think in terms of scenes than episodes.

In both the short story "The Ram in the Thicket" and the novel version, *Man and Boy*, by Wright Morris, one of the most important scenes is the one in which father and son just happen to take refuge from Mrs. Ormsby's domestic domination in a dark basement john at the same moment. They had their most important conversation, as Ormsby remembers, in that chance encounter. The devices of irony, paradox, and implication, enhanced by a control of style, produce a poignancy that is a triumph over the risk of sentimentality Morris takes. The importance of this scene for both versions of the story is suggested by the fact that it survives Morris's change in approach from short story to novel. The short story is a satire on the suburban family; in the novel, satire is only one minor, controlled element among others. For a line-by-line comparision, see my book *A Primer of the Novel*, pp. 192-95.

In both published versions of D. H. Lawrence's "Odour of Chrysanthemums," the scene in which the wife and the mother together wash the body of the miner killed in an accident is remarkable:

> [Elizabeth] rose, and went into the kitchen, where she poured some warm water into a bowl, and brought soap and flannel and a towel.
>
> "I must wash him," she said decisively. Then the old mother rose stiffly, and watched Elizabeth as she gently washed his face, tenderly, as if he were a child, brushing the big blonde moustache from his mouth with the flannel. Then the old woman, jealous, said:
>
> "Let me wipe him!"—and she kneeled on the other side and slowly dried him as Elizabeth washed, her big black bonnet sometimes brushing the dark head of her daughter. They worked thus in silence for a long time, lovingly, with meticulous care. Sometimes they forgot it was death, and the touch of the man's body gave them strange thrills, different in each of the women; secret thrills that made them turn one from the other, and left them with a keen sadnesss.
>
> At last it was finished. He was a man of handsome figure and genial face, which showed traces of the disfigurement of drink. He was blonde, full-fleshed, with fine round limbs.

Apparently, looking at the story for inclusion in *The Prussian Officer*, Lawrence wanted an opposite effect and felt that other parts needed clarification:

> She rose, went into the kitchen, where she poured warm water into a bowl, brought soap and flannel and a soft towel.
>
> "I must wash him," she said.
>
> Then the old mother rose stiffly, and watched Elizabeth as she carefully washed his face, carefully brushing the big blonde moustache from his mouth with the flannel. She was afraid with a bottomless fear, so she ministered to him. The old woman, jealous, said:
>
> "Let me wipe him!"—and she kneeled on the other side drying slowly as Elizabeth washed, her big black bonnet sometimes brushing the dark head of her daughter-in-law. They worked thus in silence for a long time. They never forgot it was death, and the touch of the man's dead body gave them strange emotions, different in each of the women; a great dread possessed them both, the mother felt the lie was given to her womb, she was denied; the wife felt the utter isolation of the human soul, the child within her was a weight apart from her.

At last it was finished. He was a man of handsome body, and his face showed no traces of drink. He was blonde, full-fleshed, with fine limbs. But he was dead.

In the first version, Lawrence cannot quite get the extraordinary situation he has imagined in focus, so he drifts into a mixture of sentimentality ("as if he were a child," "they forgot it was death") and uncontrolled eroticism ("strange thrills," "secret thrills," "keen sadness") that is discordant with the rest of the story. In the second version, Lawrence reverses the sentimentality and the eroticism by making both very aware that husband and son are dead ("They never forgot it was death," and the stress at the end—"But he was dead") and by making each aware of the negation of her role as wife or mother ("the wife felt the utter isolation of the human soul, the child within her was a weight apart from her" and "the mother felt the lie was given to her womb"). Their "strange emotions" is intentionally less provocative than "secret thrills." Both feel the "bottomless fear" and are possessed by "a great dread" as they experience the paradox of a greater physical intimacy with the "handsome body" than they could when it was alive, while simultaneously feeling each her own death by contact with "the man's dead body." "His face showed no traces of drink," another reversal from the first version, more powerfully enhances the sense that the man they knew is dead than "showed traces of the disfigurement of drink" did. Lawrence has radically reconceived and reimagined this astonishing scene.

To study revisions in a complete, narratively pivotal scene, especially the ending, see the discussion of Thomas Hardy's *Tess of the D'Urbervilles* in Hildick, *Word for Word*, pp. 82-84.

Compare Stephen's scene with the priest in James Joyce's *Stephen Hero* with the expanded version in *A Portrait of the Artist as a Young Man*.

Compare the three-page scene at Fishbein's house in "A Long Ticket for Isaac," the early draft of Bernard Malamud's "Idiots First," with the one-and-a-half-page revision, in Kuehl's *Creative Writing and Rewriting*, pp.76-79.

Compare the scene in Robert Penn Warren's verse drama *Proud Flesh* with the same scene in his later novel version, *All the King's Men*, in Kuehl's *Creative Writing and Rewriting*, pp.248-59.

79 | Have you failed to sustain the *narrative logic* of the story?

Except for deviations for the purpose of contrast or for some other controlled effect, your story benefits from a sustained narrative progression in which each event logically follows the preceding one.

Neither adherence to nor a divergence from chronological order has in itself any value. The choice depends upon a great many considerations. But with the first draft in hand, you should ask whether the logic of your narrative works and then whether you have sustained it. You may decide, as Fitzgerald did, that the nonchronological narrative logic didn't work. Several years after publication of *Tender Is the Night*, he restructured it chronologically. See his outline in the introduction to *Three Novels by F. Scott Fitzgerald*, edited by Malcolm Cowley.

The narrative logic of most fiction is basically chronological. But some writers feel as Ronald Sukenick, an innovative writer, does: "I hate chronology. . . . My fictions work on the principle of simultaneous multiplicity, or the knack of keeping several things on your mind at once. That is the central fact of our mental atmosphere." The narrative logic of Sukenick's fiction is associational—one thing is associated with another in no particular preset order, but there is a certain logic inherent in that approach which dictates that once he establishes association as the logic of his narrative, he may not lapse into long stretches of chronological progression without violating his own logic.

The narrative logic of James Joyce's *Stephen Hero* followed from his approach—autobiographical realism. If it happened to Joyce, he could and would put it in, in chronological order. That kind of logic produced these scenes, ranging from dull to brilliant: Stephen in conflict with his mother over religion (brilliant); the long scene in which Stephen and Emma are on the tram, the scene at the library, and Emma as seen by Stephen from a distance, which are all interesting; the dull episode in which the Dedalus family moves; a great moment when Stephen sees the ghost of his mother; the controlled, selective realism of the death of Stephen's sister; and the ordinary scene in which the family has a conference about their problems. The narrative logic of life produced these and all other scenes, but when Joyce revised *Stephen Hero*, following a different narrative logic, all those scenes, dull or brilliant, were cut, because had they stayed in, Joyce could not have sustained the narrative logic his *new* conception produced (portraits, one might say, of five stages in the life of an artist).

80 | Are there stretches of *narrative* summary that should be rendered as *scenes*, with dialog?

Narrative summary and scenes—each is necessary to the effect of the other. Scenes are effective partly because they follow narrative summary. We then take up narrative summary as a rest or relief from the intensity of a scene. A rhythmic alternation from one to the other is a source of pleasure. Presenting one powerful scene after another is not desirable.

One negative aspect of narrative summary is that it has the tone and feel, for the reader, of information, like blocks of background or exposition. One way to give it some energy is to lace vivid images throughout, and perhaps to include a line or two of dialog.

A natural tendency (natural because writing is hard) in the first draft is to tell the story in summary fashion ("And then she graduated from college and went to New York, where she got a job with an advertising firm, but found that the people she was working with were unbearable, and so she took her aunt up on her offer of a job in public relations for a museum in Philadelphia, wondering all the while what she was going to do with her life.") between the scenes you want very much to write (the one in which she has the terrific argument with her mother over what she wants to do with her life; and, after the narrative summary, the one in which she has a terrific argument with her aunt about her lack of enthusiasm for her job). That the first scene left you exhausted and that you are eager to get down the great dialog for the second is not an aesthetic reason for skimming over the New York work experience. On the face of it, it calls for at least a scene (dramatizing her interaction with her unbearable coworkers) and a half scene (conversation on the telephone with her aunt—a summary with key lines quoted). Here is an example of a half scene:

Frustration mixed with anger caused such waves of nausea to sweep over her Miriam had to slump against the delicatessen telephone booth to steady her hand as she redialed Aunt Lorna for the second time. Five minutes into what she had hoped would be a quick, feignedly reluctant acquiescence to her aunt's offer of the museum position, Miriam realized she had dialed out of Manhattan into a Philadelphia source of frustration and anger.

"Aunt Lorna, how can you say I sound lukewarm about the job when the very point of my calling you is to tell you that I do, I do, very, very much, want to make a career move?"

"It's just that, Miriam, after all I had to do behind the scenes to create the *possibility* of suggesting the position to you in the first place, I would be more thrilled hearing from you if you had started off by saying something like 'I've thought it over, and I'm convinced that being public relations director of the Rodin museum would be the greatest job I can imagine!' But what I heard was—"

"Aunt Lorna, maybe not for you, but for me, at twenty-three 'career move' is a heavy phrase."

"All right, all right, let's continue this conversation, Miriam, when you come down on Sunday."

Stretches of narrative summary unrelieved by scenes have a negative effect because the reader craves an illusion of life that scenes convey. You will not find such scenes in Faulkner's *Absalom, Absalom!* because to do what he is doing requires that he set up rules unique to that novel, and to have followed the rule I am explaining here would have ruined his very effective strategy, the essence of which is almost unrelieved narrative summary, enlivened by the interplay of storytelling voices.

An almost perfect example of a just proportion of narrative summary and scene is *The Great Gatsby*. Another is *Huckleberry Finn*. Another is *The Sun Also Rises* (compare with *A Farewell to Arms*).

Out of a segment of rather static material in your story, write dialog that activates that material.

81 | Are there long *dialog* passages that should be compressed somewhat into *narrative*?

If there is an overabundance of dialog, your reader will wonder why. Elements in your story should answer that question (not always a friendly one) persuasively and move the reader to be glad.

The reader's craving for scenes—something happening now, as if in real life, with the dramatic immediacy of dialog—is satiable. Too much talk, no matter how brilliantly done, can be enervating. Give it a rest. If you cast a cold eye upon six consecutive pages of dialog in a fifteen-page story, you may have to admit that only three *play*, and that the point of the other three can be more effectively carried in narrative summary. My point here is suspended so long as you are reading the amazing *J.R.* by William Gaddis, composed of 726 pages of dialog, laced with what amounts to little more than stage directions.

Drawing on the situation outlined in the previous question, here is a hypothetical example of compressing a long dialog passage somewhat into narrative. Assume that Miriam's terrific argument with her mother over what she wants to do with her life is just starting, and that it is this opening portion that will be converted into narrative:

"Mother," said Miriam, as they walked arm in arm into the spacious new dress shop, "let's not start on that subject just now, please."

"We don't have to," said her mother, detaching herself to step with exaggerated gracefulness over to the first overdressed dummy in the shop, "if you don't want to. Oh, I can see you don't like this one. Well, the shop's full of possibilities. Do you like it? I was sure you'd love it. Been wanting to bring you here since it opened. But I realize, of course, it's sometimes hard to get out of the city."

"That one's okay."

" 'Okay' isn't what I brought you here to see. 'Okay' we can see anywhere. This one . . . well, *I* think it's stunning. Miriam, your expressions always speak volumes for you. Though in your business, it may be better sometimes to mask them a little with some just plain old sociability. It's a Saturday, darling."

"I know, Mother. I remember Saturday."

"I didn't hear that—whatever you meant by it."

"I mean nothing, Mother. Nothing at all. Don't lay traps for me."

"If this shop makes you feel—"

"No, no, no, I love it, I really do. I'm just getting the feel of it is all."

"Select what you want and I'll get it for you, dear. I can see your whole mood this weekend changing if you were walking around in this one."

"My mood, Mother, is fine. But if it'll make you feel better, you can buy that one for me."

Miriam and her mother, in life, could go on and on like that, from this shop to a good restaurant for lunch to the living room of their home, possibly on into the night. But we do not need, as readers, to follow the argument every step of the way. The argument is "terrific," as I said. The reader doesn't want to be worn out when that point is reached. Here is the same scene compressed somewhat into narrative:

"Mother," said Miriam, as they walked arm in arm into the spacious new dress shop her mother wanted to show her, "let's not start on that subject just now, please."

Her mother dropped it, instantly, but Miriam was not relieved. What she expected would happen did happen. The graceful turn through the dress shop was shot through with one innuendo after another on the slightest pretext, and walking out with a new white dress, gift from her mother, only made her feel obliged to listen longer to each of her mother's attempts to bring the subject up again than she would have without hearing the rustle of the package she carried. It lay beside her as they argued, civilly, over lunch in her mother's favorite restaurant.

Sitting in the living room, wearing the new unmodish dress, she felt disarmed for the battle that inevitably came, starting as they sat side by side on the couch, unstoppable once they had squared off from each other on opposite sides of the room.

"It's your life to live, but don't think there aren't consequences that affect other people, young woman."

82 | Is an important scene presented too briefly?

"Important" does not mean necessarily the *most* important or the climactic scene. "Brief" may not refer to measured length but to the impression the reader gets of "too brief." Cervantes's *Don Quixote* is an enormous book, but the most famous scene—Don Quixote attacking the windmills—is only a page and a half, giving the impression not of startling brevity but of being just right in its length. An important scene, obviously; not necessarily the most important scene by virtue of being the most memorable; clearly not the climactic scene. Expand that scene and its effect may get lost. Many other important scenes in that novel go on and on.

One way to determine whether an important scene is presented too briefly is to compare its length with that of an obviously less important scene.

Bernard Malamud's early version of "Idiots First" offers instructive examples of this point. In the "A Long Ticket for Isaac" version, the scene in which Mendel begs the rich Fishbein for money to care for his idiot son is six times longer than the important final scene, which in revision is about equal in length. The scenes in the pawnshop and in the cafeteria are too long compared with the more interesting and climactic scene in the rabbi's house. See Kuehl, *Creative Writing and Rewriting*, pp. 69-96.

83| Should the *sequence* of scenes be restructured?

Even if you work strictly by outline, you will sometimes rush eagerly ahead of yourself to do a scene too soon. If that happens, look for an effective position for it later. What is each scene intended to accomplish? Has an earlier scene already accomplished what a particular scene is meant to accomplish? If so, cut the earlier scene, or combine the two. Bernard Malamud, in "A Long Ticket for Isaac," packed far too much far too soon into this brief scene:

> They walked up another block, crossed an intersection, and entered a small treeless perk.
> Here a stranger followed them, a dumpy man with shoulders as broad as an ox. He wore a cap and mackinaw, and his black bushy beard seemed to sprout from his whole face. Isaac saw him first and let out a mournful cry. Mendel, drained of blood, raised his white wasted arms, and with a anguished wail, flailed them at Ginzburg.
> "Gut yuntif," murmured Ginzburg, standing out of reach.
> Mendel shrieked with all the force at his command.
> "Don't be a fool," Ginzburg shouted. "You ain't got so long. Take it easy now."
> But Mendel went on shrieking, and a policeman came running.
> "What's wrong here?" he wanted to know.
> Mendel was done in, but he and Isaac pointed to Ginzburg. Ginzburg dove into some bushes. The policeman hunted frantically but couldn't find him.

Malamud worked elements from this park scene into a brief but vivid park scene shifted further into the story, into a brief, pointed cafeteria scene, and into the climactic railroad station scene. Here is the final version, retitled "Idiots First":

> They entered a small park to rest for a minute on a stone bench under a leafless two-branched tree. The thick right branch was raised, the thin left one hung down. A very pale moon rose slowly. So did a stranger as they approached the bench.
> "Gut yuntif," he said hoarsely.
> Mendel, drained of blood, waved his wasted arms. Isaac yowled sickly. Then a bell chimed and it was only ten. Mendel let out a piercing anguished cry as the bearded stranger disappeared into the

bushes. A policeman came running, and though he beat the bushes with his nightstick, could turn up nothing. Mendel and Isaac hurried out of the little park. When Mendel glanced back the dead tree had its thin arm raised, the thick one down. He moaned.

There is a minor but clear example in Fitzgerald's *The Great Gatsby*. He cut a scene from Gatsby's first party and shifted it to the second party, but broke it into two parts separated by other moments.

Compare Fitzgerald's *Tender Is the Night* with the reconstructed version (see Cowley in the Bibliography).

84 | Are your *transitions* from one place or time, or one point of view, to another ineffective?

A transition is a movement from one time, place, position, idea, or point of view to another. A transitional device is any method a writer uses to accomplish that movement.

Flaubert and his friends, to whom he read *Madame Bovary* aloud, as was his custom, liked the horseback-riding scene, but an eight-line transitional passage was more difficult to write than the scenes it linked (not unusual for Flaubert); it took three days. "There is not a superfluous word in it, nevertheless I have to cut it down still further because it drags!"

Transitions are often difficult to make because the writer must reorient the reader, trying to avoid disorienting him, unless disorientation for a specific effect is his intent.

In most contexts, a subtle transition is most effective. Kipling handles transitions throughout "The Gardener" somewhat the way he does here:

Michael had died. . . . Now she was standing still and the world was going forward, but it did not concern her. . . . She knew this by the ease with which she could slip Michael's name into talk and incline her head to the proper angle, at the proper moment of sympathy.

In the blessed realisation of that relief, the Armistice with all its bells broke over her and passed unheeded. At the end of another year she had overcome her physical loathing of the living and returned young, so that she could take them by the hand and almost sincerely wish them well.

Notice how Kipling avoids saying "And then came the Armistice," or some such thing, by slipping it in after an introductory clause that does not directly prepare for "the Armistice."

In other contexts, an abrupt change may work best, as in Faulkner's *Sanctuary*:

> Then he knew what that sensation in his stomach meant. He put the photograph down hurriedly and went to the bathroom. He opened the door running and fumbled at the light. But he had not time to find it and he gave over and plunged forward and struck the lavatory and leaned upon his braced arms while the shucks set up a terrific uproar beneath her thighs. Lying with her head lifted slightly, her chin depressed like a figure lifted down from a crucifix, she watched something black and furious go roaring out of her pale body.

Having heard about Popeye's rape of Temple Drake, Horace Benbow looks at an innocent-looking photograph of his teenage stepdaughter and unconsciously superimposes erotic images of Temple upon the girl. Neither he nor the reader is conscious of this until he is in the act of throwing up in the toilet "while the shucks set up a terrific uproar beneath her thighs," "her" being a deliberately ambiguous pronoun in this context. Faulkner deliberately does not provide a transition because he wants the reader, with Horace, to experience disorientation. Horace and the reader are suddenly into the auditory image of the rape, without transition; a transition has occurred, but so abruptly, we are into the new experience before we realize it. That is the experience Faulkner wanted us to have, one of moving without transition, as Horace does in his own mind, from one experience into another. The effect would have been destroyed had he written, after "leaned upon his braced arms," something like this: "He realized now that the story of Popeye's rape of Temple Drake had affected him so profoundly that he had unconsciously associated his yearnings about his stepdaughter with the perverse eroticism of the rape. He was conscious now of the image of Temple, lying with her head lifted slightly," etc. Faulkner uses abrupt transitional devices, along with more conventional ones, in *The Sound and the Fury* and, more briefly, in "That Evening Sun." See Question 147, flashbacks.

Wright Morris, for different reasons, wanted to orient his reader very clearly to a shift from one third-person central intelligence to another, from Mr. Ormsby to his wife, whom he calls Mother. Here is the short-story version, "The Ram in the Thicket":

> "Ohhh Mother!" he called, and then returned to the grapefruit.
> [Space break]
> *Ad astra per aspera*, she said, and rose from the bed.

It is in character for Mrs. Ormsby to speak Latin to herself rather than answer Mr. Ormsby directly. That point is made in this transitional device. But for the novel version, *Man and Boy*, Morris added an effect:

> "Ohhh Mother!" he called, and waited for her to rap on the floor.
> MOTHER [title of new chapter]
> Rapping her mule heels on the floor she said: "Modern man is obsolete, Mrs. Dinardo," and rose from the bed to peer at the bird box in the window seat.

Now Mother responds to her husband's call but only with a rap of her mule slipper; rising from the bed, she speaks aloud, but to Mrs. Dinardo, the housekeeper, who is not present. The mechanical transition between the two point-of-view sections, the "rap on the floor," expresses the lack of warm, human communications between the two consciousnesses through which we experience events in the novel. Transitional devices (or obvious omissions of transition) can in themselves be modes of expression, not just serviceable devices. Wright Morris's uses of transitions from one third-person, central-intelligence point of view to another may be seen also in *The Field of Vision*, where he alternates several times among five different characters as they sit together at a bullfight in Mexico.

In *A Death in the Family*, James Agee's intention in using a transitional device between the end of one chapter and the beginning of another was far from mechanical orientation; it was to express a poignancy about the fact that an estranged wife and husband were thinking in the same instant, just before the husband is killed in an automobile wreck, of their most intimate domestic moment. The husband has just left early in the morning:

> She saw the freshened bed. Why, the *dear*, she thought, smiling, and got in. She was never to realize his intention of holding the warmth in for her; for that had sometime since departed from the bed.
> [Chapter break]

He imagined that by about now she would about be getting back and finding the bed. He smiled to think of her finding it.

The poignancy is tempered with irony—she found the bed cold; he, dead, will soon be cold.

Ernest Hemingway makes effective use of conventional transitional devices from one chapter to another in *The Sun Also Rises*.

See "The Day the Flowers Came," p. 284.

85 | Is the pace of your story sluggish or fitful?

Pace is the rate of movement of all the parts of a story.

An author may accelerate pace by using abrupt transitions or short bits of dialog. The pace may be slowed by using narrative or summary description. The author's regulation of pace affects the reader's responses to all the other elements in the story. Pace may contribute to the sense of inevitability we feel about the way the story turns out. Pace may excite psychological tension; it may sustain narrative tension.

Have you imagined effective ways to generate pace?

D. H. Lawrence urged his typist for "Odour of Chrysanthemums," "Mind you leave out all I have crossed away. All the playing part—most of kiddies share—goes out, I think. I intend it to. The story must work quicker to a climax." The passages with the children impede the pace early by delaying the mother's going out to search for their father (who is later brought home dead).

Questions of pace should relate to the overall purpose of the story. The purpose of Faulkner's first version of *Sanctuary* (which is now the second published version) was to convey impressions, in a melodramatic context of murder, rape, and incestuous yearnings, of a man's near-psychotic mental responses to external events and his ongoing interior monolog. Given that purpose, the pace is quite effectively controlled. But when Faulkner decided to convert the story into one of predominantly external events, to get the pace he wanted, he had to cut out as much of the mental processes as he could. Here is the first version:

The station was still three quarters of a mile away. The waiting-room, lit by a single dirt-crusted globe, was empty save for a man in overalls sprawled on his back, his head on a folded coat, snoring, and a woman in a calico dress, a dingy shawl and an awkward hat bright with rigid and moribund flowers, her head bent and her hands crossed on a paper-wrapped parcel on her lap, a straw suit-case at her feet. He discovered then that he had forgotten the book. The photograph was still propped against it—the very thing which had driven him from bed to walk four and three quarters miles in the darkness—and his inner eye showed it to him suddenly, blurred by the highlight, and beside it his freshly loaded pipe. He searched his coat again, finding only the pouch.

Except for a few changes, Faulkner left the first part, up to "a straw suit-case at her feet," alone. But he cut everything after it, substituting only the simple line: "It was then that Horace found that he had forgot his pipe." The pace of the early version of the paragraph is fine for Faulkner's early purpose. To achieve his purpose for the new version, he improved the pace by cutting those last several sentences.

James M. Cain is a master of pace. In *The Postman Always Rings Twice*, a fast pace is a vital element in the lives of the characters; violence and sexual passion are thrust ahead at a phenomenal pace that is itself part of the reader's felt experience. Frank, tramp on the road, and Cora, tramp in the home, meet on the fifth page, make love on the fifteenth, and plot to kill Nick, Cora's husband, on the twenty-third, and their wish to be rich and happy together comes true on the sixty-seventh. "I acquired," said Cain, "such a morbid fear of boring a reader that I certainly got the habit"—and developed the technique—"of needling a story at the least hint of a letdown." Albert Camus learned about pace from Cain; he said he used *Postman* as a model for *The Stranger*. Pace is not then to be associated even primarily with stories of action such as Cain's; the pace of *To the Lighthouse* is just as effective as that of *Postman* because it is just right for that novel and because Virginia Woolf sustains the pace she has set in motion for it.

To see the effect upon pace of cuts and restructuring, compare Bernard Malamud's "A Long Ticket for Isaac" to the published version, "Idiots First." See Kuehl in the Bibliography.

86 | Is there insufficient *action* in your story?

There doesn't have to be *any* action in your story in the conventional sense. "Character is action," said Fitzgerald. In the fiction of Wright Morris, style itself has the qualities of pace and action. "My problem as a writer," says Morris, "is to dramatize my conception of experience, and it may often exclude, as if often does, the entire apparatus of dramatic action." Dramatic events in Morris's fiction occur offstage; onstage is enacted the drama of human consciousness. The active sensibility *is* action. That is so in the fiction of Virginia Woolf, who often worried that her novels lacked sufficient action. No single answer serves for all stories. Few stories are all action; few stories are all meditation or impressions. For each of your stories, you define "action" all over again. But if your story's effect depends, as you intend, upon action, you may want to know as you revise whether there is a sufficiency of action.

Is there a pattern to which action contributes? The pattern might be action and repose, action and repose, action and repose. The protagonist is involved in action, followed by meditation on that action, until the next action. The pattern of appeal to the reader is action appealing to emotion and imagination, followed by meditation appealing to the intellect, and the pattern follows that sequence. If such a pattern is being developed, the question "Is there sufficient action?" relates to that pattern.

See "The Day the Flowers Came," p. 284.

87 | Is the *setting* too exhaustively or gratuituously described?

Setting is the place (town or country) or location (in the town or country) where the action "takes place."

The setting is usually natural (the sea in Conrad's "The Secret Sharer") but it may be in the mind of a character (Mansfield's "Miss Brill"); often it is both (Joyce's *Ulysses*—Dublin and Stephen's mind). Exhaustive description of the setting in first and early drafts is one of several problems that follow from the very act of writing a first draft: the writer is trying to create a *finished* world in which his characters work out their predicaments or conflicts because he has not yet imagined it fully enough to see it confidently and he works under the mistaken assumption that the reader requires exhaustive description; neither reason justifies what actually appears on the page. You need only describe the setting selectively, with a few evocative details, a combination of literal statement and implication. See Question 23, the comment on moonlight in a story by Chekhov; see also Question 107, the comment on description of setting.

A gratuitous description of a setting is one that serves no function at all; the description is there simply because the writer knows the place is there and misguidedly feels obligated to describe it or because the author likes the setting so much he is eager to describe every crack in the wall—of his favorite bar, for instance. Suppose you have described, with a few evocative details, the main setting—a small-town filling station. If your protagonist, who owns the station where most of the significant events occur, goes across the street to the bank, the reader does not expect you, nor want you, to describe the bank's exterior and interior, and history, in detail. That would be gratuitous description. Unless you have a reason for describing a few details, "the bank" will suffice.

"Feelings are bound up in place . . . ," says Eudora Welty. "Location is the crossroads of circumstance, the proving ground of 'What happened? Who's here? Who's coming?' " ("On Place in Fiction," *The Eye of the Story*).

Henry James made some changes in the definitive New York edition of *The Portrait of a Lady* to describe the setting of Henrietta's (and thus Isabel's) American life in a phrase; they are now touring England and Italy. Ruts made by chariots in ancient Rome strike her as similar to "the iron grooves which mark the course of the American horse-car." James changed that phrase to "the over-jangled iron grooves which express the intensity of American life," and by implication ancient Roman life as well.

As in all his Wessex novels, a major concern for Thomas Hardy in all revisions of *The Return of the Native* through the definitive edition was to manipulate and adjust facts and features relating to the part-real, part-imagined landscape to enhance the action and the aesthetic elements of the novel.

The three published versions of D. H. Lawrence's Lady Chatterley story (See Bibliography) afford an unusual opportunity to observe the developing contrasts between the two major settings—the mechanical world of Wragby Hall and the natural world of the woods on the Chatterley Estate, with Sir Clifford representing the mechanical, the gamekeeper representing the natural worlds, and Connie in conflict over her old attachments to the one and new attractions to the other, as suggested in this passage:

> She was like a forest, like the dark interlacing of the oak wood, humming inaudibly with myriad unfolding buds. Meanwhile the birds of desire were asleep in the vast interlaced intricacy of her body.
>
> But Clifford's voice went on, clapping and gurgling with unusual sounds.

In his revisions of *One Day*, Wright Morris added elements to his description of the Mexican setting to evoke a grotesque but comic atmosphere in such a way as to express facets of the protagonist's physical and psychological predicament.

88 | Have you dumped *background details* into one or two passages?

It is usually best to distribute appropriate details strategically throughout the story.

How does background differ from *exposition*? If information about a character or about events that occurred before the story begins is essential, it is exposition. Information about the past that lends a sense of fullness to the present narrative may be called background; it is not always essential, but it should always be relevant and interesting. Background *may* come in a complete package, as it does in Robert Penn Warren's *All the King's Men* when Jack Burden in Chapter 4 tells the Civil War story of Cass and Gilbert Mastern and Annabelle Trice; that story is historical background to Jack's life, and parallels Willie Stark's in some ways, but its function is not exposition. See Question 90.

When he restructured *Sanctuary* to express a new conception, Faulkner cut out passages that told the background of the Sartoris family; as interesting, relevant background, it was not essential. For the new conception, Faulkner felt that background material about Popeye *was* essential. In galleys, Chapter 27 of *Sanctuary* opened this way:

> While on his way to Pensacola to visit his mother, Popeye was arrested in Birmingham for the murder of a policeman in a small Alabama town on the night of July 17, 1929.

No background about Popeye had been given in the novel, and none followed his arrest here. But in the version Faulkner crafted out of those galleys, the corresponding chapter (31) opens:

> While on his way to Pensacola to visit his mother, Popeye was arrested in Birmingham for the murder of a policeman in a small Alabama town on June 17 of that year. He was arrested in August. It was on the night of June 17 that Temple had passed him sitting in the parked car beside the road house on the night when Red had been killed.

Each summer Popeye went to see his mother. She thought he was a night clerk in a Memphis Hotel.

Faulkner then does an astonishing thing: he inserts eight pages about Popeye's background. Having viewed him as a creature, like Iago, of motiveless malignancy, the reader is now moved to some degree of understanding and perhaps sympathy, throwing the entire novel, including other unsympathetic elements in the lives of other characters, into a different, somewhat ambiguous, light. Faulkner frames this block of background exposition with another restatement and extension of the opening:

While he was on his way home that summer they arrested him for killing a man in one town and at an hour when he was in another town killing somebody else.

A character's background may be presented through various devices, or you may *suggest* some sense of it. Virginia Woolf meant Rachel, in her first novel, *The Voyage Out*, to impress the reader as being a reserved person. In the English version, when Terence asks Rachel, "How do you spend your day?" Rachel replies with a lengthy, detailed description that conveys her background. But Rachel hardly sounds reserved and disinclined to give in to Terence's request. Given the opportunity of the American edition, Woolf summarizes and internalizes Rachel's background. See DeSalvo in Bibliography.

89 | Do passages of inert *exposition* retard the pace of your story?

Exposition is the presentation of essential background information about characters and present action, about what has happened. Its function is to orient the reader, to enable him to understand what is about to happen.

It is important that you present significant background information, general or specific, strategically, at the most effective point in the narrative and in the most effective way. Exposition may be incidental, it may be crucial. You may offer it early, delay it, or give it all in one place; but it is usually more effective to distribute it piecemeal throughout the early part of the narrative.

Avoid blatant, dull exposition. Make information vivid with an expressive phrase or two.

As a prose stylist, George Moore was appalled to reread his most famous novel, *Esther Waters*, a quarter of a century after its publication and find such dull, inert blocks of blatant exposition as:

> Esther Waters came from Barnstaple. She had been brought up in the strictness of the Plymouth Brethren, and her earliest memories were of prayers, of narrow, peaceful family life. This early life lasted till she was ten years old. Then her father died. He had been a house-painter, but in early youth he had been led into intemperance by some wild companions.

Moore revised most such passages, and this revision is typical:

> Her life among these sectaries lasted till she was ten years old, till her father died, a house-painter, who in early youth had been led into intemperance by some wild companions.

One effective method is to present exposition through dialog. Moore made fifteen revisions in which he broke up blocks of exposition and put details into the mouths of his characters. Writing *Letting Go*, Philip Roth decided in the second draft of Chapter 1 that the third person was making his style stilted, especially in long passages of background and exposition:

> It had almost been as though the chattering Mrs. Herz knew his predicament and set out to top it. She and her husband had the problem in reverse and it was much worse. Their families had run out on *them*. Jew wed Gentile and two wounds opened, one in Brooklyn, one in Queens, and were unhealable. Even conversion made matters worse; switching loyalties apparently proved you really had none. Libby read six thick books on the plight and festivals of the Jews, she met weekly with a thoughtful rabbi in Ann Arbor—finally there was a laying on of hands, she was a daughter of Ruth . . . and in Brooklyn no one was much moved: they listened to Paul's explanation, then they hung up. A shiksa was a shiksa. Knowing the dates of the Temple's destruction didn't change her blood any.
>
> The DeWitts, mother and father of Ruth Elizabeth Herz, were not notified. A priest and two nuns already graced Mrs. DeWitt's side of the family; no Jew was needed to round things out. They hadn't needed one, why two?

By shifting to first-person narration, for many good reasons, Roth lends to the passage of exposition the dramatic immediacy of a voice talking to the reader *now*. Roth converts inert exposition into dialog, which is even more dramatically immediate.

> Fresh from their drafty little house, I could not help comparing my condition with the Herzes': what I had learned at dinner was that all that my father would bless me with, the Herzes of Brooklyn and the DeWitts of Queens withheld from their struggling offspring. Once Jew had wed Gentile wounds were opened—in Brooklyn, in Queens—that were unhealable. And all that Paul and Libby could do to make matters better had apparently only made them worse. Conversion, for instance, had been a fiasco. "Switching loyalties," Libby Herz had said, "somehow proved to them I didn't have any to begin with. I read six thick books on the plights and flights of the Jews, I met with this cerebral rabbi in Ann Arbor once a week, and finally there was a laying on of hands. I was a daughter of Ruth, the rabbi told me. In Brooklyn," she said, pouring me a second glassful of tinny-tasting tomato juice, "no one was much moved by the news. Paul called and they hung up. I might be Ruth's daughter—that didn't make me theirs. A shikse once," she said, drinking a tomato juice toast to herself, "shikse for all time." As for *her* parents, they hadn't even been notified. Over the spaghetti I learned that a priest and two nuns already graced Mrs. DeWitt's side of the family; no Jew was needed to round things out.

Later in Chapter 1, Roth frames a block of exposition with telephone dialog between Gabe and his father.

To watch Virginia Woolf's handling of exposition elements (especially details about Peter Walsh) in five very different versions of the opening of *Mrs. Dalloway*, see Hildick, *Word for Word*, pp. 116-27, and the final published *Mrs. Dalloway*.

See also George Eliot's versions of exposition passages in *Middlemarch* in Hildick, *Word for Word*, pp. 42–43.

90 | Do *digressions* interrupt or impede the flow of the narrative action, especially early in the story?

A digression is any departure from a firm narrative structure.

Filling the very first pages with rather static exposition was customary for Victorian writers, but in *The Way of All Flesh* Samuel Butler succumbed earlier than most to the tendency to carry exposition to the excess of digression. The reader is content to know that Mr. Pontifex was not only an artist but a musician, that he built an organ for the church and another for his own house with his own hands, that he could play it fairly well; but that he worshiped Handel is not in the category of necessary exposition. A whole paragraph on Handel is a digression from our interest in Mr. Pontifex to Butler's own hobbyhorse, his worship of Handel. See Hildick, *Word for Word*, pp. 66-67.

It is in character for Peter Walsh in *Mrs. Dalloway* to become "aware of all the towers which rise above the little streets, the Abbey, the Houses of Parliament, Westminster Hall. There they sit, he thought, thinking of the Government," but when Virginia Woolf added "of Institutions, of settled ways. Mantling nonsense, he thought, and—" she caught herself about to launch into a digression and struck the words out.

Readers who have experienced the force of the artistic unity of Thomas Hardy's *The Return of the Native* thus far are appalled by his empty concession to the conventions of the Victorian serial novels—he tacks on "Aftercourses," Book Sixth. For Hardy, the creator, and for readers who responded to what he created, the novel ended with the irony of Yeobright's cry, after the violent death of Eustacia and Wildeve, ". . . my great regret is that for what I have done no man or law can punish me!" Before Chapter 4, the final chapter of the extraneous Book Sixth, Hardy inserted a note in the 1912 definitive edition:

> The writer may state here that the original conception of the story did not design a marriage between Thomasin and Venn. He was to have retained his isolated and weird character to the last, and to have disappeared mysteriously from the heath, nobody knowing wither— Thomasin remaining a widow. But certain circumstances of serious publication led to a change of intent.
>
> Readers can therefore choose between the endings, and those with an austere artistic code can assume the more consistent conclusion to be the true one.

A classic example of a digression that works (so say *half* of us readers) is Chapter 42, "The Whiteness of the Whale," in Melville's *Moby-Dick*. There are fewer champions (I am one) of Chapter 32, "Cetology." Another example is Book V, Chapter 5, "The Grand Inquisitor," in Dostoyevsky's *The Brothers Karamazov*.

91 | Have you neglected to lend interest to your story through an *implied narrative?*

A major source of interest in serious fiction is the implied narrative that emerges from a pattern of implications that accompanies the stages in the development of the overt narrative. For instance, the overt story of William Carlos Williams's "The Use of Force" is very simple: the narrator tells about his struggle to force a little girl's mouth open so he can examine her for an infectious disease; she resists; he succeeds. That story is told in only three pages, but a story of equal length is implied by several brief passages, of which this is one:

The little girl screams, "Stop it! You're killing me!" The mother asks, "Do you think she can stand it, doctor!" As soon as the father says to the mother, "You get out. . . . Do you want her to die of diphtheria?" the implied narrative is set in motion; the reader gets, by implication, the story of the mother's and the father's very different handling of the girl before the doctor arrived. That's a previous implied narrative. For the more imaginative reader, the end of the story implies a future narrative: "She had been on the defensive before but now she attacked. Tried to get off her father's lap and fly at me while tears of defeat blinded her eyes." What's the story of this defeated child and her parents after this episode?

Katherine Anne Porter's "Flowering Judas" implies, from passage to passage, a complex previous story, a complex parallel story (Braggioni's conflict with Laura and with his wife), and a future story for Braggioni and for Laura separately; the story, by implication, spins off interacting narratives that have the complexity and richness of a novel.

See "The Day the Flowers Came," comment 17, pg. 276.

92 | Have you in some way defused the impact of the *climax?*

The climax is that point in a narrative where the external conflict between the protagonist and the antagonist reaches its most intense and decisive development; soon after, the conflict is resolved. Or, if the conflict is internal, between two opposing psychological forces within a character, the climax comes when that conflict reaches its most critical level of intensity and effect.

The reader has anticipated with high expectation the impact of that moment of climax; if the moment is weak for some reason, the effect is anticlimactic. Or the climax may be inherently forceful, but diminished in its impact by some failure in the writing that defuses that impact. There are many possible causes for this defusing effect. You may have prefigured the climactic event too clearly and too obviously, as early even as in the first few pages or in the first few chapters.

The way in which you have presented the climax may be out of key with the rest of the novel, as when a writer offers a melodramatic climax to a novel that has developed subtly. The impact may be momentarily great, but its effect is weak within the context of the whole novel. Often a reader will have a feeling after an earlier chapter similar to what a moviegoer feels when he says, about a strong scene, "Oh, I thought that was the end," because it has all or most of the necessary elements for the climax.

The climax of Bernard Malamud's "Idiots First" was very weak in the first version, because, first, he had defused the story of conflict and suspense by presenting scenes between Mendel and Ginzburg too early, and, second, the climactic scene at the train station was too short and Ginzburg played no part in it. Malamud's solution to the problem of weak climax—and other problems—was to make earlier contact between Mendel and Ginzburg brief and mysterious, to transfer the Mendel-Ginzburg material from the park and the cafeteria scenes to the train station for a resolution of the conflict in a scene of sufficient length between Mendel and Ginzburg. (See Kuehl, *Creative Writing and Rewriting*, pp. 69–96.)

What is the climax of Faulkner's "That Evening Sun"? At the end, Nancy, the black servant, is left alone in her cabin, waiting for her husband to come and cut her throat, as the narrator and his brother and sister and father go up to their big fine house. The climax is not external (that event will or will not happen *after* the story's end). It is internal (Quentin's, the narrator's, inner conflict), but it is a climax by virtue of there being no climax—Quentin's internal conflict never reaches a climax; if there is a climax for the reader, it comes in the realization that an irresolvable conflict has compelled Quentin to tell this story of an external conflict between Nancy and her husband. Climax, then, which seems to be one of the most cut-and-dried narrative elements, may be handled in a very complex and subtle manner.

To follow Wright Morris's struggle with the climax of the Mexico episode (it's an episodic novel in the positive sense) in *One Day*, see Kuehl, *Creative Writing and Rewriting*, pp. 98-129.

93 | Do you *begin* your story ineffectively?

An effective story begins where it *has* to. But, said George Eliot, "Beginnings are always troublesome."

Most writers find getting started very difficult. Effective beginnings are all the more crucial when you consider that getting started is often very difficult for readers, too.

Everything you find in your first draft is there because you *had* to write it. But how much of it does the reader have to read? Writing the first draft, you are only doing what comes naturally. But writing fiction is not a natural act. The problem begins at the beginning—often with a three-page weather report or a description of the setting.

To determine the type of opening, consider all your many intentions.

Usually, an opening that is specific is more effective than one that plunges into *exposition* (see Question 89). See Samuel Butler's opening of *The Way of All Flesh,* marred at first by a long digression and dull exposition, in Hildick, *Word for Word*, p. 65. For five very different versions of the opening passage of Virginia Woolf's *Mrs. Dalloway*, see Hildick, *Word for Word*, pp. 116-27.

We all know that the opening sentence of a commercial story must "hook" a reader. The master commercial novelist Stephen King opens his short story "Nona":

> *Do you love?*
> I hear her voice saying this—sometimes I still hear it. In my dreams.
> *Do you love?*
> *Yes*, I answer. *Yes—and true love will never die*.
> Then I wake up screaming.

Some literary stories, too, use the hook. Franz Kafka opened *The Metamorphosis* with: "As Gregor Samsa awoke one morning from uneasy dreams he found himself transformed in his bed into a gigantic insect."

Several years before *A Farewell to Arms*, Ernest Hemingway prefigured the famous opening of that novel in the opening, which Fitzgerald greatly admired, of the short story "In Another Country." A stylistic study of the two openings would be very rewarding. In the revision of the first paragraph of *A Farewell to Arms,* all the key words remain, but Hemingway has rearranged them to create a rhythm that enhances not only the images but the underlying elegiac tone. It is that rhythm that makes this one of the most impressive opening paragraphs in American literature. See Reynolds in Bibliography.

In making comparisons between the two published versions of Fitzgerald's *Tender Is the Night*, one will face the question of which beginning is more effective in itself and which makes the best contribution to the novel's overall effect. Malcolm Cowley, who edited the second published version, concludes: "Although the new beginning is less brilliant than the older one, it prepares us for the end and helps us to appreciate the last section of the novel as we had probably failed to do on our first reading. That is the principal virtue of Fitzgerald's new arrangement."

"Openings for us," said Ford Madox Ford, describing his collaboration with Joseph Conrad, "as for most writers, were matters of great importance, but probably we more than most writers realized of what primary importance they are."

Should you create a dramatic opening or a reflective opening? "Openings," said Ford, "are . . . of necessity always affairs of compromise." The manuscript for Ford's own novel, *Professor's Progress*, reveals his conscious effort, in four versions, to make the opening paragraph at once dramatically immediate and reflective; the fourth is an improvement over the first three, but the writer who advocated technical consciousness in all writers still had an ineffective opening.

No matter what the point-of-view technique is, there are many kinds of openings. Some novels open with a question, positive or negative; some nostalgically; paradoxically; shockingly; ironically; epigrammatically; thematically; with a generalization and an evaluation; with dialog; with a disclaimer. Read the openings of ten or twenty novels and stories you admire.

To evaluate your own opening, it may help to analyze the beginning paragraphs of a wide range of stories and novels of varying types and quality. What immediate effects do they have on the reader? What cumulative effects? Examine your responses. What assumptions do they make about the reader? What fictive techniques are used? What fiction elements are set in motion? Relate the opening paragraphs to the closing paragraphs.

See "The Day the Flowers Came," comment 1, p. 264.

94 | Does the *ending*, given what has gone before, seem inevitable?

Some stories end neatly with a moral or a sentimental touch or a decrescendo. Other stories are most effective if they are open-ended: Julio Cortazar's *Hopscotch*, or Thomas Pynchon's *Gravity's Rainbow*. R. V. Cassill says, "Almost always I had to rewrite the beginning extensively for the sake of economy and to make it conform to developments I hadn't foreseen when I began. The endings I had first written were usually too abrupt and had to be modulated and paced better." Effective openings contribute to structure and form.

Ernest Hemingway says, "I rewrote the ending to *A Farewell to Arms* . . . the last pages of it, thirty-nine times before I was satisfied. . . . Getting the words right." In an early draft, just after telling about the death of Catherine, Frederic Henry launches into a long catalog of things "I could tell," ending with this paragraph:

> I could tell you what I have done since March nineteen hundred and eighteen and when I walked that night in the rain alone, and always from then on alone, through the streets of Lausanne back to the hotel where Catherine and I had lived and went upstairs to our room and undressed and got into bed and slept, finally, because I was so tired—to wake in the morning with the sun shining; then suddenly to realize what it was that had happened. I could tell what has happened since then but that is the end of the story. [Michael Reynolds, *Hemingway's First War*, p. 47; see also other versions of the end, p. 293]

In the published version, Frederic Henry talks briefly with the doctor, then to the nurses, then ends with this brief paragraph, the style and elegiac tone of which flow from the dialog itself. One of the nurses says:

> "You can't come in yet."
> "You get out," I said. "The other one too."
> But after I had got them out and shut the door and turned off the light it wasn't any good. It was like saying good-by to a statue. After a while I went out and left the hospital and walked back to the hotel in the rain.

Does your opening prefigure key elements to come? "If I didn't know the ending of a story, I wouldn't begin," says Katherine Anne Porter. "I always write my last lines, my last paragraph, my last page first, and then I go back and work towards it." And Chekhov said that "at the end of a novel or a story I must artfully concentrate for the reader an impression of the entire work. . . ." Chekhov's stories do not often so literally illustrate his point as "Gooseberries" does.

Try to get the story's patterns started in the opening passages. At the end, give the reader the feeling that he is recapitulating certain motifs introduced in the beginning; he senses that these patterns have become much richer than they were in the opening.

Here is an example from Katherine Mansfield's "Miss Brill":

[Beginning:] Miss Brill put up her hand and touched her fur. Dear little thing! It was nice to feel it again. She had taken it out of its box that afternoon, shaken out the moth powder, given it a good brush, and rubbed the life back into the dim little eyes. "What has been happening to me?" said the sad little eyes. Oh, how sweet it was to see them snap at her again from the red eiderdown!

*   *   *

[End:] [She] went into the little dark room—her room like a cupboard—and sat down on the red eiderdown. She sat there for a long time. The box that the fur came out of was on the bed. She unclasped the necklet quickly; quickly, without looking, laid it inside. But when she put the lid on she thought she heard something crying.

Before you revise the beginning and the ending of your story, with their effect on each other in mind, it may be helpful to examine the beginnings and endings of the stories in any anthology or of ten or twelve novels. What characteristics do they all share? How do they differ in the kinds of effects on you that they seem to strive for? How do the endings relate to the beginnings? Are they mirrored or hinted at in the beginnings? Why did you want to keep on reading some stories but not others?

Endings are so crucial that external factors sometimes influence the author. In an interview in *Writers at Work* (Fourth Series, pp. 327, 336-39), Anthony Burgess expresses his ambivalence regarding the omission of the final chapter of *A Clockwork Orange* in the American edition. Appleton-Century-Crofts persuaded John Barth to write a different ending for his first novel, *The Floating Opera*; for the 1967 Doubleday edition eleven years later, Barth revised the novel, including the ending.

Compare the last four pages of the two published versions (1965 and 1977) of John Fowles's *The Magus* to observe very complex and subtle changes starting at "A wall of windows . . ." For two inept endings, the second better than the previous one, to D. H. Lawrence's "Odour of Chrysanthemums," see Keith Cushman, *D. H. Lawrence at Work*, pp. 57-62. The endings of three published versions of Lawrence's Lady Chatterley story give an impression of the great differences among those versions. See "Selected List." In the revised edition of *The Portrait of a Lady*, Henry James added several lines that have aroused opposing interpretations. See special issue, *Narrative Endings, Nineteenth Century Fiction*, v. 33, number 1, June 1978.

"Conclusions are the weak point of most authors," says George Eliot, "but some fault lies in the very nature of a conclusion, which is at best a negation."

See "The Day the Flowers Came," comment 27, pp. 282–83.

95 | Is your story or novel too long or too short?

No matter what you do, each reader will have his own opinion as to whether your story or novel is too long or too short. A badly written three-page story is very long for some readers; a very well-written twenty-five-page story can be very short for the same readers. The process is so mysterious that a reviewer or reader may well tell you someday, "I loved every bit of your book and hated to see it end, but you know it really is about three-hundred pages too long." Brief can be too long if the reader's response is negative.

The only way you can determine whether your work is the right length (and there *is* a right length for every work) is to subject its every element to the kind of close scrutiny this handbook's questions are intended to guide you through. If certain elements strike you as underdeveloped or ineffectually handled, the story is too short; if certain elements strike you as overdeveloped or ineffectually handled, the story is too long. For example, in writing *A Farewell to Arms*, Hemingway at one point had no idea where the novel was going. "I did not return to the war for three months," says Frederic Henry on page 149 of the manuscript. That line covers most of what became the ninety pages of Book II, the Milan hospital section. Hemingway clearly felt that that part of the story was underdeveloped.

V DIALOG

96 | Are there sections that have either *too much* or *too little* dialog?

Make dialog selective.
Make it immediate.
Make it active.
Make it credible.
Make it natural.
Make it appropriate to the speaker.
Make it intimate a character's mood.

Malamud allowed his characters in "A Long Ticket for Isaac," the early draft of "Idiots First," to talk too much the way people talk in real life. The dialog that's easy to listen to in real life can be very stilted and tedious on the page. If one were to catch two or three people for three hours unawares with a tape recorder, then play the conversation back to find some dramatic pattern, one would discover the banality of reality. "The vital dialogue is that exchanged by characters whom their creator has really vitalized," said Edith Wharton, "and only the significant passages of their talk should be recorded, in high relief against the narrative." The scene in Fishbein's house goes on much too long, and many of the individual speeches are too long, as seen clearly when contrasted to Malamud's revisions.

"Your uncle? How old is he?"

"Uncle Meyer—a long life to him—is now eighty years."

"Eighty," Fishbein cried. "Eighty years, and you sending him this boy? What can a man eighty do for such a boy?"

"Where is open the door, there we go in the house," Mendel answered. "Is by my Uncle Meyer open the door, but costs fifty dollars the train ticket. I got now maybe twelve. If you will kindly give thirty-eight, God will bless you your whole life, and everything you got now you will soon have double."

"Headaches I got now," answered Fishbein. "I got headaches from everybody that they come to me for money. Take my advice, mister, and don't waste your life for this boy. For him the best thing will be home where they will take care on him. Let me give you my personal card. Tomorrow morning go in this home that I will write down the name of it and leave your boy there, they should learn him a trade or something. This is what he needs more than a eighty-year uncle with his crooked foot in the grave."

"Tomorrow morning is too late," said Mendel. "Please Mr. Fishbein, what is to you thirty-eight dollars? Nothing. What is to me? To me is everything. Enjoy yourself to give me everything."

"Private contributions I am not making—only to institutions. This is my policy."

Talk is easy. *Let* your characters talk and they *will* talk. But talk is not a fictional experience. The revised version of Malamud's story is:

"Who is your uncle? How old a man?"

"Eighty-one years, a long life to him."

Fishbein burst into laughter. "Eighty-one years and you are sending him this halfwit."

Mendel, flailing both arms, cried, "Please, without names."

Fishbein politely conceded.

"Where is open the door there we go in the house," the sick man said. "If you will kindly give me thirty-five dollars, God will bless you. What is thirty-five dollars to Mr. Fishbein? Nothing. To me, for my boy, is everything."

Fishbein drew himself up to his tallest height.

"Private contributiuons I don't make—only to institutions. This is my fixed policy."

97 | Is there a lack of *proportion* among the elements of narrative, dialog, description?

Contemporary novels rely as heavily upon dialog as Victorian novels relied upon long passages of descriptive narrative summary. It is questionable whether either, no matter how well done (and many are poorly done), is necessary. Nothing is achieved in page after page of dialog or page after page of narrative summary, crammed with words, words, words, that cannot be achieved by a sense of proportion. In your own work, you will find more often than not that a great block of narrative summary cries out for the relief of a fully developed scene, composed of dialog, narrative, and description meshed. You will find that pages of talk without some action relief, without some description of who, what, and where is just that—talk. And talk is cheap.

I know how readily brilliant exceptions come to mind—pages of Henry James without dialog, pages of Hemingway dialog without narrative passages and with minimal description. If you can do that, you should. Or you can write one novel—as William Gaddis did in *J.R.*—or one after another with almost nothing but dialog, as Ivy Compton-Burnett did. But brilliant exceptions remind us that the act has been achieved, and we don't have to strive to repeat it. See end of Question 157.

This passage from Kay Boyle's "The Ballet of Central Park" offers a fair example of proportion in the use of dialog, narrative, exposition, and description:

"We're none of us brothers," said the shoe-shine boy while the others ate. "Jorge here, he's from Puerto-Rico. Giuseppe's from Italy. My mother and father, they were born in Spain." Whatever he said, it was as if music had started playing, as if he carried within him a small harp on which the sun, and the breeze, and his own sorrow played. "My name's Frederico," he kept on saying. "I was named after a Spanish poet the cops killed back in Spain."

"Would you like some popcorn?" Hilary said quickly, and she held the waxed bag out to him. In fifteen minutes the ballet would begin.

"I only eat reptiles and carrion," he said.

There was no time to stop even for the camels. Last summer, Jorge's brother had drowned up in the Bronx, he told her as they walked, with the others following close behind. It was a reservoir place where he'd fallen in, and there was a big high fence around it, like for a zoo, and nobody could get over the fence in time to get to him. "There was a cop there, and he couldn't get off his horse and get over the fence. People just stand around and don't do anything," he said.

But Kay Boyle felt that the elements she had presented in good proportion needed emphasis, sharpening of focus, organic unity. Here is her revision:

"We're none of us brothers," he said. They could smell the camels, like bad butter, on the air ahead. "Jorge there, he's from Puerto Rico. Giuseppe's people, they're from Italy. My father and mother, they were born in Spain." Whatever he said, it was as if he carried within him a small harp on which the sun, and the breeze, and his own sorrow played. "My name's Frederico. They named me after a Spanish poet the cops killed back in Spain," he said.

"If you'd liked some popcorn," Hilary said, holding the waxed bag out to him, "I haven't touched it yet." But he shook his head.

"I only eat reptiles and carrion," he said.

There was no time left even for the camels, for in twenty minutes the ballet would begin again. The smell of them, and the sound of the seals' voices, grew fainter and fainter as Hilary and Frederico climbed the steps toward the traffic of the avenue. Frederico shifted the strap of his bootblack box higher on his shoulder, and he might have been speaking of something as casual as the way the grass grew between the trees, or of the tunnel of sidewalk shade that was waiting at the top. But what he was saying was that Giuseppe's brother had drowned in the Bronx two weeks ago. It was a kind of reservoir that he'd fallen into, he said, with a big fence around it, and nobody could get over the fence in time.

"There was a cop there, and even the cop couldn't get off his horse quick enough and get over the fence," Frederico said, his voice low, the words he spoke playing like music in the beginning of the leafy shade.

Boyle integrates and orchestrates the elements of dialog, narrative, exposition, and description much more effectively in the revision. Hilary and Frederico are walking toward the camels in the zoo, so Boyle introduces them earlier. Description: Frederico's voice is much more economically described by the cutting of "as if music had started playing." "He kept on saying" contributes nothing and is cut. Exposition: that the ballet is about to begin is misplaced information; Ms. Boyle moves it into the next paragraph. Dialog: she adds "I haven't touched it yet" to prepare the ironic contrast of Frederico's reply, "I only eat reptiles . . ." Narrative: the summary of Frederico's story comes too abruptly; Boyle gives us first some immediate narrative. Description: she makes her description of the setting serve as a simile for the way Frederico talks. She cuts the simile "like for a zoo" because it's too pat (they've just left the zoo area) and because it is a false note to place Jorge's brother in a zoo context. She adds another reference to Frederico's voice like music and mingles it with a repeated reference to the shade toward which they have been walking. In the first version, the elements are all simply there; in the revision, they interact with and enhance each other.

98 | Should a scene now rendered mostly in dialog be changed to have a more narrative emphasis?

As you work to achieve proportion among the major components—narrative, dialog, description—you may test a long dialog scene to determine whether it is really effective, and you may decide that only enough of it is necessary to treat in a narrative summary. The next dialog scene may be more effective if it is preceded by a narrative summary of the scene that doesn't work.

In the galley version of *Sanctuary*, Mrs. Goodwin in her jail cell tells Horace Benbow the story of Popeye's rape of Temple Drake, and Faulkner interrupts her story with dialog between the two:

"That car passed me about halfway back to the house," she said in a flat, toneless voice. "She was in it. I don't know what time it was. It was about halfway back to the house."

"You had turned around and were going back?"

"I forgot to bring his bottle," she said. Her hand went out and hovered about the child's face. For a time it performed those needless, brooding, maternal actions with the covers as though it responded instinctively to old compulsions of habit and care while the discretion of the mind slept. Then she sat again, her hands quiet in her lap, her face bent above the child. "So I had to go back. Lee was in our room. He came to the door and looked at me and I said. Yes. What. What is it. About noon the car came and he sent word for the sheriff."

For the new version of *Sanctuary*, carved out of the galleys, Faulkner dropped the storytelling scene and took the story itself out of Mrs. Goodwin's mouth, but presented it from her point of view.

While she was sitting beside the spring, with the sleeping child upon her knees, the woman discovered that she had forgot its bottle. She sat there for about an hour after Popeye left her. Then she returned to the road and turned back toward the house. When she was about halfway back to the house, carrying the child in her arms, Popeye's car passed her. She heard it coming and she got out of the road and stood there and watched it come dropping down the hill. Temple and Popeye were in it. Popeye did not make any sign, though Temple looked full at the woman. From beneath her hat Temple looked the woman full in the face, without any sign of recognition whatever. The face did not turn, the eyes did not wake; to the woman beside the road it was like a small, dead-colored mask drawn past her on a string and then away. The car went on, lurching and jolting in the ruts. The woman went on to the house.

This is a good example for showing the nature of fiction as opposed to nonfiction. The effective presentation of information is the basic purpose of nonfiction; this scene presents information and much of it is the same in both versions, but the difference between the two versions demonstrates the nature of fiction, which is to arouse the reader's response to information as determined by the technical means through which that information is presented. Thus two different fictional experiences are presented in these two versions: the first determined by a combination of dialog and oral storytelling, the second by narrative images presented through the third-person, central-intelligence point of view.

You may decide that the effect of a dialog scene, especially at the end of a chapter, is too blatant. Here is a version of such a scene in Henry James's *The Portrait of a Lady*:

"Does she like him?"

"Yes, I think she does."

"Is he a good fellow?"

Ralph hesitated a moment. "No, he's not," he said, at last.

"Why then does she like him?" pursued Lord Warburton, with noble naiveté.

"Because she's a woman."

Lord Warburton was silent a moment. "There are other men who are good fellows," he presently said, "and them—and them—"

"And them she likes also!" Ralph interrupted, smiling.

"Oh, if you mean she likes him in that way!" And Lord Warburton turned round again. As far as he was concerned, however, the party was broken up. Isabel remained in conversation with the gentleman from Florence till they left the church, and her English lover consoled himself by lending such attention as he might to the strains which continued to proceed from the choir.

James felt that the first published version was too literal, that rich ambiguities were latent in the scene that would make it far more interesting. *More* dialog and less narrative comment were necessary to lay out those ambiguities.

"Does he like him?"

"She's trying to find out."

"And will she?"

"Find out—?" Ralph asked.

"Will she like him?"

"Do you mean will she accept him?"

"Yes," said Lord Warbuton after an instant; "I suppose that's what I horribly mean."

"Perhaps not if one does nothing to prevent it," Ralph replied.

His lordship stared a moment, but apprehended. "Then we must be perfectly quiet?"

"As quiet as the grave. And only on the chance!" Ralph added.

"The chance she may?"

"The chance she may not?"

Lord Warbuton took this at first in silence, but he spoke again. "Is he awfully clever?"

"Awfully," said Ralph.

His companion thought. "And what else?"

"What more do you want?" Ralph groaned.

"Do you mean what more does *she*?"

Ralph took him by the arm to turn him: they had to rejoin the others. "She wants nothing that *we* can give her."

"Ah well, if she won't have you—!" said his lordship handsomely as they went. [End of chapter]

The reader becomes caught up in the tracing out of the ambiguities of tone and information. To end this version with an explanatory paragraph such as the one that ends the first version given above would be to destroy the tone and the play of ambiguities. The scene ends more dramatically and with more verve.

Should direct discourse be changed to indirect discourse, or vice versa? See Question 81. Compare Virginia Woolf's English edition of Chapter

16 of her first novel, *The Voyage Out*, with her revised American edition to see changes in her handling of dialog; she cut speeches that were out of character for Rachel and Terence and she converted direct dialog into summary.

99 | Have you failed to make dialog perform secondary functions?

Dialog is first of all vital and interesting in itself. Readers want and need to listen to the characters interact in dialog. Human speech, because it is immediate and dramatic, is one of the things we turn eagerly to fiction to experience. We purely enjoy listening to John Updike's or John Cheever's or Joan Didion's characters talk to each other. But dialog can at the same time serve you as a device for doing work that is less effectively done in narrative or description or commentary. You can make normally static elements such as exposition dramatic by placing it credibly in dialog. "Be glad it burned. That house was too big for you anyway. Besides, you wouldn't be driving a new car if you weren't rolling in insurance money." You can describe a character ("I've always wanted a scar like yours"), an interior setting ("Why do you always keep the shades drawn?"), an object ("I didn't know they made red dishwashers"). You can avoid overt thematic commentary by putting a key phrase or two into the mouth of a character. "Well, I certainly don't come here because I'm lonely. I have plenty of things to do. I decided one night that I ought to make myself useful. So I come here every Saturday night to help make people's loneliness just a little bit more bearable. You know?" In context, this is obviously the ironic speech of a desperately lonely woman; we sense that the pain of her loneliness is increased by her prideful refusal to admit it. Dialog then serves here to illuminate theme.

When dialog would work just as well as narrative summary, it may become the device you need to stimulate pace. Since exposition, description, and commentary often retard the pace, by making dialog serve the kinds of secondary functions suggested above, you automatically accelerate pace.

The first published version of John Fowles's *The Magus* ended this way:

I hit her before she could speak. . . .
And suddenly the truth came to me, as we stood there, trembling, searching, at our point of fulcrum. There were no watching eyes. . . .

Then she buried her face in her hands, as if some inexorable mechanism had started.

I was so sure. It was logical, the characteristic and perfect final touch to the godgame. They had absconded. I was so sure, and yet. . . . After so much, how could I be perfectly sure? How could they be so cold? So inhuman? So incurious? So load the dice and yet leave the game? And if I wasn't sure?

I gave her bowed head one last stare, then I was walking. . . .

Seven more lines, composed of images, and that's the end. When he revised the novel for a new edition, Fowles must have decided some thematic element concerning the narrator's relationship with Alison had not been made clear. To contrast it with thematic comments on the more general situation stated above, he used dialog to express a thematic point about love and hate:

Perhaps it had all been to bring me to this, to give me my last lesson and final ordeal. . . .

I looked back towards the path. The far more natural watchers there were strolling on, as if this trivial little bit of masculine brutality, the promised scene, had lost their interest also. Alison hadn't moved, she still held a hand to her cheek, but now her head was bowed. There was a little shuddered outbreath as she tried to stifle the tears; then her voice, broken, hardly audible, in despair, almost self-amazed.

"I hate you. I *hate* you.". . .

"Then why wouldn't you let me walk away?"

"You know why."

"No."

"I knew within two seconds of seeing you." I went closer. Her other hand went to her face, as if I might hit her again. "I understand that word now, Alison. Your word." Still she waited, face hidden in her hands, like someone being told of a tragic loss. "You can't hate someone who's really on his knees. Who'll never be more than half a human being without you."

The bowed head. The buried face.

She is silent, she will never speak, never forgive, never reach a hand, never leave this frozen present tense. All wait, suspended.

Then Fowles ends with the same last few lines. The two endings are very different, and Fowles's use of dialog helps to dramatize the difference. The love-hate thematic element was submerged in the first version. Now, climatically, it is expressed.

See "The Day the Flowers Came," comment 24, pp. 281–82.

100 | Have you used too many stock *dialog* and thought tags?

A dialog tag is a phrase that tells the reader *how* a character speaks. " 'I hate you,' " she said angrily." That one and most others, is redundant or unnecessary.

Mark Harris cites, in only half a page of a novel by William Brinkley as it appeared in part in *Life*, the following: "Ensign Siegel said blankly," "Ensign Siegel said absently," "the exec exclaimed," "the exec whipped out," "the exec said ferociously," "Siegel said urgently," then "fervently," etc. (*Life*, July 2, 1956, p. 124). Harris avers endearingly, "You will no more expect the novelist to tell you precisely *how* something is said than you will expect him to stand by your chair and hold your book" ("Easy Does It Not," *The Living Novel*, edited by Granville Hicks, pp. 121-22).

Often the context has already made clear who the speaker is, and the context and the expressions have made clear how the character has said the speech.

Thomas Hardy, *Tess of the D'Urbervilles*: " 'I would rather stay here with father and you,' she said nervously reflecting." He cut the last two words; they are implied by the context.

George Eliot, *Middlemarch*: " 'No—and yes!' said Lydgate, half-dubiously." Eliot, having replaced a comma after "no" with the dash, which suggests "half-dubiously," neglected to cut that phrase.

Hemingway is famous (or notorious) for deliberately sticking many tags in, but he just as deliberately cut many out, as in "Hills Like White Elephants." Faulkner also deliberately used (as in "That Evening Sun") or avoided "he said/she said" for rhythm and other reasons. Readers tend to become oblivious to them after a while, using them only as indicators. But they are one of the most obviously artificial elements in fiction and to some degree undermine a major effect of dialog—the naturalness and dramatic immediacy of human speech. There are ways to rid ourselves of them, or at least to circumvent them. For instance, to avoid dialog or thought tags, or "stage directions," use complete sentences, as Henry James did when he revised the *Scribner's Monthly* version of "Four Meetings." First, the *Scribner's* version:

"Can she not wait upon herself?"

"She is not used to that."

"I see,"—said I, as gently as possible. . . .

Here is the revision:

"Then can't I help?" After which, as she but looked at me, I bettered it. "Can't she wait upon herself?"

Miss Spencer had a slow headshake—as if that too had been a strange idea. "She isn't used to *manual* labour."

The discrimination was a treat, but I cultivated decorum. "I see— and you *are*." But at the same time I couldn't abjure curiosity. . . .

The "he said/she said" monotony drove the elderly Henry James to such distraction that while revising most of his life's work for the New York edition he changed almost all of them to "he averred," "she put in," and such phrases. Here is the first published version of *The Portrait of a Lady*:

"What's your opinion of St. Peter's?" Mr. Osmond asked of Isabel.

"It's very large and very bright," said the girl.

"It's too large; it makes one feel like an atom."

"Is not that the right way to feel—in a church?" Isabel asked, with a faint but interested smile.

Here is the New York edition version:

"What's your opinion of St. Peter's?" Mr. Osmond was meanwhile inquiring of our young lady.

"It's very large and very bright," she contented herself with replying.

"It's too large; it makes one feel like an atom."

"Isn't that the right way to feel in the greatest of human temples?" she asked with rather a liking for her phrase.

Revising *The American*, did James go too far? "Newman declared" became "Newman roundly returned." "She said" became "she sweetly shrilled." "Said Madame de Cintré" became "she safely enough risked." "Asked very softly" became "inordinately fluted."

How a character speaks may be expressed in ways other than dialog tags. Kay Boyle makes a special effort to create a character through descriptions of *how* he speaks; see Question 97.

How do you indicate thoughts without repeatedly stating "she thought"? Virginia Woolf, in a draft of *Mrs. Dalloway*, wrote: "She's hard, he thought to himself." The reader may wonder to whom else but himself he *could* think. Or how do you think to yourself? She struck that phrase out, but in a fiction composed almost exclusively of the thought processes of several characters, what necessitates *ever* stating "he thought"? Let the context tell. Woolf was aware of her problem when she caught herself dealing out "he thoughts" too readily and reached for "he remembered," etc., when she could.

101 | Have you overused *dialect, slang,* or | *colloquialisms?*

Dialect is the distinctive way people in a specific region pronounce words. Colloquialisms and slang are words or phrases or sayings acceptable in conversation but not in formal writing.

Most editors, speaking for readers, will urge you not to spell dialect phonetically, not to overload dialog with dialect phrases.

Eudora Welty's handling of dialect and colloquialisms is among the pleasures of reading her stories. But there are problems to solve. In "Where Is the Voice Coming From?" "That's how" became "I reckon that's how." "Too late for him or me to turn by an inch" became "Too late then for him or me to turn by one hair." "It looks like the town's on fire already, wherever you go, on every street, with crape myrtle trees and mimosa trees blooming their heads off" became "It looks like the town's on fire already, whichever ways you turn, ever' street you strike, because there's those trees hanging them pones of bloom like split watermelon." But she thought she had gone to far with "I set in my cheer," and changed "cheer" to "chair."

When he revised "Guests of the Nation," Frank O'Connor generally reduced the dialect. For instance, " 'Awkins" became "Hawkins." He changed colloquialisms to neutral wording. "There were four of our lads went west this morning" became "There were four of our lads shot." "We saw Feeney and Noble go round to the houseen where the tools were kept" became "to the shed." But because his narrator is a lower-middle-class Irishman, O'Connor revised literary phrasing to oral:

"grow excited"	to	"got excited"
"produce the cards"	to	"bring out the cards"
"they'd have stayed put and flourished like a native weed"	to	"they'd have taken root"
"he says reddening"	to	"getting red"
"Noble took such a mortal start the match quenched in his trembling hand"	to	"Noble started so that the match went out in his hand"
"He talked too much"	to	"He had too much old gab"

Revising *The American*, Henry James decided his American didn't sound slangy enough: "I've been my own master all my life" becomes "I've skipped about in my shirt all my life." "Oh horrors!" became "Oh, shucks!" "Yes" became "Yes—I'll be hanged if I ain't sure!" "You are sad, eh?" becomes "You've got a sentimental stomach-ache, eh?"

Generally, in dialog, use contractions. Even Henry James usually changed "cannot" and "she would" to "can't" and "she'd." If you depart with good reason from contractions as a rule, the effect of a "cannot" will be all the more powerful.

102 | Does your character need a *speech signature* to make him or her more vivid?

In revision, writers often find that they have failed to make the reader see and hear a character, as did Fitzgerald, and his editor Maxwell Perkins, regarding Gatsby. To *show* Gatsby, Fitzgerald provided Gatsby's smile. To make us hear Gatsby, he gave him the speech signature "old man," which he changed to the now memorable "old sport." Most of Dickens's characters use a characteristic speech signature.

103 | Have you created problems for the reader by experimenting with the mechanics of *displaying* dialog?

Every departure from convention makes some sort of demand upon the reader; even readers who are predisposed to embrace different or new devices and techniques must make an effort to respond. Is the effect gained worth the effort the reader must exert? Or does the demanding device detract more than it enhances?

Don't use single quotes, as many British writers do.

Don't use dashes in front of the speech, as James Joyce and William Gaddis do.

Above all, don't present dialog with *no* indicator.

Don't try anything fancy on the assumption sophisticated readers will "figure out" what you're doing. You can probably draw on your own experience to support my suggestion. Like most readers, you probably got lost reading Hemingway's "A Clean Well-Lighted Place," which relies heavily upon implications conveyed in dialog between the young waiter and a new waiter about an old man who frequents the café:

> "He's drunk now," he said.
> "He's drunk every night."
> "What did he want to kill himself for?"

The young waiter says the first line; most readers assume therefore that the new waiter says the next line, and the young waiter therefore says the third, even though it's not logical since it is *he* who knows the answer to the question. The dialog continues with no identification of who says what. Only a few scholars are certain about what's going on, half being convinced by evidence in other manuscripts and published versions of other fiction by Hemingway that he meant both the first and second lines to be spoken by the young waiter to achieve an effect (too complicated to describe here), the other half being convinced it was an error. I offer it as a cautionary instance. Fancy effects with dialog may cause confusion and thus prove foolhardy. Don't ask for trouble.

" 'Guests of the Nation' is the only story I have admitted from my first book," wrote Frank O'Connor in his foreword to *Stories by Frank O'Connor*, "and it has been greatly revised. It was written originally under the influence of the great Jewish storyteller, Isaac Babel." If O'Connor's American editor of his stories advised him to break up this paragraph chocked too full of dialog, it was good advice:

> "What use is that pair to us?" I asked him.
> He looked at me for a spell and said, "I thought you knew we were keeping them as hostages." "Hostages—?" says I, not quite understanding. "The enemy," he says in his heavy way, "have prisoners belong to us, and now they talk of shooting them. If they shoot our prisoners we'll shoot theirs, and serve them right." "Shoot them?" said I, the possibility just beginning to dawn on me. "Shoot them,

exactly," said he. "Now," said I, "wasn't it very unforeseen of you not to tell me and Noble that?" "How so?" he asks. "Seeing that we were acting as guards upon them, of course." "And hadn't you reason enough to guess that much?" "We had not, Jeremiah Donovan, we had not. How were we to know when the men were on our hands so long?" "And what difference does it make? The enemy have our prisoners as long or longer, haven't they?" "It makes a great difference," said I. "How so?" said he sharply; but I couldn't tell him the difference it made, for I was struck too silly to speak. "And when may we expect to be released from this anyway?" said I. "You may expect it to-night," says he. "Or tomorrow or the next day at latest. So if it's hanging round here that worries you, you'll be free soon enough."

I cannot explain it even now, how sad I felt, but I went back to the cottage, a miserable man. [*Collected Stories*, p. 6; oddly, the English version was used in this 1981 collection]

Here is how it looks revised:

"What use are those fellows to us?" says I.

He looked at me in surprise and said: "I thought you knew we were keeping them as hostages."

"Hostages?" I said.

"The enemy have prisoners belonging to us," he says "and now they're talking of shooting them. If they shoot our prisoners, we'll shoot theirs."

"Shoot them?" I said.

"What else did you think we were keeping them for?" he says.

"Wasn't it very unforeseen of you not to warn Noble and myself of that in the beginning?" I said.

"How was it?" says he. "You might have known it."

"We couldn't know it, Jeremiah Donovan," says I. "How could we when they were on our hands so long?"

"The enemy have our prisoners as long and longer," says he.

"That's not the same thing at all," says I.

"What difference is there?" says he.

I couldn't tell him, because I knew he wouldn't understand. If it was only an old dog that was going to the vet's, you'd try and not get too fond of him, but Jeremiah Donovan wasn't a man that would ever be in danger of that.

"And when is this thing going to be decided?" says I.

"We might hear tonight," he says. "Or tomorrow or the next day at latest. So if it's only hanging around here that's trouble to you, you'll be free soon enough."

It wasn't the hanging round that was a trouble to me at all by this time. I had worse things to worry about. [*Stories by Frank O'Connor*, pp. 7-8]

The mechanical act of paragraphing was enough to set other changes in motion. In any case, the insertion "If it was only an old dog . . ." and the dialog dramatically imply the narrator's feelings so that O'Connor cut out "how sad I felt" and "a miserable man."

VI DESCRIPTION

104 | Have you presented description without sufficient regard to *point of view?*

Point of view determines the way you describe things. The third-person-omniscient author describes for the reader's benefit, directly.

This is an objective method.

George Moore, *Esther Waters* (1894 version):

> William lit his pipe and unlaced his boots. Esther slipped on her nightdress and got into bed. It was a large brass bedstead, without curtains. The room had two windows, one on a line with the head of the bed, the other very nearly facing the door. The chest of drawers stood between the windows. Esther had placed there the books her mother had given her, and William had hung some sporting prints on the walls.

The third-person, central-intelligence approach gives us what the main character sees and how he responds; it reveals the world filtered through his character and personality, thus revealing his character and personality. This is a subjective method. George Moore learned at some point that character animates place. Twenty-six years after he published *Esther Waters*, he revised descriptions from his own omniscient point of view so that they came out of Esther's point of view.

Third published revision (1920):

> William lit his pipe and unlaced his boots. Esther slipped on her night-dress and got into a large brass bedstead, without curtains. On the chest of drawers Esther had placed the books her mother had given her, and William had hung some sporting prints on the walls.

Having established Esther's point of view, Moore may assume the reader will take everything presented as having been perceived by Esther. But he must also omit rather mechanical descriptions and integrate them with character action: "Esther slipped on her night-dress and got into a large brass bedstead, without curtains" conveys a sense of Esther experiencing what is described. "It was a large brass bedstead. . . . The room had two windows. . . . The chest of drawers stood between the windows." That is the kind of description, direct to the reader, that characterizes description from the omniscient point of view.

The first-person narrator combines the subjective, how he feels about what he sees (perception is an act of self-discovery for him), with the objective: he wants to *show* the reader. He is both omniscient storyteller and subject of his story. Here is how Esther might tell about the room:

> While William lit his pipe and unlaced his boots, I slipped on my night-dress and got into bed. It was one of those large brass bedsteads, with no curtains. I glanced up at the sporting prints William had hung on the walls, and there on the chest of drawers were the books my mother gave me.

We sense how Esther feels about what she tells us, first because we draw on the context, and because of the deliberate way she chooses and orders what she wants to tell us.

The tone of description is colored by the mood of the narrator: melancholy, elegiac, ironic, tragic, sardonic, rhapsodic, lyrical.

In *Tess of the D'Urbervilles*, Thomas Hardy, as omniscient narrator, deliberately, with a controlled purpose, handles description in ways I usually advise not to. See Hildick, *Word for Word*, pp. 91-92.

105 | Have you neglected to present descriptions from the appropriate *physical perspective*?

Description is affected by the physical point of view: the time of day, season, spatial range or scope (close or far away; size), and the character's senses that are engaged.

Near the end of the first chapter of *The Great Gatsby*, Fitzgerald wanted Nick to give the reader vivid parting images of Daisy and Tom Buchanan to mark them off from a description of the setting in which Nick glimpses Gatsby for the first time. But the first line of a draft of his description of the setting suggests that he had not yet fashioned those vivid images of Daisy and Tom: "But before I had driven ten minutes from their door the breeze had blown them both away." That line marks off his visit with Daisy and Tom from his glimpse of Gatsby, but it rings false, seems forced to function. Fitzgerald struck it out and revised the preceding three paragraphs about Daisy and Tom so that they (as a single paragraph) climax the scene. Now he focuses directly on the setting in the new first line: "Already it was deep summer on roadhouse roofs and in front of wayside garages, where new red gas-pumps sat out in pools of light, and . . ." Fitzgerald now interrupts to let Nick tell us about his own feelings in a very general way:

> . . . and summer always promises fulfillment of my old childish desires. I wanted something definite to happen to *me*, something that would wear me out a little—for I suppose that the urge toward adventure is one and the same with the obscure craving of our bodies for a certain death.

That is the kind of digression that can wreck a finely wrought setting description that is supposed to portend something of the sort Nick is overtly, portentously *trying* to express. So Fitzgerald cut that out. Now Fitzgerald fixes upon the setting alone. Since he had to make only a few changes for sharper focus, I will give the passage as published, for it illustrates most of the aspects of physical point of view that I listed above:

> . . .when I reached my estate at West Egg I ran the car under its shed and sat for a while on an abandoned grass roller in the yard. The wind had blown off, leaving a loud, bright night, with wings beating in the trees and a persistent organ sound as the full bellows of the earth blew the frogs full of life. The silhouette of a moving cat wavered across the moonlight, and turning my head to watch it, I saw that I was not alone—fifty feet away a figure had emerged from the shadow of my neighbor's mansion and was standing with his hands in his pockets regarding the silver pepper of the stars. Something in his leisurely movements and the secure position of his feet upon the lawn suggested that it was Mr. Gatsby himself, come out to determine what share was his of our local heavens.

Nick's description accurately reflects every aspect of his physical point of view on the setting. Time: night, summer. Spatial range or scope: Nick moves back and forth, far away to close up. Nick's senses: the sound of the frogs, and by implication the sound of the sea and the smell of the summer vegetation and the touch of grass underfoot and the iron roller he sits on; and, of course, the objects he sees and the image of Gatsby in this context. To compare the two versions of the entire chapter, see Kuehl, *Creative Writing and Rewriting*.

106 | Are your descriptions of characters *too brief* or too slapdash?

"However detailed such description is," says Ivy Compton-Burnett, "I am sure that everyone forms his own conceptions, that are different from everyone else's, including the author's."

Here is a passage from the first page of George Moore's *Esther Waters* (first published version):

> A girl of twenty, short, strongly built, with short, strong arms. Her neck was plump, and her hair of so ordinary a brown that it passed unnoticed. The nose was too thick, but the nostrils were well formed. The eyes were grey, luminous, and veiled with dark lashes. But it was only when she laughed that her face lost its habitual expression, which was somewhat sullen; then it flowed with bright humour. She laughed now, showing a white line of almond-shaped teeth. The porter had asked her if she were afraid to leave her bundle with her box.

Although not brief, this description of the protagonist has a perfunctory, obligatory, slapdash quality about it that must have made Moore cringe decades later. He revised all such passages.

> A girl of twenty, firmly built with short, strong arms and a plump neck that carried a well-turned head with dignity. Her well-formed nostrils redeemed her somewhat thick, fleshly nose, and it was a pleasure to see her grave, almost sullen face light up with sunny humour; for when she laughed a line of almond-shaped teeth showed between red lips. She was laughing now, the porter having asked her. . .

By cutting and combining and avoiding the stops and starts of the first version, Moore animates the description so that the reader doesn't feel Esther is an exhibit in a wax museum.

In the first draft of *The Pistol*, James Jones's description of O'Brien was sufficient:

> A guy in the same truck but from another squad, a huge heavy-bearded black Irishman of twenty-two named O'Brien, asked him enviously where did he get the pistol?

As Jones developed O'Brien from a very minor character into a major one, he expanded the initial routine description with this addition:

> "That?" Mast said coolly, but with his mind working swiftly. "Oh, I've had that a long time. Bought it off a guy."
>
> O'Brien moved his big dark face inarticulately, wrinkling his broad forehead and moistening his lips, then flexed his hamlike hands a couple of times where they dangled from his knees. He stared at the holstered pistol hungrily, almost abjectly. Then he turned his huge dark head with the pale green eyes and stared off levelly from the back of the open truck with its hastily mounted MG on the cab roof, toward where the sea was. Mast had seen him engaged in some tremendous, almost Herculean fist fights since he had been in the company, but he did not look tough now.

The description of O'Brien in the draft is inert information, non-expressive. Once O'Brien had come alive for his creator, the description of him, though perhaps a little drawn-out, expresses a good deal about him. What is an "inarticulate" face? One whose expressions are not controlled; that aspect of O'Brien is enhanced by the expressiveness of his "hamlike hands" that flex nervously; that they "dangled from his knees" suggests an apelike aura. The first sentence enhances the effect of O'Brien's hungry, abject stare. The explicit description of O'Brien is enhanced by the suggestiveness of the third sentence: "huge dark head," Jones's variation on "big dark face," benefits from the contrast of "pale green eyes," and the stare, shifting from the pistol, out of "the back of the open truck . . . toward the sea," now suggests O'Brien's enormous longing for the pistol. Jones adds Mast's narrative line about "almost Herculean fist fights" to bring us back to the image of the huge Irishman in a more violent context, and when Mast concludes, ". . . but he did not look tough now," the reader, who has had his own experience looking at O'Brien, now experiences the narrator's evaluation of what he has shown us. In this revision, Jones gives the reader description that is never inert information; his orchestration of the components makes the passage a living, vital experience for the reader, along with Mast.

But suppose Jones had not developed O'Brien further as a character. Could he have made that brief description in the draft more effective in the *manner* of the revision? Here's one possibility:

> "Where'd you get that pistol?" Mast turned toward the voice. Pale green eyes stared out of a huge dark head. Mast recognized him as a man from another squad—O'Brien, notorious for Herculean fist fights. O'Brien stared hungrily, abjectly at the holstered pistol.

What is important is not that we get a fuller description of O'Brien in this version but that the description serve to convey to Mast the reaction his possession of the pistol arouses in the men around him.

In "The Ballet of Central Park," Kay Boyle's revisions show that she was at first too brief and slapdash in her description of the boys. The "smallest" boy in Draft 1, Jorge, becomes also the "sharpest" in Draft 2, and "quick and beautiful" with "small white teeth" in Draft 3, and in the published version, "delicate-boned and beautiful," his teeth "white in the ivory mask of his face," his eyes "thickly lashed." For contrast, Boyle makes Jorge, from draft to draft, more attractive, and Giuseppe uglier. See Kuehl, *Creative Writing and Rewriting*, pp. 46-47.

107 | Do you open the story with an overlong description of the *setting*?

"I try to leave out," says Elmore Leonard, "the parts that people skip."

The setting of a story is the time and place in which the events occur. The time may be the period (past, present, future) or a year, or the season or time of day in which a story is set. The place may be physical (in a house, on a plane, in a city) or psychological (in a character's mind). An author may make time or place indeterminable, however. Atmosphere is often conveyed in descriptions of setting; Robert Penn Warren sees setting as the "metaphoric expression of characters." The setting may be a social context—in the slums or in high society. The setting may be natural or human (psychological), but usually both. Together all these elements constitute the environment of a story, in which the narrative events and the conflicts are worked out.

Descriptions of the setting are easily overdone, often clumsy. Through a misplaced sense of obligation to describe a setting exhaustively, many young writers get into what I call the setting fallacy—that is, they start the story with a whole paragraph describing the sky, weather, or a city street as the protagonist walks, or a bar. In rewriting, the first thing to get cut is usually the first paragraph.

See the openings of Elizabeth Bowen's *Death of the Heart* and Charlotte Brontë's *Jane Eyre* to see the omniscient author evoking character through a description of weather in a place.

See the opening of Erskine Caldwell's *A Place Called Estherville* and the opening of the fourth chapter of Virginia Woolf's *Orlando* to see how the omniscient author describes weather thematically in a place.

Your handling of other major fictional elements may contribute to the reader's sense of place in your story: narrative, character, dialog, among others. Your description of a place should come in direct relation to a character's physical or mental action in the narrative. For instance, in Faulkner's fiction, place *is* character.

Interweave descriptions of the setting with depictions of characters in action ("Going to see Madeleine, Buck had to climb the town's steepest hill"). See the opening of Hemingway's "In Another Country," of William Styron's *Lie Down in Darkness*, and of Balzac's *Père Goriot* to see how description of place evokes character.

Describe the setting in the dialog, using, for instance, a curious questioner ("Does that rotten-egg smell from the paper factory *always* grip Springhill this way?"). Suggest place by the common speech, dress, ornamentation, manners, taboos, religion of the place.

The naturalistic writers demonstrated that place is destiny, as did Zola in *Germinal* and, again, Faulkner in all his fiction, especially in stories and novels about Quentin Compson. Eudora Welty talks about the importance of place in "On Place in Fiction." See also Mark Schorer, "Fiction and the 'Analogical Matrix.' "

If setting is not really important in the story you are revising, don't overemphasize that element on the mistaken premise that you ought to describe every setting fully. Don't decorate and thus distract. Use restraint, be selective, avoid excess. Inclusiveness is not what is meant by accuracy.

Avoid describing the setting in a lump; usually, this happens in the first paragraph and proves to be public information anyway. "The streets of New York City were alive with nervous energy" is information hardly any reader will require. "Five taxis and one delivery truck narrowly missed Sam and five pedestrians jostled him between Forty-second and

Forty-ninth streets'' only *alludes* to our common knowledge about New York's ''nervous energy.''

Don't present place as a mere backdrop, with picture-postcard detail, local color, or clichés: ''The president of the bank bought a hot dog from the curbside vendor, who said 'T'anks,' and, with his eye on the Empire State Building, the banker walked on.'' If the time setting is a historical period (the Civil War, etc.), avoid excessive detail derived from the research that probably overwhelmed *you*; don't punish the reader for your own self-imposed agony.

Descriptions of places you know very intimately are often too exhaustive and literal. You may transform the places you know by devices for heightening or muting or metamorphosing the major aspects of that place. Through consistency and passion of vision, writers reimagine real places, they don't just describe them as they are. In that sense, Twain created Missouri in *Huck Finn*; Faulkner created Mississippi in *Absalom, Absalom!*; Robert Penn Warren created Louisiana in *All the King's Men*; Flannery O'Connor created Georgia in *Wise Blood*; Willa Cather and Wright Morris created Nebraska in *My Ántonia* and *Ceremony in Lone Tree*; Sinclair Lewis created the midwestern small town in *Main Street*, as did Sherwood Anderson in *Winesburg, Ohio*; William Styron created tidewater Virginia in *Lie Down in Darkness*; John Steinbeck created southern California in *The Pastures of Heaven*.

Test the force of place in ten fine stories by asking whether the story could be shifted to another locale and retain its effects. Then ask the same question of your own story. If the locale is your own hometown, shift it to another, similar town; this forces you to use your imagination.

108 | Do you devote too much space to creating atmosphere?

Atmosphere is the feeling generated by descriptions of the setting, usually in correlation to the prevailing emotional tone of the characters. Mood is more a description of the character's mental state. The atmosphere of a place and the mood of a character work together. Tone comes more from the narrator's *attitude* conveyed in his style.

This atmospheric passage is from the galley version of William Faulkner's *Sanctuary*:

It was after midnight when he [Horace Benbow] left the house with the barefooted man. . . .

Just as they began to descend the hill he looked back at the gaunt ruin of the house rising above the once-formal cedar grove. The trees were massed and matted now with long abandonment; above the jagged mass the stark shape of the house rose squarely like an imperishable and battered landmark above an extinct world. There was no light in it. . . . The road descended gradually—an eroded scar too deep to be a road and too straight to be a ditch gutted by winter freshets and choked with fern and bracken, with fallen leaves and branches moldering quietly above scars of ancient wheels. . . . By following in his guide's footsteps he walked in a faint path where feet had worn the rotting vegetation down to the clay. Overhead an arching hedgerow thinned against the stars to the ultimate leaf.

I have omitted two passages of about ten lines each from the above quotation, one in which Benbow remembers the fixed image of Popeye, Goodwin, and the woman in the house, the other in which Benbow sees images of the historical past associated with the house. The entire passage is saturated with atmospheric effects, within the context of Horace Benbow's neurotic consciousness. When he revised the novel in galleys to shape a more forceful narrative, Faulkner trimmed the lines devoted to atmosphere:

Walking in single file, Tommy and Benbow descended the hill from the house, following the abandoned road. Benbow looked back. The gaunt ruin of the house rose against the sky, above the massed and matted cedars, lightless, desolate, and profound. The road was an eroded scar too deep to be a road and too straight to be a ditch, gutted by winter freshets and choked with fern and rotted leaves and branches. Following Tommy, Benbow walked in a faint path where feet had worn the rotting vegetation down to the clay. Overhead an arching hedgerow of trees thinned against the sky.

It is usually more effective, even for a master of atmospherics, to evoke atmosphere than to describe it directly. These characters and the narrative action in which they are engaged evoke, with the help of a few lines of description, the atmosphere more fully than the galley version does.

In the first chapter of *The City and the Pillar*, Gore Vidal described the atmosphere of a bar as colored by the mood of the protagonist. His revision seventeen years later reduced the space devoted to describing atmosphere and mood.

See "The Day the Flowers Came," comment 19, p. 278.

109 | Are your descriptions of characters, setting, and objects unrelated to a conception?

Descriptions should relate to your *conception* of the whole work (see Question 156.)

Ford Madox Hueffer (later known as Ford Madox Ford), editor of the *English Review*, said he had only to read the first paragraph of "Odour of Chrysanthemums" to see D. H. Lawrence's genius. But he asked him to cut the story, and Lawrence, refocusing his conception from his depiction of the world of the miner and his family to the family's reception of the dead miner's body, started cutting immediately after that first paragraph.

Here is the manuscript version:

> Already among the waggons the men were moving: those who were going up to Underwood stood aside to let the train jolt past, lifting their blackened faces to call something to the driver. Then they passed on, loudly talking, their shapeless grey-black figures seeming of a piece with the raw November afternoon, the tea-bottles rolling in their pockets, while the stumbling of their great boots across the sleepers resounded from afar.

This passage, too, Hueffer must have found impressive; but it struck Lawrence as being now isolated, incidental, or gratuitous. He trimmed it so that it related to the new conception:

> Miners, single, trailing and in groups, passed like shadows diverging home.

Having focused on the wife, Lawrence gives the reader now a single detail, suggestive of key elements to come: a "single" miner from a "group" of miners will die and a "group" of miners will bring him home to his wife, his family. "Shadows" here suggest his "single" death and the deaths of the members of the "group." See Cushman in Bibliography.

110 | Are your descriptions inconsistent with the context?

Make each description consistent with the immediate and the overall context (see Question 22).

If the purpose of description were to be true to life, to give a full sense of it, I could rip off ten pages describing this old Royal typewriter. But you know why I won't do that. It would be true to life, but it would be false to literature. We all know that what we're reading at any given moment is the product of a selection process, and we all know as we are writing that we ought to be selecting from the range of almost endless possibilities what goes down on paper. The question is what goes in, what stays out? What are the criteria, if any? Too often, there is none. So that what goes in strikes the reader very often as arbitrary or gratuitous.

If you use context as the criteria, context will tell. For D. H. Lawrence in "Odour of Chrysanthemums," the general, developing context was death, the death of the miner. In this passage, the immediate context was Elizabeth's fear that something had happened to her husband. She puts her children to bed:

> When she came down, the room was strangely empty, with a tension of expectancy. The mother took up her sewing and stitched for some time without raising her head. Meantime her anger was accumulating. She broke the spell sharply at last, and looked up. It was ten minutes to eight. She sat staring at the pudding in the fender, and at her saucepan to the inside of which bits of dried potato were sticking. Then, for the first time, fear arrived in the room, and stood foremost. The expression of her face changed, and she sat thinking acutely.

Lawrence did not describe the saucepan, the "bits of dried potato," just because, true to life, they would be there and he felt obligated therefore to describe them. He described them because within the context of submerged fear, the sight of them somehow brought that fear into the room where it "stood foremost." Within the overall context of death, the wife and the reader sense where this fear will end.

Using the same criteria of contexts, look at the following passage two paragraphs later. The wife has gone out to look for her husband:

> Something scuffled down the yard as she went out, and she started, though she knew it was only the rats, with which the place was

overrun. The night was very dark. In the great bay of railway-lines where the black trucks rose up obscurely there was no trace of light, only away back she could see a few yellow lamps at the pit-top, and the red smear of the burning pit-bank on the night.

The rats augment her nervousness, and the lack of light and the "black trucks" are derived from the context and serve to develop it further; the rather sinister lamps at the pit-top were not friendly. Now Lawrence introduces light, but it is inconsistent with the context:

She could see the street lamps threading down hill beyond the railway and the field, shining large where the road crossed the lines, and tangling like fireflies in a blur of light where she looked straight into Old Brinsley.

This is a description of lights because, true to life, they are there. But they are inconsistent with the developing context of this fiction, as Lawrence realized when he revised this first published version for later republication. He cut *these* lights because they undercut the very distinct function of the lights three sentences later:

She hurried along the edge of the track, stepping carefully over the levers of the points, and, crossing the converging lines, came to the stile by the great white gates near the weighting machine, whence she emerged on the road. Then the fear which had led her by the hand unhesitating loosed its hold, and shrank back. People were walking up to New Brinsley; she saw the light in the window of his mother's house below the road by the crossing.

And the lights of the Prince of Wales tavern make her feel her husband is inside, drinking with his friends. All the descriptions now derive from the immediate context of fear or of the dispelling of fear while also contributing to the overall context of death, either literally or ironically by contrast.

111 | Have you neglected to present description indirectly?

Characters, objects, settings, etc. are described sometimes in an overt or explicit, sometimes in an indirect or subtle manner. Describe indirectly when you can, as when one character describes another in dialog, thus raising the reader's expectations, as no direct description of the character could.

I have looked for an opportunity somewhere in this handbook to call your attention to a rather unusual example of revision or, more strictly speaking, of editing, and this opportunity will serve. In *College of One*, Sheilah Graham describes that part of her affair with F. Scott Fitzgerald in which he became her literature and creative-writing teacher; in Appendix 2, she offers a photocopy of her short story "Beloved Infidel," in which she tells about their affair; to illustrate for her several of the techniques of fiction, Fitzgerald simply revised her story with penciled-in changes. One of the interesting series of changes amounts to a recreation of himself as a character in the story.

Graham overloads the very first page and then the next with exposition and with descriptions of John (Fitzgerald, who changed his name in the story to Carter) and of John's now deceased wife, Alicia (Zelda). The point of view is omniscient:.

John O'Brien was thirty-eight, but looked thirty, particularly when he smiled. It was a charming, slow smile that lingered in his thickly lashed blue eyes several seconds, after his mouth had reverted to its normal, rather sad lines. He had the build of a lightweight boxer, broad well-developed shoulders; narrow hips, strong, well-shaped legs. He walked like a fighter with his head slightly tucked into his neck, his arms swinging, and fists closed as though ready to strike.

He had been the best looking man of his class at Yale. If you wanted to annoy him in those days, you called him "Beautiful." The lines and coloring of his face was still like a masculinized edition of Priscilla Lane.

*   *   *

. . . he married beautiful, auburn haired Alicia Sanders. They were the most popular couple of that crazy decade. You didn't count unless you knew them or said you did. No party of the intelligentsia or rich Long Island set was considered a success unless John and Alicia O'Brien were there. He was glamour boy number one and his vivid wife trailed happily along in the cloud of his glory.

Graham continues with physical description, background, and exposition, then she shifts directly to a cocktail party where John meets Mara (Sheilah Graham). I am not reproducing Fitzgerald's changes in the section quoted above; I hope you will track down a hardcover copy of the book (the reproduction of the story in the paperback edition is probably too faint).

Instead of making stylistic changes—quite effective ones—Fitzgerald might well have suggested that Ms. Graham break up the block of description and distribute it in parts throughout the story, and that she employ the device, at some points, of giving some of it energy through dialog; and he might have shown her an episode he deleted from *Tender Is the Night* in which Seth and Dinah Piper (Dick and Nicole Diver of the novel, who resemble in some ways Fitzgerald and Zelda) are described in dialog. See *Three Novels of F. Scott Fitzgerald*, edited by Malcolm Cowley, pp. 338-40.

112 | Have you written *inert* blocks of description?

Some writers assume that because they must create a world, they must do so with a fullness of detail that characterizes the world their own creator made. Nobody can sustain that assumption in actual practice, so first drafts, especially those in the omniscient point of view, contain passages produced by attempts, in bursts of activity, to be true to that preconception. In revision, the general rule of selectivity may come to the rescue.

Are sections of the narrative overloaded with descriptive detail? Have you written some descriptions out of a misguided sense of obligation to the reader? Are some descriptions gratuitous—included simply because the people or objects would, in life, *be* there in a given situation? If so, some descriptions may seem somehow separate from the narrative. Description and narrative are at best inseparable. The distinction is that description emphasizes the image and narrative the action: beads on a string. Revise to order, arrange, and coordinate a succession of descriptive details along a narrative thread.

When you find you've clustered descriptions of a character or a place, break them up, get a series of related images going, and place them strategically in a pattern throughout the story.

Abstract descriptions, using general words, describe poorly: beautiful, repulsive, terrific, big, ugly, small, boring. Abstract descriptions often don't describe but merely offer information or exposition dully. Description doesn't *report*; if it's effective, it *recreates*. "I don't observe and I don't describe," said François Mauriac, "I rediscover." Conventional descriptons of characters, scenes (landscapes, clouds), settings (houses, rooms) are often abstract and inert. In your descriptive passages, strive for a sense of movement, create a rhythm within and among the sentences, as determined by the mood, tone, and nature of what's being described. To make descriptions active, use the active voice for verbs, use concrete nouns, specific words, and be viligant about overuse of adjectives—two to a single noun are usually too many; even one is dangerous.

I stood on the threshold, dazzled by the alabaster light and the two attractive young women in white dresses who sat on a enormous couch in the middle of the large room. I could feel a nice breeze. There were white curtains over the open windows and a wine-colored rug on the floor. On the wall was a landscape painting of some sort. Tom joined me, and we walked into the room. [hypothetical first draft]

Fitzgerald had such a fine sense of activated description that he was able to make the description of Tom and Daisy Buchanan's house in the first chapter of *The Great Gatsby* work in the early draft, except for a line that I will insert in brackets and which he cut out:

A breeze blew through the room, blew curtains in at one end and out the other like pale flags, twisting them up toward the frosted wedding-cake of the ceiling, and then rippled over the wine-colored rug, making a shadow on it as wind does on the sea.
The only completely stationary object in the room was an enormous couch on which two young women were buoyed up as though upon an anchored balloon. They were both in white and their dresses were rippling and fluttering as if they had just been blown back in after a short flight around the house. I must have stood for a few moments [on the threshold, dazzled by the alabaster light,] listening to the whip and snap of the curtains and the groan of a picture on the wall. Then there was a boom as Tom Buchanan shut the rear windows and the caught wind died out about the room, and the curtains and the rugs and the two young women ballooned slowly to the floor.

Those words move. To Nick Carroway, the first-person narrator, the house seems as alive as the characters. His active sensibility activates the objects and the inhabitants, expressed in similar style.

Here is an omniscient description of a house that moves—Virginia Woolf, *To the Lighthouse*, the "Time Passes" interlude:

Nothing stirred in the drawing room or in the dining room, but owing to the old hinges and shrunken sea moistened woodwork, which wet one winter shrank in the summer, certain winds detached from the main body of wind, ventured into the house. It was not wild though. Almost one might imagine questioning, wondering, as they gently attempted the falling wall paper—would it hang, would it fall? And the chairs, and the tables and the books, and the silvery saucepans in rows on the shelf, how long would they endure, and of what nature were they? Were they, too, of the substance of wind and rain, allies, with whom in the darkness, wind and rain would commune? But passing among the sleepers, surely there must be doubt. Everything else can tarnish and perish, is dissolved again; but not there. And one would say to the grey airs of midnight and the wandering gleams of moonlight, of light which wavers up the wall and across the ceiling, phantom soft, how they had no power to smooth, to touch, or to destroy, upon which wearily, ghostily, as if they had feather-light fingers, and could disappear and come again, so now, they would fold their light garments, and die away, having looked upon shut eyes, and fingers loosely closed. They would not betake themselves to the staircase, to the window for example; they would nose and rub and fumble the pane; descending, ruffle the light cloaks in the hall, and then meditate how to chill the apples in the plate on the dining room table. . . . They tried the picture on the easel in the drawing room, they brushed the matt. They blew a little sand along the floor.

This is a good first-draft example of rather innovative omniscient, impressionistic description, but it is not description for the sake of it (it goes on for twenty-five pages this way); Woolf expresses here her vision of reality, or super-reality, a kind of metaphysical-psychological collaboration. Here is her revision of the passage:

So some random light directing them with its pale footfall upon stair and mat, from some uncovered star, or wandering ship, or the Lighthouse even, the little airs mounted the staircase and nosed round bedroom doors. But here surely, they must cease. Whatever else may perish and disappear, what lies here is steadfast. Here one might say to those sliding lights, those fumbling airs that breathe and bend over the bed itself, here you can neither touch nor destroy. Upon which, wearily, ghostlily, as if they had feather-light fingers and the light persistency of feathers, they would look, once, on the shut eyes, and the loosely clasping fingers, and fold their garments wearily and disappear. And so, nosing, rubbing, they went to the window on the staircase, to the servants' bedrooms, to the boxes in the attics; descending, blanched the apples on the dining-room table, fumbled the petals of roses, tried the picture on the easel, brushed the mat and blew a little sand along the floor. At length, desisting, all ceased together, gathered together, all sighed together; swung wide; admitted nothing; and slammed to.

Woolf wrote to Lady Ottoline Morrell: "I'm specially pleased you like Time Passes—It gave me more trouble than all the rest of the book put together, and I was afraid it hadn't succeeded." See Susan Dick's transcription of the original draft, *Virginia Woolf, "To the Lighthouse"* (Toronto: University of Toronto Press, 1982).

113 | Do your descriptions fail to activate the reader's senses?

The most effective descriptions are concrete. Concrete descriptions do not stop the action to describe a still life. They are active. They appeal to, they activate, the senses: colors, forms, textures, contrasts (light and dark, soft and hard), sounds, odors, flavors. They have a freshness of diction and of image, free of clichés, triteness, wordiness, mechanical connectives such as "which"—these dull the senses. Whether you are describing a character's bodily sensations or the mood and tone of mental states, revise to make your descriptions evoke sensory impressions through imagery.

Select your details, rather than piling one on top of another. Be economical. Prune unnecessary or excess detail. Strive for emphasis. Conventional descriptions are too often abstract, inert. Static descriptions *can* be very effective, as in the fiction of Alain Robbe-Grillet; but generally, strive for active descriptions.

In "The Ballet of Central Park," Kay Boyle changed the general phrase "ballet slippers" to the more specific "pink satin toe-shoes"

Notice the effect of Nathanael West's removal of a single detail. The "Miss Lonelyhearts and the Lamb" short-story version:

The walls were bare except for a mirror and an ivory Christ.

The *Miss Lonelyhearts* novel version:

The walls were bare except for an ivory Christ that hung opposite the foot of the bed.

West saw a mirror on the wall, but he decided the reader didn't need to see it.

In Bernard Malamud's story "Idiots First," some crumpled one- and five-dollar bills are very important to the old man. In the first version, he has them stowed in a drawer. In the published version, Malamud has added a paper bag, with this effect: bills hidden in a bag in a drawer enhance the old man's secretiveness, and when he sticks the bag in his overcoat pocket, we have a clearer sense that they are there as he goes out into the city in search of more money.

In "The Curtain," Raymond Chandler describes the green house where Philip Marlowe's rich client awaits him:

> The air steamed. The walls and ceiling of the glass house dripped. In the half light enormous tropical plants spread their blooms and branches all over the place, and the smell of them was almost as overpowering as the smell of boiling alcohol.

The passage is full of well-chosen details that appeal to our senses, but something is missing.

For the story version, Chandler knew his quick readers of *Black Mask* pulp magazine. For the novel, *The Big Sleep*, published by Knopf, a quality house, he hoped for more patient readers. The novel version:

> The air was thick, wet, steamy and laced with the cloying smell of tropical orchids in bloom. The glass walls and roof were heavily misted and big drops of moisture splashed down on the plants. The light had an unreal greenish color, like light filtered through an aquarium tank. The plants filled the place, a forest of them, with nasty meaty leaves and stalks like the newly washed fingers of dead men. They smelled as overpowering as boiling alcohol under a blanket.

The details of the first passage only deliver information rather literally, but evocative details evoke something, and the revised passage evokes the decay of the flesh of the living and the imminence of death by violence. There is an aura of an energy suppressed, about to explode. The tropical humidity evoked here is reiterated through mist, fog, and rain throughout the novel.

See Chandler's *Killer in the Rain*, introduction by Philip Durham, and Frank MacShane, *The Life of Raymond Chandler*, p. 68.

"There is nothing in the intellect," said Aristotle, "that is not first in the senses."

114 | Are some of your descriptions unintentionally melodramatic?

Melodrama is an attitude or an action in excess of the occasion which makes an excessive appeal to the emotions of the reader.

First, when should melodramatic descriptions be *intentional*? Writers very seldom set out to write melodrama, not even commercial writers who want to deliver highly charged scenes of action in police, spy, science fiction, or western novels. If an action is inherently melodramatic, melodramatic descriptions of characters, objects, and settings are not needed to enhance the effect; they are far more likely to call attention to and thus distract from the effect by straining credibility. You may intend, at some point, a sudden melodramatic surge in an otherwise non-melodramatic story, but normally, you will look in revision for phrases, lines, or passages that are unintentionally melodramatic.

The act of writing is in itself a kind of melodramatic act; it's certainly an excessive human act. You will then, quite naturally, cut loose here and there with language in excess of the occasion that you are depicting in the story itself. In "Guests of the Nation," Frank O'Connor frequently risks melodramatic action and expression because the situation is one that might be treated melodramatically from the start. But O'Connor was not really interested in the act of shooting hostages.

What O'Connor wanted to convey was the pathetic irony of men who had made friends with their captives having suddenly to shift into the role of executioners; he wanted to suggest not only how they felt then, but how the event probably marked them for life. He did not want the reader to dwell upon the event itself. But in early versions, on into the published version, the melodrama emerged in descriptions. The narrator feels certain that the man he must shoot would not, under the same circumstances, shoot him and his own comrade:

> Did either of us imagine for an instant that he'd shoot us for all the so-and-so brigadiers in the so-and-so British Army? By this time I began to perceive in the dusk the desolate edges of the bog that was to be their last earthly bed, and, so great a sadness overtook my mind, I could not answer him. . . . if you can understand, I didn't want him to be bumped off.

That O'Connor's description of the landscape is unintentionally melodramatic is suggested by his effort in every other way to tone down the action and the description of the execution. In situations such as this, one excess seems to authorize another in some other way; O'Connor's narrator probably would not have said "a great sadness overtook my mind" and "I didn't want him to be bumped off" had he not aroused himself with "the desolate edges of the bog" and "last earthly bed." Some years later, for a new collection of his stories, O'Connor cut out the lines I have quoted above. He also cut "the tragic death of his old friend" in the passage describing the narrator's reaction to Belcher's nervous laugh when his comrade is shot.

After both Hawkins and Belcher have been shot, "we had to carry the warm corpses a few yards before we sunk them in the windy bog." O'Connor cut that, too. And he cut "Noble and I . . . went back along the desolate edge of the treacherous bog without a word." O'Connor decided that his narrator had spoken far too many words in describing the bog. With these and a few other such lines cut out, the description is very simple, allowing the inherent drama of the situation to play itself out unhindered by unintentional melodrama.

115 | Are some of your descriptions unintentionally sentimental?

"Sentiment in excess of the occasion" is poet John Crowe Ransom's definition of sentimentality. It is an excessive response to a stimulus. Everyone is sentimental about something, but sentimentality is a tendency to be influenced excessively by thoughts and feelings rather than reason. Some writers deliberately play upon a reader's inclinations toward sentimentality; others deliberately avoid it and often treat it ironically or satirically, as did Ransom. When our reason tells us that the cause of a character's feelings is trivial and the author's response excessive, we may conclude that the author is being too sentimental. If you reach too high for pathos, you run the risk of falling into bathos. Oscar Wilde was revolted by the fallacy of sentimentality. "That man has no soul . . . who can read of the death of Little Nell without laughing."

Are your descriptions of your character at times too sentimental? One of the reasons why D. H. Lawrence cut passages describing the miner's children at play in "Odour of Chrysanthemums" was to avoid sentimentality. Also repeated use of the word "little" tended to plead for sympathy, so he cut it.

In "Idiots First," Bernard Malamud wanted Isaac's weeping to contribute to the cumulative sense of emotions in turmoil. The "A Long Ticket for Isaac" version:

Isaac resumed eating. Tears dripped into his coffee. Mendel tried to apologize but couldn't and looked away.

Malamud realized that "tears dripped into his coffee" was an expression of sentiment in excess of the occasion, so he revised to keep the weeping but to put it in a tougher context. The "Idiots First" version:

The tables were crowded except where a heavy set man sat eating soup with kasha. After one look at him they left in haste, although Isaac wept.

Samuel Butler, *The Way of All Flesh*:

My father came on him in the afternoon, just as the sun was setting, and saw him with his arms resting on the top of the wall looking towards the sun over a field through which there was a path on which my father was. My father heard him say "Good-bye, sun; good-bye, sun," as the sun sank, and saw by his tone and manner that he was feeling very feeble. Before the next sunset the poor old man was gone.

Before the reader reaches the last line, the saturation point of sentimentality has already been reached in this passage. Butler struck out the excessive "poor old man" (though the phrase was in character for the narrator) and substituted simply "he."

See "The Day the Flowers Came," comment 27, pp. 282–83.

116 | Do you commit the *pathetic fallacy?*

The pathetic fallacy is "the attribution of human characteristics to inanimate objects," said John Ruskin. Today, the use of the pathetic fallacy is associated with sentimentality. "Weeping, the trees looked down upon Laura."

Here is a passage from the manuscript version of D. H. Lawrence's first novel, *The White Peacock*. The narrator has been watching a swan and turns toward the orchard:

There the daffodils were lifting their glorious heads and throwing back their wanton yellow curls to sport with the sun. At the foot of each sloping, grey old tree a family of these healthy, happy flowers stood, some bursten with overfulness of splendour, some raising their heads slightly, modestly showing a sweet countenance, others still hiding their faces, leaning forward from the jaunty cluster of grey green

spears; many were just venturing timidly out of their sheaths peeping
about. I felt inclined to hug them, I wanted desperately to know their
language perfectly so that I might talk out my heart to them. They
had a rich perfume as of oranges; they laughed to me, and tried to
reassure me.

Some writers will lapse into a line or two of such personification; fewer
will leave such lines in for publication. Lawrence created a context to
justify his use of personification but in this version he must have decided
he had passed over the mark into a commission of the pathetic fallacy,
because he struck out the more excessive expressions:

There the daffodils were lifting their heads and throwing back their
yellow curls. At the foot of each sloping, grey old tree stood a family
of flowers, some bursten with golden fullness, some lifting their heads
slightly, to show a modest, sweet countenance, others still hiding
their faces, leaning forward pensively from the jaunty grey-green
spears; I wished I had their language, to talk to them distinctly.

Virginia Woolf put the pathetic fallacy to controlled use with positive
effect in the "Times Passes" middle section of *To the Lighthouse*. See
Question 112.

117 | Do you use terms or details that will eventually date your story?

Contemporary writers exhibit a rather unrestrained tendency to put
name-brand clothes on their characters and name-brand products in their
hands, and to surround them with fads and fashions and headlines and
pop-culture artifacts, not only as a way of attesting to authenticity but as
vehicles for depicting character and even presenting action. Today's
reader, such writers seem to assume, will cry, "How true to life!" They
forget that tomorrow's readers can only feel left out. Too often too much
rides on those up-to-date details. Many writers who revise their work a
decade or so after publication leap upon such details and mark them
"first to go." The story that got a lot of mileage out of references to the
Edsel goes nowhere slowly today. The story written in the same era that
was content with a general description escapes such limitations.

VII DEVICES

118 | Have you neglected to imagine the possible uses of a wide range of *technical* devices?

A device is any technique that produces or enhances the effectiveness of point of view, style, character, conflict, theme, etc.

As you read any fiction, ask yourself, What attention-getting devices does the author use? A device often functions in a rather clear-cut way that is apparent to the reader while not usually distracting him from the illusion he is experiencing.

Identify the devices you have already used. Are they effectively employed? Are they controlled within an overall design?

119 | Does your story lack the enhancements of *figurative language*?

Figurative language is language expanded beyond its usual literal meaning to achieve intensity and vividness. A figurative expression usually contains a stated or implied comparison to express a relationship between things that are essentially unlike. "Colors, scents and sounds correspond," wrote Baudelaire in his poem "Correspondences."

For the New York edition of *The American*, Henry James revised to express character in more figurative language. "Yes, this seeing of the world was very pleasant, and he would willingly do a little more of it" became "Yes, these waters of the free curiosity were very soothing, and he would splash in them till they ran dry."

". . . and it was both uncomfortable and slightly contemptible to feel obligated to square one's self with a standard" became ". . . and shouldn't hunt about for a standard as a lost dog hunts for a master." ". . . he was too short, as he said, to afford a belly" became ". . . he was too short, as he said, to afford an important digression."

120 | Is your story deficient in *imagery?*

Imagery is the collection of descriptive details in a literary work that appeal to the senses. W. H. Auden said that poetry is memorable speech; one might say that fiction is memorable images. Ezra Pound said, "An image is that which presents an intellectual and emotional complex in an instant of time." W. B. Yeats said, "Wisdom speaks first in images."

A writer uses an image to arouse emotion in the reader and to create mood. Key the imagery to specific purposes: foreshadowing, setting, mood, picturization of characters.

In *Middlemarch*, Mr. Casaubon says, very early in Eliot's long novel, that he arranges the documents of his research "in pigeon holes partly," thus setting in motion a pattern of similar images of darkness and narrowness associated with him and with Dorothea's perception of him and of her relationship with him.

Don't neglect auditory images: "Standing beside the closed piano on the morning of the funeral Stephen heard the coffin bumping down the crooked staircase" (James Joyce, *Stephen Hero*).

Create vivid images so the reader can *see* what is happening. Do your images stimulate the reader's senses, arouse his emotions, stimulate his imagination, activate his intellect?

In *Stephen Hero*, Joyce fashioned specific images to enable us to see his characters:

—In the name of God what do you wear that hat for? It's not so terribly hot, is it? he asked.
Cranly took off the hat slowly and gazed into its depths.

Joyce decided that the hat alone was not a strong enough image:

Cranly . . . was picking his teeth with a match, very deliberately and scrupulously, occasionally halting to insert his tongue carefully into some crevice before continuing the process of picking. He spat out what he dislodged.

In *A Portrait of the Artist as a Young Man*, Joyce refined and repeated the Cranly image:

Cranly dislodged a fig seed from his teeth on the point of his rude toothpick and gazed at it intently.

Joyce deemphasized the hat as a character image and focused on the toothpick and figs. "Gazed into its depths" (the hat's) becomes "gazed at it intently" (the fig seed).

In *Tess of the D'Urbervilles*, Thomas Hardy seems consciously to have crafted this image:

> He plunged amid the webs of vapour which hung about between the trees, and she could hear the rustling of the branches as he ascended the adjoining slope, till his movements were no louder than the hopping of a bird, and finally died away.

But wanting us to see and feel the "webs of vapour" image more vividly, Hardy refined it: "He plunged into the webs of vapour which formed veils between the trees . . ."

121 | Are all your *abstractions* and generalizations about character and meaning embodied in *vivid images?*

Abstractions and generalizations, especially as applied to characters, have relatively little effect on the reader. They become as inert as raw information; the reader does not experience the illusion of living them, and since illusion is the main purpose of fiction, the more you can do without abstractions, the better. Rather than describe a character in abstract, general language, conjure a visual image of your conception of him or her.

From *Stephen Hero*, here is a *conceptual image* that helps explain James Joyce's use of imagery (which has influenced a good many writers):

> By an epiphany he meant a sudden spiritual manifestation, whether in the vulgarity of speech or of gesture or in a memorable phase of the mind itself. . . . the most delicate and evanescent of moments.

*   *   *

> . . . Then all at once I see it and I know at once what it is: epiphany.
> —What?
> —Imagine my glimpses at that clock as the gropings of a spiritual

eye which seeks to adjust its vision to an exact focus. The moment the focus is reached the object is epiphanised.

For such an epiphany, here is the raw material, from *Stephen Hero*:

The babble of the young students reached him as if from a distance, in broken pulsations, and lifting his eyes he saw the high rain-clouds retreating across the rain-swept country. The quick light shower was over, tarrying, a cluster of diamonds, among the shrubs of the quadrangle where an exhalation ascended from the blackened earth. The company in the colonnade was leaving shelter, with many a doubting glance, with a prattle of trim boots, a pretty rescue of petticoats, under umbrellas, a light armoury, upheld at cunning angles.

Joyce had set that passage in the middle of long descriptions, but in *A Portrait of the Artist as a Young Man*, he epiphanized the image:

The quick light shower had drawn off, tarrying in clusters of diamonds among the shrubs of the quadrangle where an exhalation was breathed forth by the blackened earth. Their trim boots prattled as they stood on the steps of the colonnade, talking quietly and gaily, glancing at the clouds, holding their umbrellas at cunning angles against the few last raindrops, closing them again, holding their skirts demurely.

For more on epiphanies, see the definitive Viking edition of *Portrait of the Artist* edited by Chester Anderson, pp. 267-72.

Compare Wright Morris's handling of the image of the boy as a bird in his father's dream and the image of the boy showing a jar of spoiled leftover food to a group of his mother's friends early in "The Ram in the Thicket" with the same images early in the novel version *Man and Boy*. In *Earthly Delights, Unearthly Adornments*, Wright Morris says, "To make an image that is adequate to his sensations" the writer "will have to imagine more than he remembers, intuit more than he saw." The writer has at his "instant disposal the inexhaustible powers of light and darkness, the ceaseless, commonplace, bewildering interlacing of memory, emotion and imagination."

The aim of Henry James's revisions of *The Portrait of a Lady* was to create images that would provide deeper insight into the makeup and motives of his characters and to give a dramatic edge to their experiences.

To discover the way ideas about death are embodied in images, read James Agee's *A Death in the Family*.

"My task which I am trying to achieve," said Joseph Conrad, "is, by the power of the written word to make you hear, to make you feel—it is, before all, to make you see. That—and no more, and it is everything."

122 | Have you overused *metaphors* and *similes*?

A metaphor is a figure of speech that conjures an image that stimulates one or more of the reader's five senses by directly stating that one thing is like something else with the purpose of enabling the reader to experience the one thing more intensely. Metaphors and similes are two common types of figures of speech. The metaphor "John is a lion" is an implied comparison which is more immediate and dramatic than "John has some of the characteristics of a lion."

A simile differs from a metaphor in that the comparison is stated: "John is like a lion." The word "like" specifies that a similarity exists between John and a lion. "As if" and "as though" are other signals that a simile is being introduced.

The metaphor or simile image is usually visual, but it may also be auditory, or it may evoke a smell, touch, or taste, or may even be an intellectual image.

Virginia Woolf makes brilliant use of metaphor in the opening of Chapter 5 of *Orlando*. Dampness becomes a metaphor for the English character in the Victorian era:

> This great cloud hung . . . over the whole of the British Isles. . . . damp now began to make its way into every house—damp, which is the most insidious of all enemies, for while the sun can be shut out by blinds, and the frost roasted by a hot fire, damp steals in while we sleep; damp is silent, imperceptible, ubiquitous. Damp swells the wood, furs the kettle, rusts the iron, rots the stone. So gradual is the process, that it is not until we pick up some chest of drawers, or coal scuttle, and the whole thing drops to pieces in our hands, that we suspect even that the disease is at work.
>
> Thus stealthily and imperceptibly, none marking the exact day or hour of the change, the constitution of England was altered and nobody knew it. . . . But the change did not stop at outward things. The damp struck within. Men felt the chill in their hearts; the damp in their minds. . . .

Writers of fiction use similes more often than metaphors because metaphors tend to try a reader's patience. "John is a lion" may make some reader reply, "Oh, no, he isn't." A reader is more likely to accept the simile "John is like a lion."

Flaubert expressed the dilemma of all writers when he said, "Comparisons consume me like flies." For writers, constitutionally, everything is like something else or, momentarily, *is* something else—often it is, or is like, two or three things at once. The predisposition to compare, which is always active, is aggravated by the desperate necessity, in the first draft, and on through every revision, of finding ways to describe what is difficult to describe. Writers overuse, then, metaphors and similes quite naturally. Do not take the mere presence in abundance of similes and metaphors as proof that you are sure enough writing fiction. In the first draft, draw on them, let them come. In revision, be vigilant.

Often, a simple description proves far more effective than a habitual or a desperate reaching for simile: "To the little boy, the clouds were very high and the trees brushed against them as he ran home, trying to beat the rain to his front door." You don't need, in that context, to say "the trees were as tall as telephone poles" or "the trees reached so high, it was as though they touched the clouds," or "the trees were skyscrapers," or "the trees were like skyscrapers." The little boy is far more aware of their simple treeness than he would ever be of their resemblance to skyscrapers.

Revising "The Chrysanthemums," John Steinbeck added a simile that has a major effect on how his reader perceives the protagonist, Elisa. First published version:

Kneeling there, her hand went out toward his legs in the greasy black trousers. Her hesitant fingers almost touched the cloth. Then her hand dropped to the ground.

When he revised the story for inclusion in *The Long Valley*, he added:

She crouched low like a fawning dog.

Crane first wrote that Henry Fleming wished for "a little red badge of courage," but cut "little," giving greater force to the image as a metaphor; also, the diminutive "little" trivializes the title metaphor. In *The Red Badge of Courage*, Stephen Crane first wrote that the sun "was pasted in the sky like a fierce wafer." He cut "fierce" (end of chapter 9), thus creating one of the most famous similes (and symbols) in American fiction—famous partly because there is much disagreement about its meaning. "Fierce" may suggest what he meant, but the phrase "fierce wafer" itself sounds ludicrous. In *The Light That Failed*, Kipling used a similar phrase: "The sun shone, a blood-red wafer, on the water."

See "The Day the Flowers Came," comment 9, p. 269.

123 | Considering the context, should some metaphors be turned into similes, some *similes into metaphors?*

In a version of *The Red Badge of Courage*, Stephen Crane wrote:

> He saw that he was a speck, raising his tiny arms against all possible forces and fates which were swelling down upon him like storms.

"He was a speck" is a metaphor, but Crane wanted the effect of two metaphors, so he struck out the simile "like storms," and substituted the metaphor "in black tempests".

In "Miss Lonelyhearts and the Dead Pan," Nathanael West wrote:

> May 1932
> And on most days I received more than thirty letters, all of them alike, as though stamped from the dough of suffering with a heart-shaped cookie knife.

West cut "as though," thus converting a weak simile into a strong metaphor.

124 | Have you included *floating metaphors and similes* that fail to contribute to the overall design?

Metaphors and similes are most effective when the reader feels that they are appropriate to the context of the story, that they seem to be part of a pattern of figurative language, as opposed to being incidental, gratuitous. Throughout *The Return of the Native* runs a pattern of fire and light images that relate to the Prometheus myth: ". . . the deity that lies ignominiously chained within a human being looked out of him [Clym Yeobright] like a ray. . . ." Hardy sharpened the simile:

The look suggested isolation; but it revealed something more. As usual in bright natures the deity that lies ignominiously chained within a perishable human carcase looked out of him like a ray.

The simile "like a ray" is enhanced by "bright natures" and contrasted to "carcase." Hardy revised the novel to achieve a pattern of fire images for Eustacia—an image of the general idea of her romantic rebellion. Her "lurid red" soul became "flame-like."

> After a long look at him [Wildeve] she resumed with—softness.
> "Must I go on weakly confessing to you things a woman ought to conceal?"

That became:

> After a long look at him she resumed with the old quiescent warmth.
> "Must I go on confessing . . ."

Eustacia turns away from Wildeve "in pained indignation"; the phrase became "while an inner indignation spread through her like subterranean heat." "Eustacia could not wait for her companions [the Mummers] after this" became "Eustacia warmed with an inner fire could not wait for her companions after this."

Avoid mixing metaphors. If you say, "John is a lion and when he is angry he is a Mack truck on a rampage," the effect of the lion is canceled by the reader's attempt to see the truck and to relate lion and truck to each other.

Thomas Wolfe makes passionate use of metaphors and similes in his first novel, *Look Homeward, Angel*, and in all his other fiction, but without the kind of controlled pattern Fitzgerald uses in *The Great Gatsby* and Robert Penn Warren uses in *All the King's Men*.

In "Where Is the Voice Coming From?" Eudora Welty revised to increase images of heat to form a pattern. See *Creative Writing and Rewriting*, Kuehl, pp. 3-18. Compare John Hawkes's "The Nearest Cemetery" with *Second Skin*, the novel that absorbs the short story, to see how he developed patterns of cemetery images (Kuehl, pp. 266-87). See Mark Schorer, "Fiction and the 'Analogical Matrix.'"

125 | Have you failed to *prepare* early for a later event or effect?

Preparation is the insertion ("planting") of information, or some other specific element, making it part of a later action, so as to prevent the reader's feeling that the later event has occurred "out of nowhere."

In Bernard Malamud's "A Long Ticket for Isaac" ("Idiots First"), Mendel and his son Isaac go to a pawnbroker:

> Mendel breathing heavily fumbled with his watch chain, unhooked it, and silently held forth the worn gold watch, his hand shaking.

This scene is important because it is the first of several in which Mendel, with great urgency, strives to secure money for his retarded son's welfare. Also, the swift passing of time is a major stimulus of emotion in the story. But Malamud neglected even to mention the watch earlier. He adds a passage to prepare the reader for the pawnshop scene:

> He wound his old watch though the sight of the stopped clock nauseated him.
> Isaac wanted to hold it to his ear.
> "No, it's late." Mendel put the watch carefully away.

By inserting this new passage on the first page, before father and son leave their apartment, Malamud not only "plants" the watch, he introduces the motif of Mendel's death ("the stopped clock") and of time passing for Isaac ("No, it's late."). See Kuehl in Bibliography.

As you read "Good Country People," you can see how Flannery O'Connor prepares for the revelation at the end that the Bible salesman is a diabolical fraud.

Identify a key moment in your story. Have you prepared for it earlier? If not, you may have neglected to prepare other moments as well.

See "The Day the Flowers Came," comment 11, pp. 271–72, and comment 14, pp. 273–74.

126 | Have you failed to *foreshadow* major developments?

A foreshadowing is an event that prefigures a later event, so that it will be more convincing and forceful.

Here is a version of a passage in Samuel Butler's *The Way of All Flesh*:

> Vastly merry were we, but it is so long ago that I have forgotten almost all save that we were vastly merry.

Butler's narrator's purpose here early in his narrative is to give the reader an impression of Theobald Pontifex's own childhood. But the focus is misplaced; it is on Overton, the narrator, and the memory is too generalized.

> We were very merry, but it is so long ago that I have forgotten nearly everything save that we *were* very merry. Almost the only thing that remains with me as a permanent impression was the fact that Theobald one day beat his nurse and teased her, and when she said she should go away cried out, "You shan't go away—I'll keep you on purpose to torment you."

The passage Butler added not only enhances the general statement with a specific incident, but foreshadows Theobald's similar behavior when his own son, Ernest, is at his mercy.

In revision, be sure to cut a passage that foreshadows a later event or development that you have already cut out, or that you realize you never included.

See Chapter 17 of Emily Brontë's *Wuthering Heights*, where developments foreshadowed earlier occur, and where Brontë foreshadows more events to come.

Identify a major event in your story. Have you foreshadowed it earlier? If not, insert a foreshadowing passage in the most strategic place.

127 | Have you neglected to imagine uses for the device of *anticipation*?

Anticipation is the reader's feeling that something is sure to come, stimulated by an element the writer has deliberately placed to arouse that feeling.

As you bring the development of one episode to an end, you may introduce an element that anticipates an episode to come. You may satisfy that anticipation immediately or you may deliberately frustrate it for an even more interesting effect. Dickens is a master at that kind of engaging manipulation of the reader. He moves his reader from anticipation to expectation to gratification.

Indicators or suggestions of what is to come are sometimes called "preparation" or "foreshadowings," but there is enough distinction among the terms to treat them separately.

In Emily Brontë's *Wuthering Heights*, Isabella, referring to Heathcliff, who is now her husband, asks Nellie, "Do you think he could bear to see me grow fat, and merry; and could bear to think that we were tranquil, and not resolve on poisoning our comfort?" Something about that question causes the reader to anticipate that Heathcliff will do what Isabella fears. And indeed he does, almost systematically.

Robert Penn Warren in *All the King's Men*, Mark Twain in *The Adventures of Huckleberry Finn*, and Ernest Hemingway in *The Sun Also Rises* employ the device of anticipation frequently.

See "The Day the Flowers Came," comment 7, pp. 267–68, and comment 13, pp. 272–73.

128 | Have you used the device of *repetition* too little or too much?

Repetition is the repeated use of an element, with variations in a pattern, throughout a story. Repetition intensifies the reader's response by enabling him to remember elements as the story moves ahead. Similes, metaphors, motifs, character relationships, situations are repeated. Repetition is a major unifying force. For repetition in style, see Question 27.

Here is an early version of a passage from William Faulkner's *Absalom, Absalom!*:

> They faced each other on the two gaunt horses. . . . *Don't you pass the shadow of that limb, Charles*; and *I am going to pass it, Henry*) —and then Wash Jones sitting that Sutpen saddle mule before Miss Rosa's house, shouting her name into the sunny and peaceful quiet of the street, saying, "Air you Rosie Coldfield? Then you better come on out yon. Henry has done shot that durn French feller. Kilt him dead as a beef."

The action of Henry Sutpen and Charles Bon arriving at the gates to Sutpen's Hundred has such a powerful and complex effect on Quentin, the *reteller* of this epic story, that he returns again and again to this moment, and to similar "at the gate" actions that quickly followed—Wash Jones at Rosa Coldfield's gate in town; Rosa at the foot of the stairs at Sutpen's Hundred, her ascension blocked by Clytie, Henry's Negro half sister; then Rosa encountering Judith, Henry's full sister, where she stands outside her bedroom door, holding her dress intended for her wedding with Charles Bon. But Faulkner saw that the first "at the gate" instance was too vaguely described.

> They faced each other on the two gaunt horses. . . . *Don't you pass the shadow of this gate, this branch, Charles*; and *I am going to pass it, Henry*)—and then Wash Jones sitting that saddleless mule before Miss Rosa's gate, shouting her name. . . .

The simple insertions of "gate" for "limb" and "gate" for "house" may seem minor, but they focus much more sharply a major recurring event. Having returned often to this event, Faulkner knew that all Quentin and the reader needed, at the end, was the barest reference to it, so he omitted " 'Don't you pass that shadow, Charles' and Bon said 'I am going to pass it, Henry.' "

Now Shreve, Quentin's roommate, repeats the image simply, swiftly:

> Henry spurred ahead and turned his horse to face Bon and took out the pistol; and Judith and Clytie heard the shot, and maybe Wash Jones was hanging around somewhere in the back yard and so he was there to help Clytie and Judith carry him into the house and lay him on the bed, and Wash went to town to tell the Aunt Rosa and the Aunt Rosa comes boiling out that afternoon and finds Judith standing without a tear before the closed door.

No device should ever be just a device, and Faulkner's use of repetition in *Absalom, Absalom!* is a brilliant example of how a device becomes in itself a major aspect of the characters' experience. Quentin's obsession with events of the past compel him to "tell about the South" repeatedly—a compulsion he shares with his fellow southerners and which is so contagious that Shreve, his Canadian roommate at Harvard, becomes entangled in the convolutions of language and events, telling the story back to Quentin.

Similar use of repetition is of major importance in Joseph Conrad's *Victory*, F. Scott Fitzgerald's *The Great Gatsby*, and Robert Penn Warren's *All the King's Men* (some argue overuse there). William Gaddis's *The Recognitions* and Julio Cortazar's *Hopscotch* are examples of novels unified by repetition even though they seem to depict or imitate chaos.

See "The Day the Flowers Came," comment 5, p. 266.

129 | Have you failed to imagine an effective use of the device of *reversal*?

Reversal is an unexpected change in a development the reader has been led to anticipate, causing delight, or giving force to an enlightenment. (For reversal in style, See Question 28.)

In the short story "The Ram in the Thicket," Wright Morris wrote:

When he was just a little shaver, the boy had walked into the living room full of Mother's guests and showed them something in a jar. Mother had been horrified—but she naturally thought it a frog or something and not a bottle out of her own icebox. When one of the ladies asked the boy where in the world he had found it, he naturally said, *In the icebox*. Mother had never forgiven him.

Mother's reaction is exactly what a reader would expect—she is horrified. It is a strong indication of her character, as criticized rather satirically, that she never forgave her son.

In the novel version, *Man and Boy*, Morris gave Mother a rather positive power to reverse such situations. His revision of the jar strikingly illustrates an expressive and meaningful use of the reversal device.

When the boy had been just a little shaver, maybe six or seven years old, he had once walked in on one of Mother's parties, with a jar in his hands. He had walked around the room with it, showing it to Mother's guests. The glass was foggy, but it wasn't hard to see the explosive inside. Any other woman should have died, any *mother*, certainly would have died on the spot, but Mother just sat there with a charming smile on her face. She didn't speak to him, or get up and hustle him out. By her not saying a word every woman in the room got the impression that this was something the boy was growing for himself. One of his nature studies, and that she was *very* proud of him. There was simply no accounting for the way Mother could turn a blow like that. . . .

In the short-story version, the incident is a static anecdote, a one-dimensional joke. The revision offers a totally different side to Mother. The question "Did the boy do it to embarrass Mother?" is deliberately left unanswered in both versions, but the novel raises another unanswered question: Was the boy, like his father (who is remembering this incident), impressed by Mother's ability to transform a negative situation into a positive one?

A reversal of plot, situation, or the protagonist's fortune may deepen a reader's understanding of what he has experienced so far. The reversal technique offers the reader a psychological satisfaction. But overuse can wear a reader out. Readers may resent a reversal that is obviously contrived or forced.

As you read fiction, look for the writer's use of various reversal or surprise devices. A reversal device is an always popular method for ending a story or a novel, as in du Maurier's *Rebecca*, when the narrator learns from Maxim that he did not love Rebecca, he hated her. In Henry James's *The Wings of the Dove*, Densher and Kate's elaborate scheme against Milly causes a reversal in their own relationship. See the use of reversal in Emily Brontë's *Wuthering Heights*, especially Chapter 17.

See "The Day the Flowers Came," comment 13, pp. 272–73.

130 | Have you failed to use the *delay* device where it might be effective?

The delay device is the setting up of an event or effect and the deliberate postponement of the completion of it to achieve greater impact.

Here is a passage from Wright Morris's "The Ram in the Thicket":

> With the jar of cabbage and furry mold, Mr. Ormsby made a trip to the garage, picked up the garden spade, walked around behind. At one time he had emptied the jars and merely buried the contents, but recently, since the war that is, he had buried it all. Part of it was a question of time. . . . There were worms in the fork of earth he had turned and he stood looking at them. . . . he remembered the water was boiling on the stove. He dropped everything and ran. . . .

In this short-story version, the jar episode is presented in full in a single passage from Mr. Ormsby's point of view. It is one of many moments that express somewhat satirically the relationship between Ormsby and his wife, whom he calls Mother. But for the novel, *Man and Boy*, Morris revised to provide the reader with a more interesting and complex experience. Mr. Ormsby's point of view:

> With the puffy lidded jar in his hands Mr. Ormsby turned to look at the clock, saw that it was now seven thirty-eight. He stood there, his eyes lidded, calculating the amount of time he would need to dig a hole, bury the jar, and get back to the house.

Now Morris shifts to Mother's point of view, and five pages later gives the reader this perspective:

> In the window corner, she paused to watch Mr. Ormsby, a garden fork in his hand, crawl through the rhododendron at the back side of the garage. He wore his rubber raincoat, and the flap concealed something. She knew. She let him get to the back of the yard, then she hammered with her brush on the bath tub plumbing until the sound, like the pipes of an organ, seemed to vibrate the house. She was in the bedroom, at the back of the closet . . . when she heard him skid on the papers near the stove.

Not only is the jar episode now more forcefully written, Morris sets up Mr. Ormsby's mental anticipation of burying the jar; later, from Mother's point of view, the reader sees him in the act and experiences Mother's reaction. By delaying the action, Morris gives the reader the enjoyment of recognizing, and then more fully experiencing, an action set up earlier.

Morris is particularly adept, here and in most of his fiction, at dramatizing mental processes, one facet of which is the delay-and-connect sequence. In "The Ram in the Thicket," for instance: "Eyes wide, she then stared for a full minute at the yard full of grackles, covered with grackles, before she discovered them." Mother sees, there is a delay, then she connects, then she perceives, then she classifies, explains, and records. Sometimes the sequence for the reader too is perception, mystification, then clarification. The sensibility active *is* action.

See Wright Morris's *The Deep Sleep* and *In Orbit*. Robert Penn Warren uses the device throughout *All the King's Men*.

131 | Does your story need suspense?

Suspense is a feeling, simultaneously fearful and pleasurable, of being suspended between a past experience and a related but unknown, and probably surprising, experience that is to come. Preparation through the device of foreshadowing augments the effect of suspense.

Suspense for its own sake has come to be regarded as a cheap device for holding a reader, and is dependent upon a mechanical plotline. Suspense, allied with raw curiosity, is the province of popular fiction. Some noncommercial writers deliberately undermine the element of suspense to force the reader to pay attention to other values in the story, such as the quality of experience for its own sake, rendered in a complex way, from which suspense would only distract the reader. Nevertheless, most readers go on hungering for it, because suspense offers a particular sort of psychological satisfaction—the wondering what will happen next, whether the hero will make it, etc.

Do you undercut suspense by telling or depicting too much too soon? In "A Long Ticket for Isaac" ("Idiots First"), Bernard Malamud had that problem. Malamud realized the encounter with Ginzburg, the Angel of Death, had come much too early and was too realistically rendered, robbing Ginzburg of his aura of mystery and menace, and denying the reader a feeling of suspense. Although as they leave the house Mendel cautions Isaac to avoid Ginzburg, in both versions, the actual encounter with him is delayed suspensefully in the published version until the next-to-last scene. A brief encounter with Ginzburg in the park now has a more mysterious, surreal aura. The suspense is sustained until the climactic scene; Mendel struggles with the Angel of Death in the train station, a scene that did not appear in the draft version. See Kuehl, *Creative Writing and Rewriting*, pp. 69-96.

See Joseph Conrad's *Suspense* (left in suspense—unfinished—by his death). See William Blatty's *The Exorcist*, Emily Brontë's *Wuthering Heights* (focus on Chapter 17), and William Faulkner's *Absalom, Absalom!* for three different uses of suspense.

132 | Have you made too little or ineffective use of analogies?

An analogy is a comparison of two things that basically are not alike in order to show certain similarities. An analog is something comparable, to some extent, to something else. Analogy enables you to extend your reader's experience by suggesting another dimension.

In many of his works Henry James drew analogies to the theater and to painting. In *The Portrait of a Lady*, he uses analogies to painting most often, and in revision saw many opportunities to transfigure dull statements such as this: the Countess "delivered herself of a hundred remarks from which I offer the reader but a brief selection." That is a dull, static, abstract statement; it is pure information, in itself devoid of interest. As revised, the Countess "began to talk very much as if, seated brush in hand before an easel, she were applying a series of considered touches to a composition of figures already sketched in." The added dimension of the painting analogy makes the brief passage much more interesting for the reader.

Novelist-critic Mark Schorer suggests Jane Austen's *Persuasion*, Emily Brontë's *Wuthering Heights*, and George Eliot's *Middlemarch* as excellent examples of works in which analogies are impressively employed ("Fiction and the 'Analogical Matrix,' " *The World We Imagine*). See also William Gaddis's *The Recognitions*, William Faulkner's *The Sound and the Fury*, James Joyce's *Ulysses* (structural analogies to Homeric myths), Thomas Mann's "Mario and the Magician" (analogies between magicians and dictators).

Determine whether you have already used analogies or analogs. If so, determine whether they are strategically placed and effectively employed.

133 | Have you neglected to use the device of association?

The associational device is the use of an element that calls to mind another element with which it is somehow associated. The effect is to add another dimension of interest.

Wright Morris's "The Ram in the Thicket" offers a good example:

Seated on the attic stairs she trimmed her toenails with a pearl handled knife that Mr. Ormsby had been missing for several years. The blade was not so good any longer and using it too freely had resulted in ingrown nails on both of her big toes. But Mother preferred it to scissors which were proven, along with bathtubs, to be one of the most dangerous things in the home. *Even more than the battlefield, the most dangerous place in the world.*

Mother associates knives with scissors and home's dangers with those of the battlefield. This passage appears in the novel version, *Man and Boy*, also, but there Morris adds to it when he returns to Mother's point of view twenty pages later. Mother sands

> the surface where she was expecting a corn.
>   The corn—seeing the corn, she was reminded . . . of something—and closing her eyes saw Mrs. Dinardo's wide flat feet.

Ten pages later, Mr. Ormsby, in his point of view, finds in the attic "something hard, like a kernel of corn, and held it up to the light." Here, it is the reader who associates that simile with Mother's toe corn. But what Ormbsy has actually found is his son's "first gold-filled wisdom tooth." Using the association device in this complex manner, Morris has involved Mother (Mrs. Ormsby) *and* the reader in a single psychological process that is both conscious and unconscious.

We may find examples in most of Morris's fiction and in James Joyce's *Ulysses*, the Molly Bloom section, the final forty-five pages; in William Styron's *Lie Down in Darkness*, Peyton Loftis's section; and in Virginia Woolf's *To the Lighthouse*.

If you are using the central-intelligence point of view, you are trying to simulate, to some extent, the actual process of stimulus and response, perception, consciousness. Find places where the use of association may lend greater authenticity to that process.

See "The Day the Flowers Came," comment 17, pp. 276–77.

134 | Does your story suffer a lack of *allusions* where they might be useful?

An allusion is a reference to persons or places, to historical events, to mythic events, to biblical or other literary writings, or to elements presented earlier in your story.

Thomas Hardy uses allusions in profusion in *The Return of the Native*:

> Indeed, it is pretty well known that such blazes as this the heathmen were now enjoying are rather the lineal descendants from jumbled Druidical rites and Saxon ceremonies than the invention of popular feeling about the Gunpowder Plot.

Hardy began with the intention of giving to his story, set in a remote, narrow area of an English heath, a prehistorical dimension through an elaborate system of allusions to legend and to major historical events. In the draft, in Chapter 3, we see him doing just that. But he decided he also wanted the broader dimension of Greek myth. He added this passage to the one in the draft:

> Moreover to light a fire is the instinctive and resistant act of man when, at the winter ingress, the curfew is sounded throughout Nature. It indicates a spontaneous, Promethean rebelliousness against the fiat that this recurrent season shall bring foul times, cold darkness, misery and death. Black chaos comes, and the fettered gods of the earth say, Let there be light.

The Prometheus myth becomes a major analog to the story, and Hardy makes frequent allusions to it, usually associated with the doomed heroine Eustacia Vye. Hardy inserted the italicized phrases:

> Clym watched her as she retired *towards the sun*. The *luminous rays* wrapped her up with her increasing remoteness. . . .

Often, you will decide that allusions distract more than they enhance. For instance, F. Scott Fitzgerald cut an allusion to D. H. Lawrence out of "Babylon Revisited." Sometimes one allusion distracts from another. Virginia Woolf cut out of her first novel, *The Voyage Out*, a perfectly apt allusion to Nora in Ibsen's play *A Doll's House* because it diluted the effect of an even more useful allusion to George Meredith's *Diana of the Crossways*. Sometimes an allusion is too obscure, as in Frank O'Connor's "Guests of the Nation": "Well, like that in the story, a terrible dispute blew up late in the evening between 'Awkins and Noble. . . ." What story? O'Connor cut it out.

135 | Have you missed opportunities for using the device of *contrast*?

A contrast is a demonstration of the essential qualities of one thing by comparing those qualities to the qualities of something that is very different. Contrast provides one of the major sources of interest for the reader, beginning with contrasts between characters. Flaubert said he reached his "dramatic effect" in part by "contrast of character."

Contrast seems to have been one of E. M. Forster's major techniques in all versions of *A Passage to India*; given the general intention of contrasting two major cultures, it would follow that in revising descriptions of characters, settings, cultural elements, and a great range of details, Forster would revise to set up those contrasts and to refine them with each draft. For instance, Forster revised the visits to the temple and to the Marabar Caves to emphasize contrasts between Mrs. Moore and Adela Quested, as English women, and Doctor Aziz as an Indian.

If the setting or the characters of your story seem vague, consider whether the device of contrast might not set them off in sharp relief.

These novels provide good examples of contrasts between characters: between Jack Burden and Willie Stark in Robert Penn Warren's *All the King's Men*; between Heathcliff and Edgar in Emily Brontë's *Wuthering Heights*; between Axel Heyst and Lena in Joseph Conrad's *Victory*; among Benjy, Quentin, Jason, and Caddy in William Faulkner's *The Sound and the Fury*; Between black (Jim) and white (Huck) in Mark Twain's *The Adventures of Huckleberry Finn*; between old and young in Turgenev's *Fathers and Sons*; between ways of life in Hemingway's *The Sun Also Rises*; between past and present and one setting and another in Wright Morris's *The Field of Vision*.

136 | Have you made insufficient use of *irony*?

Verbal irony is a contrast between what a character says and an implied opposite. "Nobody can call *me* a bigot, but don't you think blacks ought to stay in their place?" Dramatic irony is a contrast between what a character intends to do and an opposite result of what he does. "Wanting to show the thirsty old black man that not all whites are bigots, he took him six blocks down the street to where there was a 'For Colored Only' water fountain."

Irony is a major device in literary fiction and one of the chief sources of pleasure for the reader, as sentimentality is a major device and source of pleasure in commercial fiction. Often, serious writers use irony to control sentimentality. The writer who wants to convey the complexity of human behavior may use the device of irony because it requires of the reader an ability to see an event through a double perspective: what is literally happening and how the writer intends that happening to be seen differently. We experience literally what the character says about bigotry and blacks staying in their place; we experience literally the character wanting to prove to the thirsty old black man that not all whites are bigots by taking him six blocks to drink out of a "For Colored Only" fountain. The reader who stops there on the literal level is in the same position as the self-deluded character himself. The further act of interpreting the dialog and the action gives added force to the dialog and the action because they become double experiences; having gotten the ironic point, the reader in a flash reexperiences the dialog and the action.

But because irony calls attention to itself as being a collaboration between author and reader, usually to the exclusion of the character, it has a certain artificial quality about it. You cannot use it often without risk; when you use it, use it with caution. It must strike the reader as right, in context, and necessary, and not as easy or obtrusive.

Writers who use irony often abuse it. There is, for writer and reader, a sense of superiority and power in the use of irony. Readers who enjoy it, crave it; writers sometimes lose control in their eagerness to provide it. It can distort a moment in a story or the entire story, especially if used ineffectively at the end.

On the other hand, some writers do not make sufficient use of irony because they don't understand how it functions or because they do not have an ironical perspective on life or on the story. Those commercial writers who deal in sentimentality use irony only as an isolated effect, far removed from passages of sentimentality. But the early version of a story that is without irony may well benefit from a limited, controlled use of it, to provide an element of complexity or distance that may be lacking. Finding a place for one touch of irony, you may discover that a pattern of ironic effect would make the crucial difference in a story that isn't working. Irony can put a story in a new perspective so that you become aware of possibilities for revision.

An ironic vision of life informs Carson McCullers's *The Heart Is a Lonely Hunter*. Four people who do not understand their own spiritual and psychological dilemmas, and do not communicate with each other separately, talk at length, fervently, to a man they know is a mute but who they are convinced understands them. He does not understand them at all; and he, in turn, tells his innermost thoughts to a mute who is retarded. Charles Dickens's notes for *Bleak House* show him eagerly exploiting opportunities for irony. A pattern of ironies runs through Fitzgerald's *The Great Gatsby*; see especially those related to the automobile accident.

137 | Have you neglected to make use of *paradox* in style or situation?

A paradox is a startling contradiction, or seeming contradiction, that stimulates a fresh perspective.

In Wright Morris's "The Ram in the Thicket," Mr. Ormsby and his wife always referred to their son as "the boy"; today a boat is being named after him because he died a hero in World War II:

> The U.S.S. *Ormsby* was a permanent sort of thing. Although he was born and raised in the town hardly anybody knew very much about Virgil, but they all were pretty familiar with his boat. "How's that boat of yours coming along?" they would say, but in more than twenty years nobody had ever asked him about *his* boy. Whose boy? Well, that was just the point. Everyone agreed Ormsby was a fine name for a boat.
>
> . . . "The" boy and "The" *Ormsby*—it was a pretty strange thing that they both had the definite article, and gave him the feeling he was facing a monument.

The simple paradox here is that nobody knew the boy when he was alive but now that he is dead, he is very well known, but only in connection with the boat that is to be named after him. In the novel version, *Man and Boy*, Morris deemphasizes this minor paradox and takes the focus away from the father's awareness that nobody "ever asked about his boy" to express a more complex and profound paradox.

> *The* Boy and *the* Ormsby—it was a very strange thing that they both had the definite article. There was something impersonal and permanent about both of them, and this was why it had never worked to call him Son. *The* son, perhaps . . . There goes the *Ormsby*, men would say, without ever knowing, as he knew, how absolutely right it was.

The key terms in the paradox are now "impersonal" and "permanent," as opposed to conventional feelings about the dead—very personal emotions and a sense of the transience of life. The father achieves an act of consciousness in which he sees that the most permanent love, even for one's own son, is the impersonal love a person might feel for a ship.

Morris's fiction, in both style (he uses the word "naturally" in many paradoxical ways in the novel) and situation, is heavily paradoxical. See especially *In Orbit*. Other writers who stress paradox are Oscar Wilde in *The Picture of Dorian Gray* and G. K. Chesterton in *The Man Who Was Thursday*.

138   I Do you use *personification* inappropriately?

Personification is the attribution of human feelings, qualities, or actions to nonhuman creatures, inanimate objects, or even abstract concepts. See the discussion of *pathetic fallacy*, in Question 116.

Here is a passage from Virginia Woolf's first draft of *Mrs. Dalloway*:

> In Westminster, whose temples, meeting houses, conventicles, and steeples of all kinds are congregated together, there is, at all hours and half hours, a sound of bells. . . . Thus when Mr. Walsh walking with his head down, and his coat flying loose came out by the Abbey the clock of St. Margaret's was saying two mintues later than Big Ben that it was half past eleven. . . . St. Margaret's spoke as a woman speaks, there was a vibration in the core of the sound, so that each word, or note, comes fluttering, alive, yet with some reluctance to inflict its vitality, some grief for the past which holds it back, some impulse nevertheless to glide into the recesses of the heart and there bury itself in ring after ring of sound, so that Mr. Walsh, as he walked past St. Margaret's, and heard the bells toll the half hour felt . . . only all that surrounded it, only its futility.

I quote at length to show how a personifying sensibility is apt, in the first draft, to run amok. This is the first page of the first draft of a novel in which time, Big Ben, is a charged image; the original title was "The Hours." Woolf was so little in control that she rewrote it five very different ways; she omitted the first description of St. Margaret's bells from the second draft, delaying reference to the striking of the hours until the fifth paragraph:

> For having lived in Westminster—how many years now? over twenty,—one feels even in the midst of the traffic, or waking at night, Clarissa was positive, a particular hush, or solemnity; an indescribable pause; a suspense (but that might be her heart, affected, they said, by influenza) before Big Ben strikes. There: Out it boomed. First, a warning, musical; then the hour, irrevocable. The leaden circles dissolved in the air.

Woolf has shifted from an omniscient opening (which tends to encourage the impulse to personify) to inside her character's mental processes (and she has opened with a focus not on Peter Walsh but on Mrs. Dalloway). See Hildick, *Word for Word*.

There is personification in most of the fiction of Charles Dickens. *Little Dorrit* and *Bleak House*, for instance, rely upon personification. Rudyard Kipling's *The Jungle Book* and Richard Adams's *Watership Down* offer examples of allegorical personification.

139   Do you make awkward use of *allegory*?

Allegory is the consistent narrative use of stylized or idealized human or animal characters, places, or events that personify or stand for moral, romantic, religious, philosophical, or political concepts.

Very few writers today set out to write allegory in its purest form as seen classically in John Bunyan's *Pilgrim's Progress*. The embodiment of abstract human virtues and vices in human or animal characters dramatized in a narrative action works today in fantasy and science fiction, but the appeal there seems to lie more in the creation of strange worlds and creatures than in the working out of ideas and values.

Many short stories and novels have allegorical aspects or elements or dimensions or they are intended to have some sort of allegorical effect. The question of awkward use then has to do with whether these secondary allegorical elements work in context. Are they cosmetic, as when Stephen Crane omitted the names of his soldiers in *The Red Badge of Courage* to give them general qualities for an allegorical effect, or are they substantive, as in Melville's *Moby-Dick*, which is not strictly speaking an allegory, but which has strong allegorical dimensions? Problems arise when writers employ allegorical elements without having a clear understanding of classical allegory or without thinking through the function of allegorical elements within the full context of their story.

140   Do you make inappropriate use of *satire* or *humor*?

Satire is the controlled use of humorous exaggeration to promote specific reform of social, religious, or political errors. Humor is the comic depiction of human foibles.

The writer in both satire and humor makes the reader feel superior (even though readers are often also the target). Among the differences between satire and humor are that with humor the laughter is indulgent and the attitude is compassionate and tolerant, but in satire the laughter is malicious and the attitude is critical and intolerant. Both satire and humor draw on some of the same devices to get their effects: reversal and surprise; understatement *or* exaggeration; contrast; irony; implication.

If your intention is to write satire, the question you must ask yourself is whether what you have in the first draft really is satire or whether it is only the extended, prolonged expression of invective or a sarcastic attitude, or an elaborate put-down; or whether it is some lesser form of humor such as lampoon, burlesque, travesty, parody, mockery, black humor, even farce. None of those forms are satire, although any of them may be employed as transient devices.

But the classic examples of satire adhere to this description: satirical fiction ridicules mankind generally or an actual person, group, class, nation, system of thought, movement in art, or social, political, or religious institution through a serious moral vision in a tone either of gentle amusement and delight or of a ferocious moral indignation, the aim of which is to expose, to diminish, or to destroy the target so that the reader gains insight into specific excesses, follies, and vices; the reader may then perhaps help correct them through reform. Satirists are often basically conservative; some would restore the original vitality of withering institutions. In the greatest satire, as in great tragedy, the target and the issue must have stature. If your story does not fit this description, consider whether you have written some other form of humor in this first draft and then whether you want to strive to achieve a work that reaches the stature of satire.

Satire is a very difficult mode; the great works are few: Swift's *Gulliver's Travels*, Voltaire's *Candide*, Rabelais's *Gargantua and Pantagruel*, Cervantes's *Don Quixote*, Thackeray's *Vanity Fair*, Sinclair Lewis's *Babbit*, Evelyn Waugh's *The Loved One*, Joseph Heller's *Catch-22*. The problem today is that we have very few authentic models for satire. Great satire destroys a false vision of life as it suggests a better one. But many writers today mistake the ability to detect evil or corruption for a vision of life. Their targets are topical and lack magnitude.

Suppose that your intention is not to write a satire, but that you discover in your first draft a passage the tone of which is satirical. Ask then whether it works, contrasting as it does with the very different intent of the story as a whole.

A good example of the satirist learning his craft in the act of revision lies in the difference between the short story "Catch-18" and the novel version of the first chapter of *Catch-22*. The story version is full of words, phrases, lines, and events that misfire as either satire or simple humor.

Humor raises problems similar to those of satire. If your intent is to write a humorous story or novel, ask, line by line, as you revise, Is this really humorous? Is the humor fresh, or is it trite, too imitative? If the humor is meant to be only incidental, ask whether it works where it appears or whether it disrupts a different mood. No matter how witty or funny a line or passage is in isolation, the question is whether it works in context.

Like satire, humor is very difficult to achieve. Reading satire or humor in manuscript, I often get the impression that some writers think satire requires only indignation or contempt, and that humor requires only an intention to be funny. Behind good satire there is a deadly serious moral vision; behind quality humor there is a very tough, complex mind. Writers who aren't by temperament or craft really satirists or humorists write satire and humor as if on a holiday from hard work and the demands of craft. I hasten to say that it is quite possible that what your lyrical story needs is a touch of humor or a stab of satire.

Revising the short-story material in "The Ram in the Thicket" for the *Man and Boy* novel version, Wright Morris decided that some passages were too broadly humorous, almost slapstick. For instance, see his revisions of the basement scene to cut out the slapstick so that the subtler humor may be heard.

The humor in Henry James is often so subtle many readers cannot get attuned to it. Here we see the later James converting mere description in the first published version of *The Portrait of a Lady* into humorous observation: "Lily knew nothing about Boston; her imagination was confined within the limits of Manhattan." That became: "Lily knew nothing about Boston; her imagination was all bounded on the east by Madison Avenue."

141 | Have you not yet imagined a *charged image* that can lend a unity of effect to your story?

A charged image is the controlling, dominant image-nucleus in a story.

As the reader moves from part to part, the charged image discharges its potency gradually. After the reader has fully experienced the story, fully perceived it in a picture, that focal image continues to discharge its electrical power. The device of the charged image offers the writer one way of achieving coherence, synthesis, organic unity. "Literature is language charged with meaning," said Ezra Pound. "Great Literature is simply language charged with meaning to the utmost degree." "Meaning'' may be taken as a fusion of emotion and idea in the imagination. The important elements in a story are condensed and compressed into this charged image; it can evoke all the other elements—theme, character, setting, conflict, style, and so on. Yeats said he wanted to create images that beget other images. In a story, the developing elements become integrated finally into a single image, which is really a tissue of many images (Croce's phrase).

The charged image in F. Scott Fitzgerald's *The Great Gatsby* evolved gradually. The first version of Chapter 1 ends with a vague image. What is missing is the now famous green light at the end of Daisy's dock. The light did not come into the novel until the middle of the book when Gatsby and Daisy talk for the first time: ''You always have two green lights that burn all night at the end of your dock.'' Since the green light symbolizes Daisy most of all, Fitzgerald cut one light and inserted it at the end of Chapter 1:

> . . . it was Mr. Gatsby himself, come out to determine what share was his of our local heavens.
>
> I decided to call to him. . . . But I didn't call to him, for he gave a sudden intimation that he was content to be alone—he stretched out his arms toward the dark water in a curious way, and, far as I was from him, I could have sworn he was trembling. Involuntarily I glanced seaward—and distinguished nothing except a single green light, minute and far away, that might have been the end of a dock. When I looked once more for Gatsby he had vanished, and I was alone again in the unquiet darkness.

Fitzgerald repeats the green-light image in the final passages of the novel. The symbolic image of the green light at the end of Daisy's dock is enhanced by other key images in that novel: Wilson's green face, the ''fresh, green breast of the new world.''

Gatsby's reaching toward the green light is a symbolic gesture—his very soul reaches out not for Daisy herself but for what she represents to him, his ''platonic conception of himself.'' In revising this scene, Fitzgerald provided the reader with an image that enables him to grasp the essentials of Gatsby's character, to illuminate him by comparison with Daisy and all other characters, most importantly Nick, who witnesses this scene and writes about it; to understand the theme—how our dreams elude us, for instance; to respond to the settings for the interior and exterior scenes; to understand the conflict between two concepts of selfhood; to understand how the style itself works—it is somewhat poetic, with a tone of romantic irony. If you follow the charged image of the green light through *Gatsby*, you will notice how Fitzgerald develops the Doctor T. J. Eckleburg image as a direct contrast.

Not all fiction has a charged image, nor should you expect to create one for each story. Here are a few examples of charged images (not all readers will agree):

Cervantes, *Don Quixote*: Don Quixote and Sancho Panza on the road approaching the windmills (the entire scene is only a page and a half in a book of about a thousand pages; it is probably the best-known image from fiction worldwide). Mark Twain, *The Adventures of Huckleberry Finn*: Huck and Jim on the raft on the Mississippi River between visits ashore. Virginia Woolf, *Mrs. Dalloway*: the sound of Big Ben striking the hours. Albert Camus, *The Stranger*: the sun flashing on the Arab's knife, Meursault pulling the trigger of the revolver. William Faulkner, "A Rose for Emily": the strand of iron-gray hair on the pillow. Katherine Anne Porter, "Flowering Judas": Laura at the table, cleaning Braggioni's pistols as he plays the guitar and sings to her. Carson McCullers, *The Heart Is a Lonely Hunter*: Mick Kelly, Jake Blount, and Doctor Copeland in the mute's room. Wright Morris, *In Orbit*: Jubal on his motorcycle entering the small town, followed by a tornado. See "The Day the Flowers Came," comment 12, p. 272.

142 | Do you neglect to use *objective correlatives* where they might convey a sense of subjective states?

The term is T. S. Eliot's: "The only way of expressing emotion in the form of art is by finding an 'objective correlative'; in other words, a set of objects, a situation, a chain of events which shall be the formula of that *particular* emotion; such that when the external facts, which must terminate in sensory experience, are given, the emotion is immediately evoked" (see Eliot in Bibliography).

Direct description of a character's extreme subjective state is very difficult, sometimes impossible. D. H. Lawrence found something in his characters' objective world that correlates with their subjective state in *The Rainbow*. The draft version is simply a description of Will and Anna stacking corn in the moonlight, an impulsive activity of two lovers who had been walking at night. The revised passage renders an action, but the wording and the rhythm of its phrasing are an objective correlative to the passion of Anna and Will synchronized by the regular rhythm of the act of corn stacking.

> She took her new two sheaves and walked toward him, as he rose from stooping over the earth. He was coming out of the near distance. She set down her sheaves to make a new stook. They were unsure. Her hands fluttered. Yet she broke away, and turned to the moon, which laid bare her bosom, so she felt as if her bosom were the sea heaving and panting with moonlight. And he had to put up her two sheaves, which fell down. He worked in silence. The rhythm of the work carried him away again, as she was coming near.

See *The Rainbow*, Chapter 4, pp. 116-20, and Chapter 11, pp. 318-22, of the Viking Compass edition.

Since the term is Eliot's, see his poem "The Love Song of J. Alfred Prufrock" for his own use of the device. In *The Cannibal*, John Hawkes externalizes in images the neuroses of the German people of World Wars I and II. In E. M. Forster's *A Passage to India*, the cave becomes an objective correlative for Mrs. Moore's subjective state, enabling the reader to understand her collapse after the visit.

Identify passages in which you attempt to describe a character's subjective state. If the description does not satisfy you, try to find objects or actions in the objective world that may correlate somehow to those feelings.

See "The Day the Flowers Came," comment 4, p. 266.

143 | Have you imagined obvious, overt, or literary symbols?

Symbolism is the use of one object, image, event, or character to represent or suggest another.

The use of symbolism enables a writer to show relationships among people, nature, society, the intellect, and the spirit. Symbols may be incidental, or a story may be united by a symbolic design. Symbols, like charged images, help to focus ideas and feelings so that the story's impact is stronger, deeper, more lasting.

We've passed through several decades of overuse of symbols. The habit of symbol hunting in literary study, aided of course by overinfatuation with symbols on the part of some writers, has led to an antisymbol attitude among readers. "Who can't make up symbols?" asks James M. Cain. And some readers may ask, "And who wants to hunt them down once writers do make them up?" This attitude ignores the vital importance of symbols and symbolic patterns when they are used effectively.

I urge you to use symbolism very judiciously. Parallels, repetitions, and motifs can create effects similar to but less obvious than symbolism as it is too often used. Some writers and readers feel symbolism was almost the death of the novel. Mary McCarthy's exasperation with literary symbolism comes out in a famous anecdote she told about an eager young writer who rushed up to her one day to tell her that she had just written a short story that her writing teacher thought was wonderful. "He's going to help me fix it up for publication . . . we're going to put in the symbols" ("Settling the Colonel's Hash").

Learn the various uses of symbolism so that you can use it—not abuse it—more effectively: symbolic allegory (*The Scarlet Letter*), symbolic expressionism (*Absalom, Absalom!*), symbolic use of landscape (and seascape, as in Conrad's fiction). The symbolic imagination does not come into play easily.

If you feel a profound necessity for the use of a symbol, try to use the natural object, as Ezra Pound suggests; don't create an artificial or private (known only to you or to your character) symbol that stands for something. Perhaps you can relate the symbol naturally to the character, as Crane did in *The Red Badge of Courage*; the title symbol is directly related to the protagonist—it refers to the heart which produces the courage and the blood.

Here is a draft of the final passage of F. Scott Fitzgerald's *The Great Gatsby*:

> And as I sat there brooding on the old unknown world I too held my breath and waited, until I could feel the motion of America as it turned through the hours—my own blue lawn and the tall incandescent city on the water and beyond that the dark fields of the republic rolling on under the night.

Missing from this draft is the green light at the end of Daisy's dock, the focal symbol of the novel. In conjunction with the eyes of T. J. Eckleburg (suggested by a jacket sketch showing Daisy's eyes hovering over an amusement park), the green light is also a *charged image* that unifies the novel's various elements (see Question 141).

And as I sat there brooding on the old, unknown world, I thought of Gatsby's wonder when he first picked out the green light at the end of Daisy's dock. . . . Gatsby believed in the green light, the orgiastic future that year by year recedes before us.

The symbolic importance of the green light is very clear now. It is symbolic of Gatsby's romantic idealization of Daisy, who represents his American Dream of fame and fortune and other dimensions of the promise of America that he could not even articulate. But even in the first draft of the first chapter, Fitzgerald had already expressed the mythic dimension of the dream in the color green in the phrase "a fresh, green breast of the new world," and in the final passage the addition of "Gatsby believed in the green light" gives the symbol a significance that transcends embodiment in Daisy and suggests a universal quality of hopeful idealism.

One of the most obvious symbols in everyday life is the cross as the symbol of Christianity because Christ died on the cross. In literature, one of the most obvious symbols is the letter A in *The Scarlet Letter*, representing Hester's adultery. In John Hawkes's "The Nearest Cemetery," the cemetery is the symbolic focus for the numerous allusions to death. The symbolism of fire pervades Hardy's *The Return of the Native*. In three major, published versions of Lawrence's *Lady Chatterley's Lover* (the first and second are *The First Lady Chatterley* and *John Thomas and Lady Jane*) the reader may follow the author's various attempts to endow the two settings—the mechanized, civilized world of the manor and the natural world of the woods—with symbolic effect.

For an excellent explanation of symbolism, see novelist-critic Edmund Wilson's *Axel's Castle*.

As you read symbolic novels or stories, ask yourself what factors seem to determine the use of symbolism. Try to distinguish instances of symbolism from parallel or motif. The following novels obviously and heavily employ symbolism: James Joyce's *A Portrait of the Artist as a Young Man* (compare with *Stephen Hero*) and *Ulysses*, William Faulkner's *The Sound and the Fury*, Joseph Conrad's *Heart of Darkness*, Glenway Wescott's *The Pilgrim Hawk*, Franz Kafka's *The Trial*, Thomas Mann's *The Magic Mountain*, Virginia Woolf's *To the Lighthouse*.

If you have consciously used symbolism, evaluate each instance. Determine whether you have controlled the symbolism. Have you used it only incidentally, or have you imagined a pattern or interrelation of symbols? Should you eliminate some or all instances of symbolism?

See "The Day the Flowers Came," comment 22, pp. 279–80.

144 | Have you neglected to develop appropriate parallels to enhance elements in your story?

A parallel is an element that is similar to, but not necessarily symbolic of, another. It is an element that moves alongside another element; they mutually enhance each other's effect, sometimes through contrast or comparison.

A parallel is something like a motif, with the difference that although a parallel may contribute to the overall design, of which motif patterns are a part, it does not necessarily contribute to a pattern of parallels; a parallel may simply serve the function of emphasis, as there is a parallel between Gatsby's lower-class background and Wilson's and Myrtle's in *The Great Gatsby*, but that parallel is too general to contribute to the motif pattern of breed (Myrtle's mixed-breed Airedale pup is a motif) and class (Gatsby's low-class taste in shirts is a motif). Parallels are sometimes mistaken for symbols; the green light at the end of Daisy's dock is a symbol, but Fitzgerald does not always make the color green symbolic; sometimes green is used simply to call the reader's attention to objects that have some parallel value.

The value of parallels themselves is that they contribute to the overall effect of simultaneity and unity. This distinction of the function of parallel as opposed to motif and symbol is then useful, more useful to the writer striving to make all elements relate to and reinforce each other than it is for the critic or scholar who is more concerned with the thematic values of motifs and symbols.

In Wright Morris's "The Ram in the Thicket," Mother's need for "one room in the house where she could relax and just let her hair down" (the bathroom) parallels her husband's and her son's use of the basement john, where they take refuge from the tension Mother generates in all the rest of the house. The little boys in the novel version, *Man and Boy*, who write to Mother in response to her lecture against male birds "to say that they were now shooting only male birds" parallels her own son's shooting of birds.

To see parallels at work, see Mark Twain, *The Adventures of Huckleberry Finn*; Ernest Hemingway, *The Sun Also Rises*; F. Scott Fitzgerald, *The Great Gatsby*; Wright Morris, *In Orbit*; John Hawkes, *The Cannibal*; Thomas Mann, *Doctor Faustus*; James Joyce, *Ulysses*. See "The Day the Flowers Came," comment 11, pp. 271–72; for indirect parallel, comment 17, pp. 276–77. For parallelism in style, see Question 29.

145 | Have you overloaded your story with *motifs?*

A motif is an element that is repeated, usually with variation, throughout a story. A motif may be a recurring subject, idea, or theme. In "The Making of *The Magic Mountain*," Thomas Mann stressed the importance of leitmotif in that novel. It "was always like a symphony, a work in counterpoint, a thematic fabric; the idea of the musical motif plays a great role in it." The leitmotif is "the magic formula that works both ways, and links the past with the future, the future with the past. The leitmotif is the technique employed to preserve the inward unity and abiding presentness of the whole at each moment." In *The Genesis of a Novel*, he also described the dangers of overuse of motif. Having written Chapter 17 of *Doctor Faustus*, he said "I had escaped the tangle of motifs in the expositional part of the book and saw clear action before me."

Some writers consciously employ motifs; others leave such enhancements entirely to chance. For instance, one is seldom aware that James M. Cain uses motifs in *The Postman Always Rings Twice*. Motif is a major unifying device, but you should avoid overloading your story with motifs, or repeating a single motif too often. One way to repeat a motif inconspicuously is to reiterate it in dialog.

Motifs should not be confused with symbols, although symbols may be part of a pattern of motifs. Another term that might prevent confusion between motif and symbol is *parallel* (see Question 144).

Coming after a space break in Chapter 1, the following rather flat passage from a draft of F. Scott Fitzgerald's *The Great Gatsby* does little more than advance the narrative, rather mechanically at that:

> A little later we went inside and almost immediately Miss Baker's body asserted itself with a restless movement of her knee and a flutter of slender muscles in her brown arms. She closed the magazine, stood up, leaned backward like a West Point cadet and said she was going to bed.
>
> "It's almost ten," she remarked inaccurately.

Here is the published version:

> Inside, the crimson room bloomed with light. Tom and Miss Baker sat at either end of the long couch and she read aloud to him from *The Saturday Evening Post*—the words, murmurous and uninflected, run-

ning together in a soothing tune. The lamp-light, bright on his boots and dull on the autumn-leaf yellow of her hair, glinted along the paper as she turned a page with a flutter of slender muscles in her arms.

When we came in she held us silent for a moment with a lifted hand.

"To be continued," she said, tossing the magazine on the table, "in our very next issue."

Her body asserted itself with a restless movement of her knee, and she stood up.

"Ten o'clock," she remarked, apparently finding the time on the ceiling. "Time for this good girl to go to bed."

In context, the revision does a great variety of work, but Fitzgerald deliberately adds the motif of color. "Crimson room" repeats "a bright rosy-colored space" and "wine-colored rug" from the passage in which Nick first entered the house. "Autumn-leaf yellow of her hair" introduces yellow as a color motif. Gatsby's car, which kills Myrtle and thus causes Gatsby's own death at the hands of her husband, is yellow. Cars are a major motif. Daisy asks Nick whether people in Chicago miss her. "The whole town is desolate. All the cars have the left rear wheel painted black as a mourning wreath." Other key colors introduced in this chapter, "white," "silver," and "blue," are repeated with significant effect throughout the novel.

Have you imagined a pattern of motifs? Such a pattern helps to set up the reader's anticipation and provide the writer with a means of emphasis and focus.

For examples of masterful use of motif throughout, see Emily Brontë, *Wuthering Heights*, Chapter 17 especially; Ford Madox Ford, *The Good Soldier*; Carson McCullers, *The Heart Is a Lonely Hunter*; James Agee, *A Death in the Family*; Albert Camus, *The Stranger*; Ralph Ellison, *Invisible Man*; and Wright Morris, *In Orbit*. See also E. M. Forster, "Pattern and Rhythm," Bibliography.

See "The Day the Flowers Came," comment 9, p. 269; comment 22, pp. 279–80.

146 | Do the metaphors and other figurative elements fail to relate clearly and coherently to the *overall design*?

Any device gains force if it is used several times as part of a controlled design, and the design itself contributes to the living force of organic unity. A figurative device, for instance, used once, effectively or not, has only a transitory effect and thus arouses the suspicion that no part of a work is related to another, that each moment in a fiction exists in a kind of effect-vacuum. Ask yourself whether each device contributes to an overall design. That is one way of determining whether an overall design exists at all in your first draft.

In several versions of a remembered episode set in Mexico in Wright Morris's *One Day*, Cowie, the protagonist, made no clear link between that experience and the events twenty years later with which the novel mostly deals. But as Morris got to know Cowie better, Cowie began to see relationships. An automobile accident brought him, injured, to a Mexican household, where he became infatuated with a young woman but ended up being the catalyst for bringing her and her lover together. The metaphor of the "meaningful accident" appears to Cowie in the second ending Morris wrote for the episode; he refined it for the published version.

Morris succeeded in relating the Matamoros episode to an overall design of metaphors that he had developed before and would continue to develop, in which the "meaningful accident" is a key element. The novel opens with a different automobile accident that sets off a chain of events that Cowie's imagination is now able to find meaningful. Several other so-called accidents occur. As Morris was writing the novel, he learned that President Kennedy had been shot; he wrote into the novel the various reactions of his characters to that event. The accidental intrusion of reality freed his novel, as Cowie's accident freed the Matamoros lovers. See Kuehl, *Creative Writing and Rewriting*, pp. 98-129.

147 | Is your use of *flashbacks* crude?

"Flashback" is a term adopted from the technique of the movies for presenting a scene from the past, usually departing from focus on a main character. In the movies, the word "flash" was a misnomer until about the late 1960s because a slow dissolve usually acted as a transitional device into a flashback. In fiction, there are two literary models, fast and slow.

Too often flashbacks are used mechanically, crudely, obviously. The device works best in the movies, but it can be used subtly and become the major vehicle for a very complex vision, as in Laurence Durrell's *The Alexandria Quartet* and in Faulkner's *Absalom, Absalom!*, *Sanctuary*, and *The Sound and the Fury*.

This kinetic way of experiencing the flux of time is part of the whole experience. Writers have used this device in complex and profound ways, so that one experiences, in the technique itself, the vision of the work. Flashbacks, the more subtly they are used, cause deliberate discontinuity in the plot sequence to achieve effects that would not be possible with continuity; this technique is based on sound psychological insights into the workings of the mind, emotions, perceptions. Discontinuity in technique is often an expression of the same quality in the lives of the characters, or it may be a more direct expression of the author's vision of life, which may differ from that of his characters.

William Faulkner's *Sanctuary* provides many interesting examples of flashback. In the galley version, Horace Benbow is the protagonist and the mode of narration is predominantly his rather neurotic-erotic stream of consciousness broken up by Faulkner's narration. At the beginning of Chapter 2, the point of view is central intelligence, in which we gradually flash back, by a process of association in Horace's mind, to a scene in which he taunts his stepdaughter, Little Belle, about her behavior with men. In this version of the novel, Horace frequently flashes back to earlier events and sometimes flashes back and forth within a flashback, a technique very appropriate to the psychological focus upon Horace. But Faulkner decided to streamline the narrative and thus to eliminate most of Horace's retrospections. Faulkner revises the scene with Little Belle to give it a double immediacy by having Horace tell about it to Mrs. Goodwin in the moonshiner's house.

Horace's telling the woman about that scene is effective in the first published version because the focus is more on narrative, and people often tell parts of the narrative to each other, but we still get a sense of the psychological dilemma of Horace, who is now a subordinate character. And Faulkner kept one of the more remarkable examples of flashback within a character's mind in the last paragraph of Chapter 23 in which Horace has been looking at Little Belle's photograph; he goes into the mind of Temple Drake as she is being raped. This is a clinical example of transference—lusting for his stepdaughter would horrify him, so he transfers that lust to Temple Drake. See Question 85, transitions.

There is a difference of effect between that kind of flashback within the mind of a character and the author's use of it in narration. Faulkner is a master at moving into a flashback without providing a transition, and he uses that device in *The Sound and the Fury* as well.

Flashbacks are used effectively, in various ways, in Joseph Conrad, *Lord Jim*; Thornton Wilder, *The Bridge of San Luis Rey*; and William Styron, *Lie Down in Darkness*.

See "The Day the Flowers Came," p. 281.

148 | Have you neglected to discover places where the technique of *juxtaposition* might be used effectively?

Juxtaposition is the placing of two elements side by side to create a special effect.

The writer so deliberately chooses two words or images or events, which have no special impact separately, and so carefully places them side by side that they spark an emotion or idea which exists only in the reader's mind. The effect of juxtaposition may be violent (as in Faulkner) or subtle (as in Henry James). In the movies this technique is called "montage." The Russian director Sergei Eisenstein describes montage in this way: "Two pieces of film of any kind, placed together, inevitably combine into a new concept, a new quality, arising out of that juxtaposition." Juxtaposition or montage is a technique that involves the reader as a collaborator in the creative process.

There is a minor example in James Joyce's *A Portrait of the Artist as a Young Man*: Stephen's statement of his theory of beauty is juxtaposed to the metal rattle of a dray on the street for ironic counterpoint.

Wright Morris uses this device often in "The Ram in the Thicket," the short-story version of *Man and Boy*:

That gun had been a mistake—he began to shave himself in tepid, lukewarm water rather than let it run hot, which would bang the pipes and wake Mother up. That gun had been a mistake—when the telegram came that the boy had been killed Mother hadn't said a word, but she made it clear whose fault it was. There was never any doubt, as to just whose fault it was.

By juxtaposing a major element—"That gun had been a mistake"—with a trivial element—"he began to shave himself in tepid, lukewarm water"—

Morris enhances the effect of each; he also juxtaposes past and present, thought and action. But Morris may have felt that the repetition of "That gun had been a mistake" and of the juxtaposition device—"when the telegram came"—was too much, that the second use undercut the effect of the first. For the novel version, he cut the second juxtaposition.

Another kind of juxtaposition in both the story and the novel, and in many of Morris's novels, is the juxtaposition of point-of-view characters.

Sometimes a writer uses juxtaposition too mechanically or in a way that seems too contrived, or that undercuts the very effect he is setting up, as Faulkner did in the end of *Sanctuary*. See the final pages of both published versions. Popeye says, "Fix my hair, Jack," and that is juxtaposed to the scene in which Temple walks in the Luxembourg Gardens; Faulkner's revision allows the juxtaposition to sink in, not simply shock.

You may find major uses of juxtaposition in John Hawkes, *The Cannibal*; Faulkner, *Absalom, Absalom!*; William Burroughs, *Naked Lunch* and *Nova Express*; and Wright Morris, *In Orbit*.

There are, of course, accidental juxtapositions in most first drafts, but generally, juxtaposition is a consciously used technique that produces both conscious and unconscious responses. To avoid unintended effects, evaluate all juxtapositions.

Locate any juxtapositions you may already have created. Question their effectiveness. Using them as touchstones, find places where a weak effect may have stronger impact if enhanced by juxtaposition.

See "The Day the Flowers Came," comment 15, p. 274.

149 | Have you neglected to consider the use of devices from *other written forms* and *other art forms*?

As you consider the various problems raised by your first draft, imagine the possible use of a device from other written forms in your story or as an overall device through which to recast your story. Here are some successful examples:

Letters: Samuel Richardson, *Pamela*; John Barth, *Letters*
Diary: Jean-Paul Sartre, *Nausea*; James Joyce, *A Portrait of the Artist as a Young Man* (used in the last part, not used at all in the early *Stephen Hero* version)

Journal: Daniel Defoe, *A Journal of the Plague Year*; Kenneth Patchen, *The Journal of Albion Moonlight*

Notebook: Rainer Maria Rilke, *The Notebooks of Malte Laurids Brigge*; Dostoyevsky, *Notes from Underground*

Report: Donald Barthelme, "Report"

Confession: Italo Svevo, *Confessions of Zeno*; Yukio Mishima, *Confessions of a Mask*

The typography of poetry: William Faulkner, *The Sound and the Fury* (in part—see the 1984 corrected-text edition, p. 172)

Consider also the use of devices from other art forms to achieve some special effect:

Graphic devices: Laurence Sterne, *Tristram Shandy*; James Joyce, *Ulysses*; Steve Katz, *The Exaggerations of Peter Prince*

Painting: Alain Robbe-Grillet, "The Secret Room" and other works

Photography: Paul Theroux, *The Family Arsenal*; William Faulkner, *Sanctuary* (first version, in part, published 1981)

Movies: Faulkner, *The Sound and the Fury* (use of flashbacks); David Madden, "The Singer"

Theater: William Faulkner, *Requiem for a Nun*

Lecture: Herbert Wilner, "Dovisch in the Wilderness" (see his essay on the writing of this story in Ray B. West, *The Art of Writing Fiction*)

If you have already used, in part or for the whole, one of these devices from other written or art forms, ask yourself whether it has really worked. The very use of one of these devices can cast a spell over the user, making him feel he has handled the device and all other elements well, blinding him to problems the use of it has created. Even though such devices as letters or journals or diaries were often used in the very infancy of the novel, they persist in striking readers, as they did in the beginning, as rather artificial pretexts, no matter how enjoyable their use proves to be. The best test of their use is to ask, Is this the most effective form or device for this particular story? The reader must feel that your use of letters, for instance, was inevitable, that no other device or form would have worked.

150 | Have you used *dreams* ineffectively?

Everyone, for various reasons, finds dreams fascinating. And so, writers often use dreams for various purposes in fiction, forgetting what their own experience has taught them—that telling someone else your fascinating dream is almost never any more effective than subjecting a person to your home movies (everybody loves home movies, too, but only their own). You know from experience that you do not knowingly expose yourself to the prospect of listening to someone tell you about "this weird, incredible dream I had last night." Why then, in the face of this two-way experience, is the history of fiction loaded with dreams?

The use of dreams, for whatever reason or effect, seldom achieves what the writer intends, especially if the dreams go on and on, and, in a novel, appear frequently. Used for a specific purpose, they often have the opposite effect; because all dreams are so open to a wide range of contradictory interpretation, they often seem gratuitous to the reader despite your very specific intent. But they are sometimes clearly effective, as in the opening of Wright Morris's "The Ram in the Thicket." In the novel version, *Man and Boy*, the opening is the same, except for a few word changes, but in the short-story version Morris overcomplicated the dream.

A dream at the beginning of a story or novel sets the tone and provides images that symbolize, or dramatically *seem* to symbolize, aspects of the story. The reader thinks you are trying, very emphatically, to tell him something, so he will give greater weight to those initial dream images or symbols when he encounters them later than to other elements in the story. Is that really what you want? If not, cut the dream. If so, make sure the dream does not suggest more than the story can satisfy. Wright Morris decided that not even the length of a novel could develop the images he had introduced in the short-story version, so he cut a crucifixion image (which also blatantly recalled a key image in T. S. Eliot's "The Love Song of J. Alfred Prufrock").

For an interesting satirical, surrealistic use of dreams, see Nathanael West's first novel, *The Dream Life of Balso Snell*, and the epilogue of Evelyn Scott's *Escapade*.

"And then Mark woke up." If your manuscript comes back viciously twisted, or not at all, either machinery in the postal system has mangled it or the editor had read one *dream-device story* too many. Some writers remember the dirty look or the long lecture their creative-writing instructor gave them when they had a conference about their dream story, usually their first story.

The contrived *surprise-ending* story is often a "and then he woke up" story; the problem is that the reader, whether he likes for a moment the twist or not, has the feeling that every element of the story he has enjoyed so far (or slogged through, hoping for a point of some sort) has been written only to enable the writer to deliver his knockout punch. The dream device is so disappointing or infuriating that it is difficult even to recall the one or two stories in which, long, long, ago, it must have worked so impressively that its repeated use continues.

An even more repugnant variation on the kind of letdown dream stories provide is learning at the end that a character who has behaved in some bizarre fashion is in reality, after all, insane. No matter how effective a story may be up to this revelation, all its elements seem mechanically subordinate to the climactic effect, which itself is hollow.

In such stories, the writer is always conscious of moving toward the shocking revelation. Some very good stories have been ruined by this failure of creative intelligence.

Surprise endings, bizarre dream stories, and revelations of insanity convince the writer that he has used his imagination; as he writes toward the ending, imagining how the reader will react, his imagination is shut off in the creation of all the story's other elements.

151 | Have you neglected to imagine ways to use experimental devices?

An experimental device is any unconventional or innovative, seldom-used device or any conventional device used in a new or fresh manner or context. Most of the devices described in this handbook were once used experimentally; each has become rather conventional in the best sense, but each may, by exaggeration or a new context, be used experimentally.

Some few writers are more experimental in their methods than not. They are like the poet Hart Crane, who sought "New thresholds, new anatomies!" Other writers are experimental only when there is an inner necessity in the conception of the story itself. "I am interested in formal experimentation, yes," said Joyce Carol Oates, "but generally this grows out of a certain plot. The form and the style seem naturally suited to the story that has to be told." See her story "How I Contemplated the World from the Detroit House of Correction and Began My Life Over Again."

The most conventional writers can benefit from a study of experimental fictions. Some of the techniques may be adapted to become central elements in a more conventional work, just as techniques of the avant-garde theater (*Marat/Sade*, the experiments of the Open Theater, the "happenings" theater pieces of the sixties off-off-Broadway) were quickly absorbed into mainstream Broadway musicals, and avant-garde movie techniques became conventions of mass-appeal movies and even of TV commercials.

Here are some experimental techniques and works in which they are used:

Collage: William Burroughs, *Naked Lunch*

Impressionism: Virginia Woolf, *The Waves*

Automatic writing; Jack Kerouac, *The Subterraneans*

Surrealism: Anaïs Nin, "Ragtime"; Djuna Barnes, *Nightwood*

Expressionism: Faulkner, *Absalom, Absalom!*; Dickens, *Bleak House* (see Chapter 48, the Roman in the ceiling mural pointing down at Tulkinghorn's murder and his corpse)

Negative statements only: Madeline Gins, "Brief Autobiography of a Non-existent"

Lyrical interludes: Willard Motley, *Knock on Any Door*

Metafiction: John Barth, *Lost in the Funhouse*

Fantastic satire of forms: Tommaso Landolfi, "Gogol's Wife" (biography)

Juxtaposition of many literary techniques: James Joyce, *Ulysses*

Dream rhetoric: James Joyce, *Finnegans Wake*

Dadaism: Louis Aragon, *Anicet*

Black humor: Kurt Vonnegut, Jr., *Mother Night*

Montage: Lautréamont, *Maldoror*

Innovative use of language: Gertrude Stein, *Tender Buttons*

Structural innovation: Julio Cortazar, *Hopscotch*

Objectivism or phenomenalism: Alain Robbe-Grillet, *Jealousy*

Antinovel: Samuel Beckett, *The Unnamable*

Satire of conventions and other devices: Laurence Sterne, *Tristram Shandy*

Point of view (Unanimism): Jules Romains, *The Death of a Nobody*

One confusion that arises in talking about avant-garde fiction is that the terms are often used for works that simply deal with taboo subjects or controversial ideas in a style that is aggressive or outlandish in attitude, or for works that attempt to be satirical but that end up being merely sarcastic or mean-spirited.

For an excellent description of "innovative" fiction, see Philip Stevick, ed., *Anti-Story: An Anthology of Experimental Fiction*. See also David Madden, "Innovative Techniques," *A Primer of the Novel*, pp. 197-210.

152 | Have you created *unintentional ambiguities*?

An ambiguity is an element (statement, action, or symbol, for instance) that lends itself to more than one interpretation.

Look for *unintentional ambiguities* in your story that may create obscurity. Such ambiguities may reveal a confusion in your own mind about what you're doing. Unresolved conflicts between one possibility and another often result in ambiguity. Uncontrolled ambiguity allows writer and reader to indulge in subjective responses, often to the point of obscurity.

Each of the devices described in this handbook may produce ambiguity, deliberate or accidental. The reader who fails to respond to a particular device misses what that device was designed to imply, convey, or conjure up, and that missing element may cause that reader's experience in the story to be affected by the frustrations of ambiguity. That is another good reason why the writer must strive to maintain control of style and of all techniques and devices.

Faulkner's swift and complicated revision of *Sanctuary* in galley stage resulted in some unintentional confusion and ambiguity amid the controlled confusion and the instances of intentional ambiguity.

See also the next question.

153 | Have you missed places where you might cultivate an *expressive ambiguity* that is appropriate to the overall conception?

Controlled, deliberate ambiguity enables the reader to explore possibilities and experience the tensions among them, causing a deeper involvement in the story. Unintentional ambiguity is often the result of confusion in the author's mind as to the meaning of his ideas or the author's inability to express his ideas clearly or to use devices effectively.

William Empson listed seven types of ambiguity: (1) "a detail is effective in several ways at once"; (2) "two or more alternative meanings are fully resolved into one"; (3) "two apparently unconnected meanings are given simultaneously"; (4) "alternative meanings combine to make clear a complicated state of mind in the author"; (5) "a fortunate confusion, as when the author is discovering his idea in the act of writing''; (6) ''what is said is contradictory or irrelevant and the reader is forced to invent interpretations''; (7) ''full contradiction, marking a division in the author's mind'' (*Seven Types of Ambiguity*).

Some writers deliberately cause mystifications for a special effect (Thomas Pynchon, William Gaddis, Joseph Heller, Conrad); in lesser writers, ambiguity may cover shortcomings. Other writers create mystery as an end in itself. Beyond that there is willful obscurity, often on the premise that in trying to cope with the obscurity, a cooperative reader happens onto multiple and profound meanings and emotions not otherwise possible (Djuna Barnes's *Nightwood* and some of the works of Joyce, Faulkner, and John Hawkes). Just as the writer experiences pleasure in making obscurities clear, he also enjoys providing the reader with occasions for doing that on his own.

The purely subjective vision often overindulges in obscurity in a floundering dive for deeper aspects of self. Readers often resent the feeling that the writer has simply not bothered to make essential matters clear, or has sacrificed clarity for some other, lesser value. But these negatives may be turned into positives. Some innovative writers work on the assumption that willful obscurity may enable the imagination to explore possibilities and to push into far-out realms where transformations may occur.

Readers sometimes suspect that Henry James's ambiguities are often unintentional; but that the master nodded knowingly toward ambiguity is clear when we compare the first edition of *The Portrait of a Lady*, for instance, with the 1912 New York edition. When Lord Warburton, who has asked her to marry him, comes back into Isabel's life after she marries Osmond, Isabel ''hardly knew whether she was glad or not.'' Warburton, on the other hand, ''was plainly very well pleased.'' That is neither ambiguous nor obscure. But James wanted Isabel and the reader together to discover gradually an ambiguous sense of what she feels and what Warburton's intentions are, so he revised: Warburton ''was plainly quite sure of his own sense of the matter.'' In the first version, James gave Isabel very little to struggle with; in the revision, Isabel and the reader strain to figure out what Warburton's attitude is and how Isabel feels about it. The struggle pays off in an experience richer in possibilities.

Revising the English edition of her first novel, *The Voyage Out*, for the American edition, Virginia Woolf clarified some things that needed it, but deliberately made others ambiguous: the causes of Rachel's emotional instability, for instance. Knowing and understanding, like Rachel herself, less, the reader becomes more complexly involved. That was the aim of Woolf's revisions.

VIII GENERAL CONSIDERATIONS

Occasional rereading of the entries in this section in sequence may be helpful.

154 | Viewing the story as a whole, do its elements fail to cohere in a *unity of effect?*

Unity of effect is the organization of all a story's elements so that they interact and enhance each other, resulting in a total effect on the reader. Chekhov said, "A shotgun introduced on page one must go off before the end of the story." *Pattern*, or *design*, the repetition through complications of the central incident or idea, contributes to unity of effect. As we sense the pattern or design of the story we feel that it is moving forward at the same time that the main line of interest is being sustained. Pattern or design has to do with the organized relationships between the various elements or aspects of the story. Each part functions in its relationship to the whole. The effectiveness of a pattern is that the reader follows it to its completion. Through a careful concern with these elements, form evolves and we have a sense of unity when we have finished the story.

Form enables the reader to keep before him as the story moves a comprehension of the whole. Form has to do with the total structure of the story, as enhanced by the writer's style, which is his own personal way of ordering, selecting words for certain effects. It is through style and structure that we sense the *texture* of a story; texture pertains to a story much in the way it pertains to texture in a tapestry, to a painting, or to a musical composition. *Motifs* and *leitmotifs* contribute to design. Form and unity in a story work against chaos in the reader's responses; the reader doesn't like to feel that the elements of your story are there gratuitously or accidentally.

As you revise your story, ask what kind of *unity* is achieved; mechanical *or* organic; or symbolic or psychological; tonal; thematic; structural; spatial; temporal. You may create unity through a mythic pattern, as in James Joyce's *Ulysses*; a symbolic pattern, as in Melville's *Moby-Dick*; a pattern of coincidences, as in William Gaddis's *The Recognitions*; a contrasting set of patterns, as in Tolstoy's *Anna Karenina*. Narrative patterns may converge, as in a Hardy novel, or in Joyce's *Ulysses*. The Aristotelean concept of unity is still useful; a concept of drama, it consists of a unity of place, time, and action—a single action in one place, in one day.

Some experimental writers strive to create a work free of pattern, design, and unity, but the nature of all writing is that it is inherently patterned in defiance of any willful imitation of chaos. Chaos on paper is order merely impersonating chaos. A so-called nonunified story may have powerful isolated effects, but unity intensifies each effect by relating each to all others.

In all fiction, some principle of integration or unity is at work; the effect on the reader is intensity and lasting experience. Form and structure generate energy, life, emotion, and they shape meaning. "Form alone *takes*, and holds and preserves substance," said Henry James. "A novel is a living thing, all one and continuous, like every other organism." A kind of dynamism arises from the conscious cultivation of the tensions between content and form. "Cut a good story anywhere," said Chekhov, "and it will bleed."

155 | Is your story based on a *notion*?

By notion, I mean that kind of clever premise that comes often and easily to the inventive mind. Notions can usually be formulated into the superficial question: "What would happen if . . . ?" A notion is a launching pad. A mere notion, as opposed to a genuine conception, may be all that comes at first. When notion-mongering freezes the imagination, many *possibilities* are missed. See next question.

156 | Do any elements fail to relate in some way to an overall conception?

A conception offers the reader a different kind of experience from that provided by a notion. A conception is a total gestalt-like grasp of the story that enables the author to control the development of the situation, the characters, theme, plot, form, style, and techniques. It orders, interprets, and gives form to the raw material of the story and infuses it with vision and meaning. Most stories begin with a mere notion; many never transcend notion into the realm of conception. A genuine conception frees the imagination to explore possibilities.

Have you imagined your story from a notion into a conception? "Notes, scraps of paper, reverie, all that might go on for years," said Albert Camus. "Then, one day, I have the idea or conception that makes all these isolated fragments coagulate together. There then begins a long and painful putting them into order." The revision process is the cultivation of self-imposed limitations. A concept helps to set those limitations. "Every student must have a form of expression," said Joyce Cary, "and he must learn it by purely technical conceptual education."

As you read a story or novel, consider whether it is written out of a notion or a conception. Even though Thomas Hardy did not have a conceptual intellect, his revisions of *The Return of the Native* reveal a conceptual imagination (see Paterson in Bibliography). William Faulkner's *Sanctuary* was in the galleys stage when his conceptual imagination brought about massive changes in the novel. Both versions are now published. Three different conceptions of D. H. Lawrence's Lady Chatterley story produced three versions.

To watch the conceptual imagination at work, read Wright Morris's *In Orbit*, Michael Tournier's *The Ogre*, William Gaddis's *The Recognitions*, and James Joyce's *Ulysses*.

See "The Day the Flowers Came," pp. 262, 283.

157 | Do you merely use devices mechanically or is technique an agent of discovery?

Technique is any method a writer uses, consciously or unconsciously, to stimulate a response in a reader.

The use of a technical device to handle a localized problem or to achieve an effect in isolation from all other considerations in the story is a mechanical act. On the other hand, the use of a device in coordination with all other devices and elements enables you to discover facets of the story that you would not otherwise; used in that way, one effect of the device is to enable the reader also to discover some facet of your story.

Everywhere in this handbook, I have advised, explicitly and implicitly, against the mechanical application of *any* technique. Always foremost in mind should be the intention of creating, imagining an organic unity, not the expeditious handling of a problem in isolation. "I know exactly how I get my effects," said Ford Madox Ford, "as far as those effects go."

The writer's use of technique enables him to explore and discover possibilities about his characters, about his plot, about his theme, that would remain submerged were he relatively insensitive to the subtle uses of technique. It's impossible to write a story without using technique, but a few writers create mainly out of inspiration and a kind of subjective preoccupation, while most are more aware and in control of what they're doing through conscious use of techniques. Style differs somewhat from technique in that style, the arrangement of words for specific effects, is the medium through which techniques are employed. Style is one aspect of the larger realm of technique.

Novelist-critic Mark Schorer has argued that "technique is discovery." Writers do not grasp as easily as they might the meaning of Schorer's statement in "Technique as Discovery," an essay of major value to writers. "When we speak of technique, then, we speak of nearly everything. For technique is the means by which the writer's experience, which is his subject matter, compels him to attend to it, technique is the only means he has of discovering, exploring, developing his subject, of conveying its meaning, and, finally, of evaluating it."

This comment by novelists Caroline Gordon and Allen Tate enhances Schorer's insight: "Material and method become in the end the same thing, the one discovering the other" (*The House of Fiction*). Novelist-biographer Peter Quennel argues that "the technical difficulties of writing help to determine an author's mode of expression; and, while he is considering and trying to solve them, he may find that the theme he has selected discloses novel possibilities." Ford Madox Ford urged writers, "Consciously strive for an art that will appear artless."

To understand these statements, and to write in light of them, the writer must achieve a disciplined balance between the demands and tensions of freedom and restraint; he must discover that one's best work is created within the limitations that are imposed upon him by himself and by the forms in which he works. "Even in most imaginative flights," wrote T. E. Hulme, "there is always a holding back, a reservation. Be always faithful to the conception of a limit" ("Romanticism and Classicism"). Art is the cultivation of self-imposed limitations. In every good writer there will always be a conflict between inspired romanticism and experimental classicism—between the Thomas Wolfe and James Joyce in him, the Dionysian and the Apollonian.

A knowledge and command of techniques will enable the writer to experience in technical triumphs the joy he normally associates with flights of inspiration. I think of Henry James, James Joyce, Virginia Woolf, Ernest Hemingway, Katherine Mansfield, F. Scott Fitzgerald. Inspiration comes almost as easily to nontalented as to talented writers. I'm not suggesting that a proficiency in technique substitutes for inspiration, but knowing the words for and the concepts of writing techniques brings power and control.

Paul Valéry said, "Literature is the art of playing on the minds of others. . . . Given an impression, a dream, a thought, one *must* express it in such a way as to produce the maximum effect in the mind of a listener—an effect entirely calculated by the Artist." The poet "will take care not to hurl on to paper everything whispered to him in fortunate moments by the Muse of Free Association. On the contrary, everything he has imagined, felt, dreamed, and planned will be passed through a sieve, weighed, filtered, subjected to *form*, and condensed as much as possible so as to gain in power what it loses in length. . . ."

"Questions of art," said Henry James, "are questions of execution." Robert Frost said, "No tears in the writer, no tears in the reader. No surprise for the writer, no surprise for the reader. . . . What do I want to communicate but what a *hell* of a good time I had writing it? The whole thing is performance and prowess and feats of association. Why don't critics talk about those things?"

In the revision process, most writers would do well to become eclectics, open to the great range and variety of techniques and devices. One of the earliest novelists seems to have had this conception of himself, in a refreshingly arrogant, egoistic way: "I am, in reality, the founder of a new province of writing," said Henry Fielding, "so I am at liberty to make what laws I please therein." *Tom Jones* came out of that province.

Over the years, one learns a delight in *making* as well as in *expressing* oneself. Expressing is remembering, but making results in something made, which is separate from oneself and is cherished by others. If you can truly *make* a story—as opposed to simply expressing yourself—it becomes the property of other people; perhaps that's why some writers say they seldom reread their fiction after publication—they become estranged from it, dispossessed of it. The difference between *expressing* and *making* turns up in the process of rewriting.

Fiction that is a work of art can be reread over and over. Self-expression seldom can. There are parallels between the writer's eagerness to rewrite and the reader's eagerness to reread. The creative process and the reading process are never-ending.

Diderot's "Rameau's Nephew" is the result of a technical inspiration to write a novella composed solely of dialogue. Henry James in *The Awkward Age* and Ivy Compton-Burnett in most of her novels went almost that far. James, who had failed as a playwright, discusses the expressive intent of his dialogue device in his preface to *The Awkward Age*, reprinted in *The Art of the Novel*. That device enabled him to discover aspects of his story that no other device could have done.

See "The Day the Flowers Came," pp. 262, 283–84.

158 | Have you failed to employ the technique of selectivity?

It's impossible *not* to be selective. But what is meant by selectivity as a technique of fiction is conscious and deliberate selection as opposed to the natural selection that occurs, consciously or not, in the writing in the first draft. Again, *context* is crucial, and point of view. They help you determine what stays, what gets cut, and what should be added.

Henry James advised the writer to "try to be one of those on whom nothing, no, nothing is lost." But he also observed, "Life being all inclusion and confusion, and art being all discrimination and selection . . . life persistently blunders and deviates . . . life . . . is capable . . . of nothing but splendid waste."

Of "The Killers," Hemingway said, "That story probably had more left out of it than anything I ever wrote."

159 | Have you included *irrelevant* or *superfluous* material?

Your answers to this question enable you to employ the technique of selectivity. What is irrelevant? A major question to ask as you revise. "Much irrelevance is introduced into novels," says Elizabeth Bowen, "by the writer's vague hope that at least some of this *may* turn out to be relevant, after all. A good deal of what might be called provisional writing goes into the first drafts of first chapters of most novels. At a point in the novel's progress, relevance becomes clearer. The provisional chapters are then recast. . . . To direct . . . an author's attention to the imperative of re*.*vance is certainly the most useful—and possibly the only—help that can be given."

Some material may be relevant but excessive, too much of a good thing. For instance, if your story deals with a detective, *any* material about police work is theoretically relevant, but in your early drafts you may have included a superfluity of such material, well done in itself but a drag on other elements (pace, etc.). What is relevant and what is superfluous are determined generally by the nature of fiction itself and specifically by the built-in requirements of the particular story you have conceived.

160 | Have you failed to make all the story's elements, at any given point, function *simultaneously?*

Simultaneity is a sense that in any given moment all the elements are active in the reader's consciousness. The writer's coordination and control of all the elements, a coherence of the parts, a synthesis of all things into a single effect, enables the reader to experience a sense of simultaneity throughout the story. He feels at the end a sense of *inevitability*: everything has happened as it has because it *has* to.

Simultaneity is an effect that is very seldom discussed by writers or critics. The reader is always experiencing this phenomenon unconsciously; it is an aesthetic emotion that underlies all the reader's experiences as a kind of flow. It is *not* there when a work is mechanically constructed, when one thing is literally added to another, with no cumulative sense of organic unity. The techniques that most obviously promote the sensation of simultaneity are a patterned repetition and variation on key phrases, key images, and parallel elements. A sense of simultaneity may explain that sudden conscious feeling of exhilaration a reader has once or twice in the reading of a work. It explains, in part, why a reader can read a novel that is a work of art over and over again, long after the surface elements of character and story are extremely familiar so that one is not reading to see what happens next, or for some such reason. See the next question.

161 | Have you failed to achieve a quality of *inevitability* for all the elements in the story?

Inevitability is the feeling we have that what happens in a story *must* happen because of the way the elements and techniques have been set in motion. "Before everything," said Ford Madox Ford, "a story must convey a sense of inevitabililty."

One effect of unity is that when the reader reaches the end, he has a feeling of inevitability about the way events have turned out. The ending seems inevitable if, in the beginning and from time to time as the story moves forward, you prepare the reader.

162 | Do the story's form and technique, especially point of view and style, fail to express *theme*?

Theme is a story's main idea, or its underlying meaning. "What does it all mean?" the reader wonders. Sometimes "theme" is used to mean "subject matter," but not in this handbook. How are form and technique expressive of theme? Characters and events express theme, but technique and style may also be expressive of them. Theme, like symbolism, is sometimes overstressed by readers (especially teachers). Eventually, every element of fiction expresses some aspect of theme, but a preoccupation with theme usually distracts from more important, transcendent human elements. "I wasn't, and am not *primarily* concerned with injustice," said Ralph Ellison, "but with art."

Closely related to the *subject-matter fallacy* is the fallacy of theme-dominance or the communication, didactic, moral, or propaganda fallacy: "The main purpose of fiction is to convey a message."

Allen Tate's definition of the *communication fallacy* (or the heresy of communication) applies to fiction as well as to poetry: it is "the use of poetry to communicate ideas and feelings which should properly be conveyed by non-poetic discourse . . . relying on attitudes external to the aesthetic experience." The writer, some people are convinced, must communicate a moral or lesson, or an attitude about social evils. "The writer expresses," said Eugene Jolas, "he doesn't communicate." W. H. Auden always asked young writers, "Why do you want to write poetry?" "If the young writer answers, 'I have important things I want to say,' then he is not a poet."

Wimsatt and Beardsley describe the *affective fallacy* as "a confusion between the poem and its *results* (what it is and what it *does*)." Too many writers today seem distracted by what they want their work to do thematically, and neglect what it *is*. Other writers strive to bring an imagined world into being, to make the word flesh. "A poem should not mean," said Archibald MacLeish, "but be."

A work of the imagination is first of all an experience, meaning-and-emotion fused in each moment. Theme must emerge from the reader's emotional and intellectual experience in reading the story. "A novel should be an experience," said Joyce Cary, "and convey an emotional truth rather than arguments.'' Few writers want the reader to read the whole story or novel just to get the theme, point, message. A story is not a carrier pigeon with a message clamped on its leg. It is the experience of watching a pigeon fly from here to there.

Some writers are more motivated by thematic intentions and more conscious of them throughout the creative process than others; unfortunately, many reviewers and teachers, like Sunday-school instructors, are so preoccupied by the meaning of it all and by trying to answer the question ''What was the writer trying to say?'' that readers have been trained to be more attentive to signals in the story that point to meaning than responsive to aesthetic elements; they may not even know such elements are functioning in fiction.

Some writers, on the other hand, are moved primarily by character, story, images, and techniques in themselves to write a particular story, and meaning follows quite naturally from those concerns. When a writer tacks on a moral or a thematic statement, he demonstrates failure to embody meaning in the formal aspects of the work, or, having no conscious interest in a meaning reducible to a neat ''man's inhumanity to man'' statement, he surrenders to a nagging sense of obligation to supply one. Such overt theme-mongering is often easy to identify in the first draft because the writer is sometimes trying to tell himself what it all means so that he can present the meaning more subtly in revision.

You may have to ask yourself, What exactly *is* the theme of this story? Is it now expressed fully enough? If not, how can that now be done? Find ways to embody aspects of theme in characters and their relationships, events, images, point of view, and style, among other possibilities.

In his revisions of *The Return of the Native*, Hardy worked especially hard and in detail to dramatize through character, action, and style the Promethean theme of romantic rebellion. See Paterson in Bibliography.

The three published versions of Lady Chatterley's story differ not only as to the amount of theme-mongering D. H. Lawrence indulges in, but as to the particular thematic emphasis as well.

In revising *Women in Love*, D. H. Lawrence realized that thematic statements, his own or his characters', would have little effect stated baldly. He used the device of having a character speak these ideas but in revision carried it one step further by allowing other characters to interact with him in dialog and in doing so continue to reveal facets of their character and their relationships in a dramatic fashion. The dialog continues at an engaging pace. Lawrence's handling of his characters in dialog becomes as expressive of his overall themes as the ideas carried *in* the dialog. See Ross in Bibliography.

A major theme in Wright Morris's *One Day*—inspired partly by the intrusion of the assassination of President Kennedy upon the work-in-progress—is the "meaningful accident." Morris's handling of that rather unusual theme in revision can be seen in Kuehl's *Creative Writing and Rewriting*, pp. 98-129.

One of the monumental philosophical novels of the twentieth century is Thomas Mann's *The Magic Mountain*. Even so, Mann was worried at first that "the theme afforded a dangerously rich complex of ideas," and that he might lose himself in "shoreless realms of thought." See Mann's "The Making of *The Magic Mountain*."

To follow Mann's thematic preoccupations throughout the writing of *Doctor Faustus*, see his *The Genesis of a Novel*.

See "The Day the Flowers Came," comment 26, p. 282.

163 | Does the *moral* rise like a flag on a pole at, or near, the end of your story?

This is an easy problem to identify. It may be symptomatic of the underdevelopment of other elements of the story. Throughout their lives, most writers continue, in the first draft especially, to commit this fallacy. Fear of being misunderstood or a compulsion to make the point here at the last opportunity seizes them and they run the message, moral, or theme up the flagpole for all to salute. For the experienced writer, it becomes clear quite readily in the revision process that the theme or message has been already more than adequately expressed through character, action, and various techniques, such as point of view and style, and the writer strikes that passage out as he has already struck the weather report out of the first paragraph.

John Fowles wanted an overtly thematic ending for *The Magus*, but the revised version published a decade later shows that he decided it should be less blatant.

164 | Are your *intentions* unclear?

Writers sometimes work out of unclear or mistaken intentions. Have you made your intentions as clear as possible to the reader to avoid as much as possible the reader's tendency to judge your work by your success or failure in achieving what *he* thinks your intention is?

The critic or reader who analyzes, evaluates, judges a work on the basis of what he perceives to be the writer's intention commits the intentional fallacy. Both negative and positive critical comment derived from misconceptions of intention are a source of excruciating pain for most writers, because only the writer can know what his intentions are. What, then, *are* your intentions in the work you are revising?

Graham Greene's intentions in *The Heart of the Matter* seemed clear enough to himself: "The character of Scobie was intended to show that pity can be the expression of a monstrous pride." But he was distressed to discover that his intentions were misinterpreted by reviewers, critics, and readers. Most of the revisions he made for his collected-works edition of that novel were intended to make his intentions clearer (See Question 9).

The ability to articulate one's intentions for oneself and the anticipation of having those intentions misinterpreted, based on frustrations over reception of one's work in the past, is clearly demonstrated in Evelyn Scott's preface to her fourteenth novel, *Bread and a Sword*. Your desperate expectation of being misunderstood need not compel you to write a preface to your fiction, but Scott shows in this twenty-five-page preface just how articulate about intentions a fiction writer is capable of being.

165 | Are some elements now blurred that ought to be more sharply focused?

In *Understanding Fiction*, which has continued to have an enormous influence since its appearance in 1943, Cleanth Brooks and Robert Penn Warren discuss three kinds of focus: *interest*, *character*, and *narration*. Questions of focus confront the writer "as he begins to put his story into shape." Whose story is it? The answer lies in "the relation between the character and the events"; it is "a fundamental principle of organization" in a story—"the core of meaning" (p. 658).

Even though Nick Carroway's consciousness is the focus of *The Great Gatsby*, Fitzgerald focused on Nick's responses in several passages where the focus should have been on Gatsby *through* Nick's sensibility, as here, very near the end:

And as I sat there brooding on the old unknown world I too held my breath and waited, until I could feel the motion of America as it turned through the hours—my own blue lawn and the tall incandescent city on the water and beyond that the dark fields of the republic rolling on under the night.

Notice that Nick's prominence in the revised version is deemphasized:

And as I sat there brooding on the old, unknown world, I thought of Gatsby's wonder when he first picked out the green light at the end of Daisy's dock. He had come a long way to this blue lawn, and his dream must have seemed so close that he could hardly fail to grasp it. He did not know that it was already behind him, somewhere in that vast obscurity beyond the city, where the dark fields of the republic rolled on under the night.

See Kuehl in Bibliography.

The first published version of Fitzgerald's *Tender Is the Night* suffered from uncertainty of focus. He restructured it to focus on Dick Diver. See Cowley in Bibliography.

Revisions of "Odour of Chrysanthemums" show that D. H. Lawrence's focus shifted from the family and environment of the miner to the dead miner himself. See Cushman in Bibliography.

166 | Do you fail to make the reader feel that you have a *compulsion to tell a story*?

Just as the possible functions of the imagination are seldom discussed these days, because the public misconceives what *imagination* is and how it functions (or may be trained to function), *story* also is deemphasized when the techniques of writing are seriously discussed. Anybody can imagine a story, and who cares about stories anyway, goes the attitude. The term "storytelling" is seldom heard nowadays. Perhaps that is because the oral aspect of the tradition of fiction is now virtually mute. What writer today can remember hearing the request "Tell me a story"? How many writers ever uttered that request themselves?

The notion of a writer's having a compulsion to tell a story may strike most writers as rather quaint. But it's only "rather" quaint because it's still a vital reality for some writers; having a compulsion to tell a story, they *have* responded eagerly to the request "Tell me a story." The storyteller-listener dynamic is carried over into writing fiction. So that the reader feels, and in reading some writers—William Faulkner, Flannery O'Connor, Joyce Carol Oates, to mention a few—gladly responds to the power of that compulsion. "The eagerness of a listener quickens the tongue of a narrator," writes Charlotte Brontë in *Jane Eyre*.

If you don't have a compulsion to tell a story (not the same as a desire to *write* a story or to *be* a writer), there's not much you can do about it in the revision process, but if you have it, you know it; and the point of this question is to remind you that an awareness of the dynamics of the storyteller-listener relationship enables you to deal more effectively with some of the questions of technique raised in this handbook.

When Ernest Hemingway died, the aspect of his work that Robert Frost was prompted to recall was its oral quality: "I remember the fascination that made me want to read aloud 'The Killers' to everybody that came along." On the printed page, the writer strives to make the reader experience a quality of immediacy. You may test and demonstrate that quality by reading a draft of your work aloud to yourself or to a friend. "Draw your chair up close to the edge of the precipice," said F. Scott Fitzgerald, "and I'll tell you a story."

One of the most overwhelming examples of the compulsion to tell a story is William Faulkner's *Absalom, Absalom!* Not only does the main character, Quentin Compson, share the author's compulsion but Quentin's father, Miss Rosa Coldfield, and Colonel Sutpen himself, as the "hero" of the tale, do too. And most interestingly, Quentin's Canadian roommate at Harvard, Shreve, picks up from Quentin "the virus of suggestion," to borrow a phrase from Henry James, the most literary of compulsive storytellers. Shreve's vicarious compulsion, much like the reader's own, competes in energy with Quentin's.

167 | Have you failed to imagine ways to create tension?

When two or more elements pull the reader simultaneously in different directions, the reader feels a tension that sustains his emotional involvement in the story. The author may set up a tension between literal and metaphorical meaning; between characters; between techniques themselves. What May Sarton says of poetry may be suggestive for fiction writers:

These are some of the tensions I experience in the process of writing a poem, tensions which discharge a load of experience in a most beneficent and exciting way when the piece of weaving on the loom turns out to be a real poem: (1) tension between past and present; (2) between idea and image; (3) between music and meaning; (4) between particular and universal; (5) between creator and critic; (6) between silence and words. Parallel with them are the tensions within daily life: (1) between the living and the dead; (2) between the public and the private person; (3) between art and life.

168 | Have you limited your *imagination* in some way?

This question is intended as a reminder of the discussion of the imagination's possible functions in the Introduction (pp.000). The most severe limitation of your imagination results from a failure to know how it works, how to cultivate it, to expand and then control it. To misconceive what it is and how it works is also limiting.

To think of the use of the techniques described in this handbook as requiring imagination in its various functions is to set the imagination free of limitations; at some stage, of course, you set limits yourself for your own specific purposes. Paradoxically, one of the most limiting effects on the imagination is the cherished notion that total freedom is the source of the finest creative works.

"I would like to write a book of the life of the mind and of the imagination," said Sherwood Anderson. "Facts elude me. . . . When I deal in facts, at once I begin to lie." Ellen Glasgow said, "I suppose I am a born novelist, for the things I imagine are more vital and vivid to me than the things I remember."

The next six questions deal with matters that limit the imagination.

169 | Do you commit the fallacy of *imitating* life?

The writer's assumption that his story is effective *because* "it really happened" usually produces a first draft full of problems.

The imitation fallacy assumes that art and life are synonymous. The process is, however, marvelously reciprocal, for life imitates art quite frequently, and sometimes quite terrifyingly. In *Love in the Ruins*, Walker Percy imagined a sniper on the roof of the Howard Johnson Motel in New Orleans; not long after the novel appeared, a sniper killed people from the roof of the Howard Johnson Motel in New Orleans.

The writer who is a creator (as opposed to a journalist in disguise) does not feel good about his work because "it's just like life" but because it *heightens* our awareness of ordinary life; it doesn't slavishly imitate it.

170 | Have you committed the *subject-matter* fallacy?

The *subject-matter fallacy* is the assumption that an interesting subject makes an interesting story. This notion blinds the writer to technical problems in revision. When the artist or the hack is so bemused by the timelessness, the controversy, the strangeness, the importance of his raw material that he neglects the dictates of art, he is involved in the act of writing a subject-dominated story. Obvious examples of such entrapping subjects are war, racial conflict, sex, drugs, and oneself. The Naturalists fostered this notion that the writer's function is to reproduce "a slice of life," one subject at a time. In the mere act of doing that, the writer feels that what he is writing is justified, whether it is artistically well done or not.

If you were to read ten stories on any given subject (religion, love, war, crime), they would differ mainly in the techniques used in handling the same subject. A reading of passages from several stories on the subject of love, dealing with "that first golden moment" when the boy meets the girl, would reveal different assumptions about the audience, a spectrum of quality, and a spectrum of techniques. Look, for instance, at stories in *True Confessions*, *Playboy*, and *Redbook*, and at Henry Miller's *Tropic of Cancer*, Lawrence Durrell's *Justine*, Nabokov's *Lolita*; du Maurier's *Rebecca*, Charlotte Brontë's *Jane Eyre*, Wolfe's *Look Homeward, Angel*, Joyce's *Ulysses*, and Lockridge's *Raintree County*.

171 | Have you mistaken the power of *inspiration* for achieved effect?

In the middle of my first stress test, the nurse asked her fifth or sixth question. "So do you just set aside several hours each morning for writing?" I said yes. She declared, "That doesn't seem very creative." To her, creativity means thunderclaps of pure inspiration, a powerful feeling, image, or idea that activates a writer's urge to write and stimulates his imagination.

One cause of a dislike of rewriting is the popular preconception that inspiration—with its coy comings and goings—is the main source of creative energy. In the popular concept, the writer works mainly by inspiration. That's why cartoons and movie images show the writer so often frozen at the typewriter like a statue, staring into a space, frowning— either he has a writer's block, or he's waiting for inspiration like a bolt of lightning to strike his forehead; then he will leap into action. Most writers work long hours every day. After the feverish rush of the first draft, the energy that starts them off is seldom inspiration—it is willpower, discipline, and love of the craft itself. But pretty soon, the writer *is* inspired—by some technical or stylistic solution to the problems raised in the revision process. Henry Miller's rhapsody on writing is a typical expression of a widespread attitude: "Rocketing out into the blue, grasping at flying ladders, mounting, soaring, lifting the world up by the scalp, rousing the angels from their ethereal lairs, drowning in stellar depths, clinging to the tails of comets." But even Henry Miller, reputed to be a major example of the inspired writer, urges writers: "*Concentrate. Narrow down*. Exclude." "Work according to program and not according to mood. Stop at the appointed time!"

When a writer is too subjective, he works stretched on a me-rack that produces the *inspiration fallacy*, or the conviction that the writer is able to plug into the Muses' Switchboard and receive divine inspiration from a divine power source. Such writers often seem obsessed with what Plato called "poetic madness." Although Wordsworth spoke of "emotion recollected in tranquility," the Romantics made frequent use of the Muses' Switchboard. On the me-rack, writers, especially young writers, sacrifice themselves to the two-headed god Subjectivity/Self-Expression.

In his study of *The Return of the Native*, John Paterson concludes that Hardy "tended to leave too much to the poor chances of inspiration." Stephen Spender, the poet, said that everything in writing is work except inspiration. Katherine Mansfield recorded in her *Journal*, "Wrote 'The Dove's Nest' this afternoon. I was in no mood to write; it seemed impossible. Yet when I had finished three pages, they were all right. This is proof (never to be too often proved) that once one has thought out a story nothing remains but the *labour*." Some writers are able to endure all that labour because of what W. B. Yeats called "the fascination of what's difficult."

172 | In this story, do you struggle on a me-rack of autobiographical subjectivity?

"And because I found I had nothing to write about," said Montaigne, "I presented myself as subject." For Montaigne, the result was splendid. But usually, to place your own psyche and your own experiences at the center of your creative universe, for any or most of your fiction, is to place yourself on a rack, hands and feet bound. In writing, you then stretch yourself to the point of excruciating pain with the intention of *expressing* yourself, as the cant phrase has it. Such self-inflicted pain excludes all other considerations—about other people and about the techniques of writing.

In that state, every painful utterance takes on the authority associated with an intense experience. That experience is so real, honest, and authentic, how can the words that express it fail to be? Words written under those conditions seldom are real, because writing is an artificial, unnatural act, which only the conscious art of fiction can make *seem* real. When you make your own navel the center of the universe on the me-rack of subjective autobiography, *anything* you write will later suffice to remind you of the highly charged emotions and thoughts you had while you were on the me-rack; such experiences are *real*, though they are self-induced, subjective experiences. Everything has the force and authority of cosmic significance, but for you alone. No technique described in this handbook can possibly have any relevance; consequently, nothing written on the me-rack can have any relevance for most readers. Exceptions (Jack Kerouac, Henry Miller, etc.) wait eagerly in the wings to encourage you to strap yourself to the rack and to believe that what you write there will change everybody else's universe.

The *autobiographical fallacy* comes into play here. Whether you write about your own subjective experiences while delving deep into your psyche or about more external experiences or events in your life, everything seems of almost equal value to you; consequently, the task of revision is to find devices and techniques (perhaps of point of view) that will put those experiences in a more objective framework of some kind.

Samuel Butler's *The Way of All Flesh* is autobiographical; Ernest Pontifex is modeled after Butler himself. But Butler imagines a persona, the elderly Overton, who expresses, with restraint, his own insights and opinions as *he* tells Ernest's story. Two innovative autobiographies are suggestive for fiction: Henry Adams creates a somewhat similar split which gives him distance in *The Education of Henry Adams* by telling his story in the third person; and, closer to Butler's technique, Gertrude Stein in *The Autobiography of Alice B. Toklas* tells her own story by pretending to be Alice B. Toklas telling *her* own story, which is mostly about Stein.

The problems of autobiographical fiction arise in these novels: Thomas Wolfe's *Look Homeward, Angel* and his other novels; Fitzgerald's *This Side of Paradise*; the novels of Henry Miller.

173 | Does the claim *"it really happened to me"* blind you to artistic faults?

The compulsion to report on actual events results in the *it-really-happened fallacy*. There is an even greater suffocation of imagination in the it-really-happened-to-me fallacy. The me-rack fallacy and it-really-happened fallacy threaten the health of the imagination in our subject-dominated culture. The writer who is a creator does not claim, "This really happened" or "This really happened to me," but, "This really happened in my *imagination*."

The writer who writes out of the conviction that the center of the universe is his own navel may at some point strike the reader as making a hysterical discovery of the obvious. One of the consequences of self-indulgence on the me-rack is to give the trivial cosmic significance out of the conviction that *everything* that happens to *me* causes the very planets somehow to wobble in their orbits. Another version of this fallacy is the waking-up-in-the-morning fallacy; again, the description is full of exaggerations, mainly because it is the great *you* getting up or because you, the writer, are too full of a sense of the importance of this day for your fictive character. About one out of two stories by young writers begins with the hero waking up. The editor of a well-known literary magazine says, "Almost any story that begins with someone waking up in bed is bound to be dull." Almost. Consider Kafka's "Metamorphosis." I hasten to repeat that a work of fiction is often great partly because of the way it violates guidelines.

174 | Have you committed the fallacy of expressive form?

Me-rack writings produce the fallacy of expressive form, the conviction that "sufficiently intense feeling on the part of the poet will regularly produce adequate expression in the poem. This dependence upon imagination . . . deprives the poet of any external criteria, which are necessary if he is to know whether his work functions effectively for his readers." (The definition is from Beckson and Ganz, *A Reader's Guide to Literary Terms.*)

The writer commits the fallacy of expressive form when he writes out of the misconception that "emotion in the author will produce emotion in the reader.'' This fallacy is related to but is not quite the same as the me-rack fallacy. You do not have to write about yourself to commit the fallacy of expressive form.

175 | Have you failed to imagine all the *possibilities* or missed any opportunities your story raises?

Too few writers revise out of multiple possibilities. Overreliance on inspiration tends to shut down the imagination, so that it ceases to explore unrealized elements latent in the first draft. The notebooks for *Crime and Punishment* record many possibilities that Dostoyevsky did not develop. The revisions of Henry James reached for every possibility and seized every opportunity. As your imagination explores possibilities, be alert to opportunities for developing your basic story elements; when you've finished a first draft, ask yourself whether you have left any missed opportunities behind.

What happens in the writing of the first draft is that your story takes on the quality of a real experience—*this* is how it happened, this is the *only* way it could happen. Thus, the imagination becomes closed to possibilities. To avoid that, interrogate your story for possibilities and alternatives.

We must credit experimental writers for keeping formal or structural possibilities alive for more conventional writers, but the inspired writer who thinks of himself as a totally free experimentalist takes no risks. It is only in taking risks within a context of self-imposed control that one sees all the possibilities of one's story and avoids missing opportunities for creating effects that make the reader experience its deepest essence.

176 | Are there *sensational* or repulsive *elements* that distract from the overall effect of your story?

If the predominant effect you want your story to have is sensational, with some elements of the repulsive, your answer, obviously, will be no. But in some first drafts of stories that are intended to be subtle, a sensational element obtrudes to distract the reader from a range of quieter effects. A sensational element may work as contrast, but it may stick in the reader's mind as the story's most memorable moment—a result you may not want. Under critical scrutiny such moments usually prove expendable. A fixation on such moments puts constraints on the workings of your imagination in the rest of the story.

See "The Day the Flowers Came," comment 18, pp. 277–78.

177 | Do your characters and the story's events fail the test of *credibility*?

"Not likely," is the defiant answer of the writer who has drawn upon real life. But the test is not in life, it is in the reading, and the work of art written about actual events or people exists within a frame of reference entirely different from life. What happens in your story must survive the test of the elements of fiction, and those elements, depending on how you have handled them, determine the answer to the question. In fiction, that is credible which works in harmony with *all* the story's elements. Conceivably, in some particular context, the simple act of taking a bath may lack some edge of credibility, while on the same page you may convince the reader that the same character has slit his throat. So credibility is a much more complicated question than whether a character is real or an event really happened or *could* happen.

The original *Sanctuary* by Faulkner was a more credible story. For instance, the character of Popeye was more credible in the first version. Both versions have been published.

"Lawrence's first problem in revision of Lady Chatterley's story," says Mark Schorer, "was to achieve maximum plausibility within the terms of his aspiration."

See "The Day the Flowers Came," comment 2, p. 265, comment 14, pp. 273–74, and comment 20, p. 279.

178 | Are there too many *coincidences* in your story?

The manipulation of coincidences has long been a characteristic of bad commercial fiction (and it makes for bad serious fiction, too). A coincidence has, in life, its own dramatic power to interest us; we strive in vain, however, to make sense of that interest. When a coincidence appears in fiction, it seems, even when it doesn't, to *stand in* for the more normal action readers expect fiction to provide; the reader then suspects a failure of character, of plot, of ingenuity. The effect is especially negative if a main line of action is resolved by a coincidence, or a character's dilemma is solved by one. Yes, you will find Dickens full of coincidence, but his genius transcends whatever criticism, and it has been severe, he has gotten for the proliferation of that element in his work. As a general practice, then, avoid the temptations of the coincidence.

The deadly convergence of patterns of coincidences upon human beings is part of the vision of human experience Thomas Hardy conveys in *The Return of the Native*. It has a similar function in "The Day the Flowers Came," See p. 264.

179 | Do *unintentional flaws* mar your story?

One is enough to lose your most faithful reader. Most first drafts contain several at least, but you need to assume the worst to keep your vigilance high. Inaccuracies, imprecision, incongruities, inconsistencies, unintentional ambiguities, redundancies—the list is longer.

The writer who has had simple errors pointed out to him (along with the rest of the world and posterity) by witty reviewers will rejoice upon discovering such errors in the revision stage. When Fitzgerald had Doctor Diver "deliberately poking at the cervical of a brain" in the first edition of *Tender Is the Night*, he made a blatant mistake. "Cortical" perhaps, "cortex" most probably was what he had in mind. Almost as face-scalding is to have an editor to whom you have submitted a story or novel tell you that the Grand Canyon is not, never was, never will be in South Dakota.

Intelligence is no safeguard in the first draft against "howlers," as George Eliot, known for her intellect, discovered after she wrote, "He tried to heal the wound he had made by petting her." Eliot did not have to suffer seeing that in print. She corrected it: "He tried that evening by petting her to heal the wound he had made in the morning."

Writing the first draft in haste, you may drift unconsciously into rhyme as Thomas Hardy did in *Tess of the D'Urbervilles*. "The wind blew through Sue's white muslin too . . ." In *The Way of All Flesh*, Samuel Butler searched out and cut redundancies. "He was perfectly well shaped but unusually devoid of physical muscular strength." He cut "muscular" as redundant.

See "The Day the Flowers Came," p. 262.

180 | Have you chosen an effective *title*?

Ernest Hemingway said that a title has to have "magic." Hemingway saw potential magic in "The World's Room," "An Italian Chronicle," "They Who Get Shot," "The Carnal Education," "The Sentimental Education of Frederic Henry," and "Love in Italy," but real magic in *A*

Farewell to Arms. Many other writers whose titles are considered particularly effective did not start off well. Is there more magic in "Hearts Resurgent" or *Jude the Obscure*? "Catch-14," "Catch-18," or *Catch-22*? "The Boy Who Killed His Mother" or *Tender Is the Night*? *The First Lady Chatterley*, *John Thomas and Lady Jane*, or *Lady Chatterley's Lover*? "The Old Pyncheon Family" or *The House of Seven Gables*? "The Godgame" or *The Magus*?—John Fowles himself remains unsure.

"I'm terrible about titles," says Eudora Welty. "I don't know how to come up with them. They're the one thing I'm really uncertain about." Walker Percy says, "A good title should be like a metaphor: It should intrigue without being too baffling or too obvious."

It is certain that every story or novel you publish will have an oral life at least to this extent: readers will say your title, breathe life into it. Titles have a runic, iconic, talismanic, touchstone, charged-image effect. Think of the titles you have intoned: *The Sound and the Fury*, *A Catcher in the Rye*, *Steppenwolf*, *The Grapes of Wrath*, *The Heart Is a Lonely Hunter*—if you love it, there's a certain thrill in saying the title of it.

181 | Does your work-in-progress belong in a different genre?

A frequent criticism of novels that are generally admirable is that they seem to be forced expansions of novellas or of short stories (or a forcing together of several originally unrelated stories). If the market for stories has drastically shrunk since the 1950s, the market for novellas never has been hospitable. That is especially unfortunate if you agree that the art of fiction is better realized within the scope of the novella than within that of the novel.

Katherine Anne Porter might well have considered expanding the story of Laura in "Flowering Judas" into a novel, and possibly did, then rejected the idea because the effect she wanted, and achieved, would, at greater length, dissipate. There are so many and such complex implications in Faulkner's "That Evening Sun" that it contains the material of a novel, and perhaps that novel is *The Sound and the Fury*.

If you feel your short story fails, consider, then, whether it shouldn't be expanded into a novella. Examination of most of the short stories that were expanded with artistic success into novels, even very long ones, may suggest that they failed in the short form. Some were published before, some after, the writing of the novel began; some of the stories never were published. Joyce's *Ulysses*, Mann's *The Magic Mountain*,

Moore's *Esther Waters*, Woolf's *Mrs. Dalloway*, Hawkes's *Second Skin*, Faulkner's *The Sound and the Fury*, Morris's *Man and Boy*, and many other novels have short-story forms.

Should your novel be compressed into a short story? A few instances of this process are on record, but many novels have had greater force compressed into novella length (roughly from 35 to 150 printed pages).

Would your short story or novel work more effectively as a *play*? Unlike any other playwright, Tennessee Williams wrote numerous short stories, and a surprising number of his plays began in that form. For instance, "The Yellow Bird" became *The Glass Menagerie* and "Three Players of a Summer Game" became *Cat on a Hot Tin Roof*. For interesting combinations of prose and play forms, see John Steinbeck's *Burning Bright* and Faulkner's *Requiem for a Nun*; for the latter, see also Polk in Bibliography.

Would some of the material you have cut out of your novel serve as the basis for short stories? Many writers have to resist the temptation to think of the novel as a colossal gift package you can put a lot of good things into. Writers engage in salvage operations, putting material cut from earlier fictions into the one in progress, and setting aside for possible future use material cut from the work at hand. Whole stories, as many as seven or eight, are among the things writers cut out of their novels. Thomas Wolfe is an extreme example. Many Fitzgerald and Faulkner and Hemingway stories are at least early explorations or later elaborations of the novels.

182   Have you neglected your *reader*?

Be always aware of the relationship between you and your reader. "Only connect," said E. M. Forster, if I may use in this context his epigraph to *Howards End*. The writer has a compulsion to establish a relationship with his reader, to set up and control his responses.

The process of revision is to a great extent a process of working out the complex relationship between writer and reader. The art of revision parallels in many ways the art of reading.

Frank O'Connor said, ". . . the rest is rereading and rewriting. The writer should never forget that he is also a reader, though a prejudiced one, and if he cannot read his own work a dozen times he can scarcely expect a reader to look at it twice. Likewise what bores him after the sixth reading is quite liable to bore a reader at the first, and what pleases him after the twelfth may please a reader at the second. Most of my stories have been rewritten a dozen times, a few of them fifty times." William Styron, in *Writers at Work*, said, "Every day I pick up the story or whatever it is I've been working on and read it through. If I enjoy it as a reader, then I know I'm getting along all right."

The writer has many responsibilities to the reader, but some writers insist that such responsibilities require a two-way relationship: "We ought to have readers," says Mark Harris, "who do as much goddamn work as we who write." "People do not deserve to have good writing," said Emerson, "they are so pleased with bad." "Easy writing," said S. J. Perelman, "makes hard reading." "Literature is an occupation in which you have to keep proving your talent," said Jules Renard, "to people who have none." "The novelist does not as a rule rely sufficiently," said André Gide, "on the reader's imagination." "Our doctrine is," said Trollope, "that the author and the reader should move along together in full confidence with each other. . . ." "No one can write decently," said E. B. White, "who is distrustful of the reader's intelligence, or whose attitude is patronizing." In his essay on *The Magic Mountain*, Thomas Mann said, "I shall begin with a very arrogant request that it be read not once but twice." "What a writer should try to do," said Hemingway, "is to make something which will be so written that it will become a part of the experience of those who read him."

The relationship between writer and reader is a measure of the distance between them; the way that distance is handled is through techniques, such as point of view and style. Henry James said that the writer makes "his reader as much as he makes his characters." Between the writer and the reader there has always been a secret collusion, collaboration, communion, which determines the degree of involvement that is achieved. The writer must understand his audience if he is to induce it to use its imagination. Some writers have always respected the demands of and made concessions to the audience; some have catered to its prejudices and assumptions. Each writer has, consciously or not, an ideal reader, sometimes a reflection of himself.

The difference between the act of creation and the act of reading must be taken into account. How do these contrasts end up complementing each other, and what might result if some of the conflicts could be resolved? There needs to be a psychology of reading, understood by both reader and writer, student and teacher.

To involve the reader, the writer appeals to and often manipulates the reader's response to aspects of the nature of fiction. The reader comes to the form with certain conventional expectations; if the writer is to surprise the reader, or to jolt his perspective by violating these conventions, the conventions themselves must be employed, so the writer who hopes to do away with conventions entirely undercuts his relationship with the reader to that extent. Each work, of course, sets up its own peculiar expectations and anticipations, and the reader enjoys having them either realized or reversed.

The writer wishes to move his reader. He may persuade the reader intellectually; he may move him to laughter or to tears; he may charm him; he may encourage sensory, instinctive responses; he may deliberately make the reader uncomfortable; he may offer him a "voyeuristic" experience. There is an infinite range of individual differences among readers in this realm of possible emotional and intellectual and purely literary responses.

There needs to be training in the art of reading, not simply in the limited pleasures of deciphering codes, puzzles, and hunting symbols and motifs. "A good novel needs all the attention the reader can give it," said Ford Madox Ford. "And then some more." The act of reading in its various aspects parallels in many ways the act of creating. The phrase "the willing suspension of disbelief" describes the reader's initial act that makes all else possible. Conrad said, ". . . the demand of the individual to the artist is, in effect, the cry 'Take me out of myself!' meaning really out of my perishable activity into the light of imperishable consciousness."

See "The Day the Flowers Came," comment 27, p. 282.

183 | Do you *assume* too much or too little of your reader, creating confusion?

The most mysterious area in the reader-author relationship is taste. Of all the forces outside the story that affect the reader's responses, taste is the most powerful. Many kinds of environmental and educational forces converge with personal makeup to create an individual's taste in literature. Some fiction demands that readers rise above their own individual feelings, predispositions, and prejudices to an objective self. But Henry James said, "I am at a loss to imagine anything that people ought to like or dislike." He also said, "We must grant the writer his donnée" (the basic elements he has chosen to work with); and many readers have no taste for James's own donnée.

Critics have stayed out of the murky realms of taste, but a deeper understanding of the process whereby it is shaped will illuminate a great deal about the creative process itself. Readers ought to remember that often the touchstones of the present are the tombstones of the future. Taste often prevents a person from entering new realms of fiction—where everything is possible.

Because he has strong tastes of his own, each writer makes certain assumptions about his reader's tastes and morality. Writers should try to understand the way these assumptions operate. Are they implicit or explicit, and with what results, technical and otherwise? The reader comes to a work of fiction with certain expectations, and when the writer's assumptions and the reader's expectations coincide, the reader has a pleasurable experience.

The reader's anticipations, expectations, and assumptions affect his experience of your story. Unconsciously, though sometimes consciously, every writer makes assumptions about his readers' knowledge, attitudes, tastes, and perceptiveness. The commercial writer writes, in a style which he thinks his readers will find acceptable, out of certain assumptions about the kinds of readers he imagines will buy his book; working out of these assumptions, he deliberately appeals to certain attitudes he thinks his readers have about love, violence, morality, politics, religion, education, sex, masculinity, femininity, etc. Often the popular writer shares, honestly, these attitudes and assumptions with his readers.

In *Catch-22*, in the first dialog between Yossarian and the Chaplain, Joseph Heller establishes that the Chaplain brings to his hospital visits all the predictable assumptions about the situation and the men in it. Yossarian seldom makes the conventional assumptions; usually, he reverses the reader's assumptions. Heller's revisions of "Catch-18," the story version, for the first chapter of the novel, are one indication of his careful preoccupation with reversals of the usual assumptions.

Examine your assumptions about the kind of readers you expect your story will have. Writers are often mistaken in their assumptions. Have you assumed too much or too little about your reader's responses? Consequently, do you imagine you've said what isn't actually on the page?

As you read a story or novel, try to detect the assumptions the writer seems to be making about you and the rest of his readers.

See "The Day the Flowers Came," p. 284.

184 | Is your story *uninteresting?*

W. Somerset Maugham said, "I have never met an author who admitted that people did not buy his book because it was dull." On her way down to visit Thomas Hardy, Virginia Woolf read *The Mayor of Casterbridge*.

When she told Hardy that, all he wanted to know was, "And did it hold your interest?" Readers often fail to finish a novel because, they say, "It just didn't hold my interest."

Writers would do well to think about the nature of what's *interesting*, from both psychological and aesthetic perspectives. Like the phenomenon of taste, it is a neglected area of concern and investigation. We acknowledge that taste and interest work in mysterious ways, but there must be a more productive response to the problem than throwing up one's hands. "Interestingness is a criterion no serious critic has dared to apply to art," said David Daiches, "but I can see no reason why it should not be applied."

185 | Have you failed to affect your reader emotionally, imaginatively, and intellectually?

A general study of the revisions writers of fiction have made suggests that they strive first to affect the reader's emotions, and in affecting their emotions by the use of certain techniques and devices, such as point of view, context, and implication, to stimulate their imaginations (though with varying degrees of control), and then, usually as an aftereffect, to stimulate their intellects.

At every point in the progression of a work of fiction, emotions, imagination, and intellect are simultaneously affected; but one observes here a revision clearly intended to affect a reader emotionally, there a revision clearly intended to stimulate the imagination, and less often a revision overtly intended to arouse an intellectual response.

These kinds of responses are both conscious and unconscious; most readers are more conscious of their own emotional responses than they are of the extent to which their imaginations or intellects are being directly affected. It is helpful for the hypercritical writer in the revision process to ask whether and to what extent a given passage is likely to have one of these effects on the reader.

"Begin again." Albert Camus

IX REIMAGINING "THE DAY THE FLOWERS CAME"

What would happen if a man woke up one morning, alone in his house in suburbia, and florists began delivering flowers of condolence for the deaths of the man's wife and two children—and he had not learned that they are dead? The notion came to me suddenly in a class I was teaching, while we were discussing this passage from Keats's "Ode on a Grecian Urn."

> Who are these coming to the sacrifice?
>   To what green altar, O mysterious priest,
> Lead'st thou that heifer lowing at the skies,
>   And all her silken flanks with garlands drest?
> What little town by river or sea shore,
>   Or mountain-built with peaceful citadel,
>   Is emptied of this folk, this pious morn?
> And, little town, thy streets for evermore
>   Will silent be; and not a soul to tell
>   Why thou art desolate can e'er return.

Through the classroom window, I saw snow begin to fall—and the notion for the story came. Moments after it struck me, I felt a compulsion to tell my students the basic situation.

But it was not until five years later that I finally came up with a genuine conception, as opposed to an easy, clever notion, that embodied the situation, character, form, style, theme, and technique of the story. The story seemed too contrived, too commercial, but I sensed a serious dimension that I couldn't quite articulate. It took only two hours to write; I submitted it to *Playboy* that day, and it was accepted two weeks later.

(Four stories I thought better, which have since been published, were rejected by *Playboy* at the same time.)

Even though it was reprinted in *Best American Short Stories, 1969* and in several other places, when I decided to include it in a volume of my short stories, *The Shadow Knows*, I made some major revisions, which I will reproduce in the margin; I will also make some new changes.

As you read the story the first time, try to ignore the marginal comments and revisions and try to anticipate the changes I made. Then examine the comments and revisions in the margins and ask, What is the effect of each change in the immediate context? What is the effect of each change upon the story as a whole? Is there a pattern to the changes, causing a cumulative effect?

THE DAY THE FLOWERS CAME

J. D. opened his eyes. A woman was talking to him. A man began talking to him. Through the pain in his head, in his eyes, he saw his own living room ceiling. Who were these people? Why was he on the couch?

1. When I wrote "two glasses" I was just as mystified as J. D. My own explanation is that he absentmindedly poured a drink for Carolyn, who had left him alone. This act initiates the progressive isolation of J. D. from all other people. Also, the extra glass is a note of mystery to catch the reader's interest early.

1. On the coffee table sat an empty Jack Daniel's fifth and two glasses. Why two? The voices went on talking to him. "Yes?" he asked.

   Chimes. As he raised himself up to answer the front door, a magazine slipped off his chest and flopped onto the pale rose carpet. *True*. Light through the wide window clashed on his eyes. The chimes. He stumbled to the wall, pulled the drape cord, darkened the room. Light flickered from the television set in the corner. The man and the woman who had been talking to him were talking to each other in a family situation comedy series. The husband was greeting a neighbor at the door. But J. D. still heard chimes.

2. As I give dramatic readings of this story around the country, many reader-listeners express doubt that flowers would be delivered on Labor

2. Going to the door, he wondered why he wasn't at the office. Labor Day. Where were Carolyn? Ronnie? Ellen?

   The sudden smell of flowers, thrust at him in red profusion as he opened the door, made J. D. step back. "Carolyn, flowers!" No, she was gone. With the kids.

Day. You may question the plausibility of other elements. Why do you suppose I haven't changed those elements to conform to actuality?

"This the Hindle residence?"

"My wife's in Florida."

3. REVISION:

Taking the urn the young man reverently handed him, J. D. tried to remember whose birthday or anniversary fell on Labor Day.

As the young man started back down the walk toward his truck, J. D. read the printed message: "My deepest sympathy."

As though he had blundered into a stranger's private grief, J. D. yelled, "Hey, come back here, fella."

"Something wrong?"

"Yeah, I'm afraid you've got the wrong house."

"You are Mr. Hindle, aren't you?"

"Yes, but you must have the wrong Hindle," said J. D., his tone expressing respect for the anonymous dead. "There's been no death in this family."

3.   The young man hooked the basket handle over J. D.'s arm and started back down the walk.

A printed message: "My deepest sympathy."

"Hey, come back here, fella."

"Something wrong?"

"Yeah, wrong house."

"You just said you were Mr. Hindle."

"Nobody dead here, pal. Wrong Hindle, maybe. You better check."

J. D. handed the young man the basket. He took it and walked back to his truck.

Sunlight on endless roofs below glared up at J. D. as he paused a moment on his porch, which was at the crest of a roll in the Rolling Hills Homes community. Blinking, he went in and turned off the TV, picked up the bottle and the glasses and started to the kitchen to find coffee. As he passed the front door, the chimes sounded.

The young man again with the flowers.

"I checked and double-checked, Mr. Hindle. They're for you."

"Listen, nobody died here. The card's unsigned and the whole thing's a mistake, OK?" J. D. shut the door and went on to the kitchen. Through the window over the sink, he saw the delivery boy get into his truck without the flowers.

They stood on the porch, red, fresh, redolent. About to leave them there, J. D. saw

J. D. handed the young man the urn.

a familiar car come down the street, so he took the roses and set them just inside the door.

Every morning since they had moved into this house three years ago, J. D. had found coffee in the pot as dependably as he had seen daylight in the yard. This morning, daylight hung full and bright in the young

4. This is not a description of the coffee pot and the tree for their own sakes; it's an image meant to convey a visual conception of J. D.'s sense of being alone in the house, as compared with his habitual situation.

4. birch tree, but the pot was empty. When he found the coffee, he realized he didn't know how to operate the new-model percolator. When he finally found the instant coffee, he was exhausted. The drinking he had done last night had a double impact because it had been solitary, depressing.

5. The color pink is handled in various ways to evoke a sense of Carolyn's presence even as she is absent from the house. I repeat such details not only to give a sense of unity to the story but to reveal aspects of character and mood. I now think, though, that I overused the color pink. And "immersed in a glimmer of pink" is overwritten.

Now, how did the damned *stove* work? The latest model, it left him far behind. The kitchen was a single, integrated marvel—or

5. mystery—princess pink. The second outfit since they had built the house. For Carolyn, it had every convenience. On the rare occasions when J. D. entered the kitchen, he simply dangled in the middle of the room, feeling immersed in a glimmer of pink that was, this morning, a hostile blur.

He let the hot water in the bathroom washbowl run, filled the plastic, insulated coffee mug, spooned instant coffee from the jar into the cup and stirred viciously. The first sip scalded his tongue; the second, as he sat on the edge of the tub, made him gag. Perhaps four teaspoonfuls was too much.

6. As often as possible, I try to make my style active, to

6. In the hall, he slipped on Ronnie's plastic puzzle set strewn over the already slickly polished floor, and the pain of hot coffee

give it muscle. I tried to make many things happen immediately in this sentence. In the first draft I wrote it this way. "J. D. walked into the hall. Carolyn had polished the floor recently. It was slick. He slipped on Ronnie's plastic puzzle set. The hot coffee he was carrying spilled down the front of his shirt. The pain of it made him shudder." (I try to make style itself, the arrangement of phrases, create a sense of movement.)

that spilled down the front of his shirt made him shudder.

His feeling of abandonment seemed more intense than his feeling of contentment yesterday as he watched Carolyn and the kids board the plane. Sitting on the couch, he tried to see their faces.

Chimes startled him.

A different deliveryman stood on the porch, holding a green urn of lilies, using both hands, though his burden looked light.

"What do you want?"

"You J. D. Hindle?"

"Yes."

"Flowers."

"In God's name, what *for*?"

"I think there's a card."

J. D. set the coffee cup on the hall table and took a card out of its tiny white envelope: *"We extend our deepest sympathy to you in your recent bereavement. James L. Converse, Manager, Rolling Hills Homes."*

"Wait a moment, will you?"

Leaving the man holding the lilies, J. D. went to the telephone in a confusion of anger and bewilderment and dialed Converse's number. His office didn't answer. Labor Day. His home didn't answer. Gone fishing, probably.

"Everything OK?"

"I can take a joke," said J. D., taking the flowers. He tipped the deliveryman. He set the lilies beside the roses.

7. INSERT:
Good ol' Bill Henderson must be working on his masterpiece, thought J. D. Not just one more stupid practical joke. He's put-

7.   But as he showered, the more he thought about it, the less he felt inclined to take a joke like this.

ting *everything* into this one.

(The story's major scene—the one later with Bill—has to be anticipated, not only so it isn't a shock to the reader, but so the reader will be willing to believe in J. D.'s behavior in that scene. I agreed with the editor of my collection of stories that I should plant the idea of J. D.'s charge against Bill in the reader's mind, so he would be more receptive to it when it comes. I transplanted a few lines from that scene to this one.)

8. Overuse of the passive voice will put the reader to sleep. He gets the feeling that everything has already happened, rather than that it is happening now. Notice what the passive voice did to the immediacy of this sentence in

Out of razor blades. In this world's-fair deluxe bathroom exhibit, he knew there was a blade dispenser concealed in the fixtures somewhere. When he found it, he would probably be delightfully amazed. Since Carolyn always saw to it that his razor was ready, he had had no occasion to use the dispenser. But he remembered it as one of the bathroom's awesome features. He

8. pushed a button. Pink lotion burped out onto his bare toes. He ripped a Kleenex out of a dispenser under the towel cabinet. It seemed that the house, masterfully conceived to dispense with human beings, had not really existed for him until this morning, now that its more acclimatized human beings had temporarily vacated it.

Where were his underclothes, his shirts, his trousers—which Carolyn had waiting for the first draft: "The button pushed by him caused pink lotion to burp out on his toes."

9. This is one of the motifs meant to create a sense of J. D.'s isolation. It is related to the line in the final paragraph: "He looked for the man in the moon, but the moon appeared faceless." (I tried to transform the "man in the moon" cliché by giving it another dimension, a kind of poignancy in this context.) With these motifs, I tried to reinforce some of the emotional values I wanted to express.

him on the mobile valet gizmo every morning? In the first three houses they had had—each representing a major step in the insurance company's hierarchy—he had known where most things were and how to operate the facilities. He remembered vividly where his shirts used to hang in the house in

9. Greenacres Manor. As second vice-president, perhaps he spent more time away now, more time in the air. Coming home was more and more like an astronaut's reentry problem.

His wrist watch informed him that two hours had been consumed in the simple act of getting up and dressing himself—in lounging clothes, at that. As he entered the living room again, he heard a racket in the foyer. When he stepped off the pale-rose carpet onto the pinkish marble, water lapped against the toe of his shoe. The roses lay fanned out on the marble. A folded newspaper, shoved through the brass delivery slot, lay on the floor. When J. D. picked it up, water dripped on his trousers.

He removed the want-ad section and the comics and spread them over the four-branched run of water, stanching its flow.

He wished the chill of autumn had not set in so firmly. How nice it would be to sit on the veranda and read the morning paper leisurely in the light that filtered through the large umbrella. He opened the drapes a little and sat in his black-leather easy chair. The cold leather chilled him thoroughly. He would have to turn the heat on.

On page two, as he clucked his tongue to alleviate the bitterness of the second cup of instant coffee on the back of his tongue, he read a news report twice about the death of Carolyn Hindle, 36, and her children Ronald H. Hindle, 7, and Ellen Hindle, 9, in a hurricane near Daytona Beach, Florida. Survived by J. D. Hindle, 37, vice-president of—

"I'm sorry, all lines to Florida are in use."

"But, operator, this is an emergency."

"Whole sections of the Florida coast, sir, are in a state of emergency. Hurricane Gloria—"

"I *know* that! My wife—"

"And with Labor Day . . . Do you wish me to call you when I've contacted the Breakers Hotel, or do you wish to place the call later?"

"Call me."

J. D. flicked on the television and gulped the cold instant coffee. It was a mistake. They had mistakenly listed survivors instead of victims. Or perhaps they were only—the phone rang—missing.

10. At this point, I originally wrote a scene in which J. D. talks with the president of his company, who tries to reassure him, but he was one character too many, so I cut their telephone conversation.

10. "Mr. Hindle, on your call to the Breakers Hotel in Florida, the manager says that no one by the name of Carolyn Hindle is registered there."

"Well, she *was* a little uncertain in her plans."

"She didn't say exactly where she would be staying?"

"No, she left rather impulsively, but—Listen, could you ask if she *has* been there?"

"I did, sir. She hasn't."

That opened up the entire state of Florida. On television, games and old movies, but no word of the hurricane. He would have to take the day off and try, somehow, perhaps through the Red Cross, to track her and the children down. Chimes.

On the porch stood the first delivery boy, long-stemmed roses again in a basket.

"This time I'm certain, Mr. Hindle."

J. D. accepted them. On the card was written in lovely script: *"They are just away. Our heartfelt sympathy. The Everlys."*

J. D. picked up the roses that had spilled, put them in their basket and hooked both baskets of roses over his arms and carried the urn of lilies with them into the living room. Still, there was something wrong. Flowers so soon, so quickly? He looked up the newspaper's phone number and dialed it.

"I'm just the cleaning lady, mister. They put out the paper, then locked up tight."

Just as J. D. placed the receiver in its cradle, the ringing phone startled him.

"Mr. J. D. Hindle?"

"Yes."

"Western Union Telegram."

"Read it, will you?"

"Dearest Jay: The kids and I are having wonderful, wonderful time. We all miss you. But we may return sooner than planned. Love and kisses, Carolyn, Ronnie and Ellen."

"I knew it, I knew it! God, God . . . When was that telegram sent?"

"This morning."

"What time, exactly?"

"Hour ago. Eight o'clock. You want me to mail it?"

"What?"

"Some people like to keep a record."

"Yes. Please do. And thank you very much."

The flowers smelled like spring now and he bent over them and inhaled, his eyes softly closed. Then, glancing down at the newspaper on the floor, he became angry. He dialed the home of the editor of the suburban paper.

11. I want J. D.'s anger at the editor to prepare you for his anger with Bill later

and to parallel, re-inforce it.

"Are you certain?"

"Listen, Mr. Garrett, it's *your* accuracy that's being questioned. That telegram was dated today and sent an hour ago. Now, I want to know where your information came from. What town? Why? This house is full of flowers."

"Well, if we're in error, Mr. Hindle, we'll certainly print a correction in tomorrow's paper. Meanwhile, I'll investigate the matter immediately and call you back when I've tracked something down."

"I'll be waiting."

12. I try to create for my stories a *charged image* that will refer to all the other elements in the story and illuminate them. I wanted the chimes, the telephone, and the flowers to become fused by the final paragraph into a composite charged image that acts as a reference point for every other element. Here is one telephone-chimes-flowers cluster.

12.   Chimes, J. D. picked up the flowers again and carried them to the door. The odor was good, but they breathed all the oxygen, and the overtone of funerals still emanated from them. He would unload them all on whichever deliveryman it was *this* time.

13. Bill's entrance is an instance of the reversal device. J. D. has answered the chimes and greeted a flower deliveryman three times. Along with J. D., I want the reader to expect another deliveryman; the reader's interest is reactivated, I hope,

13.   Bill Henderson stood on the porch holding a tray covered with a white cloth. "Nancy sent you something hot, Jay."

"That was sweet of her, Bill. Excuse me." J. D. set the flowers outside on the porch. "Come in." J. D. was smiling. He was aware that Bill noticed he was smiling.

"We were about to risk our lives on the freeway today, to visit Nancy's people, when we saw the newspaper. Jay, I—"

when Bill (whom the reader has anticipated from the earlier plant) enters. Although readers like to have their expectations gratified, they also enjoy having them reversed.

"Thanks, Bill, but save it. It's a mistake. A stupid mistake. I just heard from Carolyn."

"What? You mean she's OK? She called?"

"Yes. Well, she sent a telegram from Florida an hour ago. Didn't even mention the hurricane."

"That's odd. Must be on everybody's *mind* down there."

"Yeah, a little inconsiderate, in a way. She might know I'd be worried about that."

"Maybe the telegram was delayed. The hurricane and all."

"What're you trying to say?"

"Nothing."

"Why can't it be the *newspaper* that's wrong?"

"Well, it just doesn't seen likely."

14. The editor of my collection convinced me that to make J. D.'s exaggerated reaction to Bill plausible would take too much preparation. So I recast the scene.
REVISION:
"Look, let's shut up about it, OK? I've had a hangover from drinking alone last night."
"Why didn't you call me? We could have had a few hands of poker."
"Yeah. Why didn't I? It was a strange night. And now all this flood of flowers this morning. My stomach's in knots. You know, at first there,

14. "I gave that editor hell. He's going to call back. Look, let's shut up about it, OK? I've got a hangover from drinking alone last night."

"Why didn't you call me? We could have had a few hands of poker."

"Yeah. Why didn't I? It was a strange night. And now all this flood of flowers this morning. My stomach's in knots. Have a cup of coffee with me before you hit the highway."

"OK, then I guess we may's well go ahead with our trip."

Bill, with the flowers and all, I even got it in my head that it might have been one of your sick jokes." The look of astonishment that came to Bill's face made J. D. add quickly, "But when I saw the piece in the paper, I knew how stupid I—"

"My God, J. D., you think I'd do a terrible thing like that for laughs?"

"That's what I'm trying to get across to you. I feel damn guilty for even *thinking* ... Well, I sure gave that editor hell. He'll be calling back in a little bit. Listen, have a cup of coffee with me before you hit the highway."

15. This is a good example of revision to achieve implication. Here is the first-draft version of this passage: "Lifting the white cloth from the tray made J. D. imagine his wife and children on a morgue slab. He felt an eerie sensation in his stomach, but the sight of the smoking food dispelled the image." What is bluntly stated in this version

15.   Lifting the white cloth from the tray, J. D. felt an eerie sensation in his stomach that the sight of the smoking food dispelled. "I'm going to eat this anyway, OK? Not enough coffee for both of us. You have this and I'll make some more instant for myself."

Running the water in the bathroom basin again, waiting for it to get steaming hot, J. D. heard the telephone ring.

"Hey, Bill, you mind getting that for me?"

J. D. spooned coffee into the plastic mug and watched it stain the water. Steam rising made his eyes misty. Bill was a blur in the bathroom door. J. D. blinked the tears from his eyes. Bill's face was grimly set.

is implied in the published version.

16. REVISION:

"Listen, let's go in the living room."

"Hell with the living room. What did he say?"

"The story ... checks out ... through Associated Press. Jay, I'm sorry...."

"Bill," said J. D., looking straight into his eyes. "What are you doing here?"

"What do you mean, Jay?"

"I mean, how is it you came in right after the newspaper arrived?"

"Listen, Jay, you know here lately, you've been—"

"It wouldn't be because you wanted to see how it was getting to me, would it, Bill? I mean, you're not *that* goddamned—"

"Jay, you better get out of this house. You're not used to being alone here."

"I've got to find out what the hell's going on here!"

"Nancy and I'll stay home," said Bill, backing out of the bathroom. "You come on over with me and—"

"What's the matter with *you*?"

16. "That was the editor. He thought I was you, so he started right in with his report. The story . . . checks out . . . through Associated Press. He made other inquiries and found out that the . . . bodies are being shipped back tonight by plane."

J. D. slung the cup and coffee into the tub and with the same hand, clenched, slugged Bill in the mouth.

"What's the matter with you, Jay? Didn't you want me to tell—"

"You damned liar! You made the whole thing up. I see the whole thing now. It was you, back of it all. Your masterpiece. Not just one more stupid practical joke. You put *everything* into *this* one."

"You think I'd do a terrible thing like that just for laughs?"

"Not until now, I didn't. Why else would you come around? You had to see how it was getting to me. OK, I fell for it. All the way. So far, I'm still sick, and I'll *be* sick all day."

"Jay, you better get out of this house. You're not used to being alone here. Nancy and I will stay home. You come on over with me and—"

"You're the one that better get out of here, before I kill you!"

Staring up at J. D., Bill got to his feet. Without looking back, he walked out, leaving the front door open.

Still so angry he could hardly see or walk straight, J. D. went into the living room and flopped onto the couch, satisfied that all the pieces of the puzzle were now in place. The mixture of emotions that had convulsed him now was a vivid anger that struck at a

"Look, just leave me alone, Bill."

"Jay, if you think I—"

"I don't know, I don't know anything. But if you did, I fell for it, OK? All the way. I'm still sick, I'll be sick all day."

"I'm not leaving, Jay, as long as you've got in your head—"

"All right! It's a mistake! Some cruel mix-up somewhere! But leave me alone, will you?"

"Yeah, I think I'd better go, Jay." Bill walked out, leaving the front door open.

J. D. flopped onto the couch. The mixture of emotions that had convulsed him was now a vivid anger without a target. (The last line is perhaps overwritten.)

17. To evoke a sense of the presence of Carolyn even though she's absent from the scene, I have Mrs. Merrill come to offer condolences; we associate her primarily with Carolyn and her role as housewife and mother, and so Carolyn's presence is evoked. I wanted this asso-

single object. Seeing the tray of food, no longer steaming, on the footrest of his leather chair, he leaped to his feet and took the tray into the bathroom and with precise flips of his wrist tossed the eggs, toast, coffee, jelly, butter and bacon into the toilet and flushed it. Over the sound of water, he heard the chimes.

17.   With the tray still in his hands, he went into the foyer, where the door still stood open. Among the flowers he had set out on the porch stood a woman, smartly dressed. She held a soup tureen in both gloved hands. The sight of the tray surprised her and she smiled awkwardly, thinking, perhaps, that she had come at the end of a line and that J. D. was ready for her. She started to set the tureen on the tray, saying, "I'm Mrs. Merrill, president of your P.T.A., and I just want you to know—" But J. D. stepped back and lowered the tray in one hand to his side.

ciational device to make Carolyn live for the reader even though she's absent from the immediate narrative; she's part of an implied narrative.

"A stupid, criminal joke has been played here, Mrs. Merrill. I won't need the soup, thank you. Come again when my wife is home. They're having a wonderful time in Florida."

"With that horrible hurricane and all?"

"Yes, hurricane and *all*."

J. D. shut the door and turned back and locked it.

He closed the drapes and lay down on the couch again. His head throbbed as though too large for his body. Just as his head touched the cushion, the telephone rang. He let it. Then, realizing that it might be Carolyn, calling in person, he jumped up. It stopped before he could reach it. As he returned to the couch, it started again. Maybe she was finally worried about the hurricane, about *his* worrying about it.

18. I agreed with the editor of my collection that this passage was too gross and highly unlikely. What do you think of this new scene? REVISION:

"Hello."

"Is this the Hindle residence?"

"Yes...."

"May I speak with the lady of the house, please?"

"She isn't at home."

"May I ask when she *will* be."

"Who is this, please?"

"My name is Janice Roberts, Mr. Hindle, and I'm with Gold Seal Portrait

18. "Mr. Hindle, this is Mr. Crigger at Greenlawn. It is my understanding that you have not yet made arrangements for your dear wife and chil—"

Seeing three red-clay holes in the ground, J. D. slammed the receiver in its cradle.

Chimes. J. D. just stood there, letting the sound rock him like waves at sea. Among the flowers that crowded the porch stood the first delivery boy.

"If you touch those chimes one more time . . ."

"Listen, mister, have a heart, I'm only doing what I was told."

"*I'm* telling you—" Unable to finish, J. D. jerked the basket of flowers from the young man's hands and threw it back at him. He turned and ran down the walk, and J. D. kicked at the other baskets, urns and pots, until all the flowers were strewn over the lawn around the small porch.

Studios. We *are* going to be *in* the Rolling Hills area in a few weeks, and your name has been selected for a special award."

"Miss—"

"For half price you may obtain a family portrait, either eight by ten or ten by twelve, and now, all we ask of you is that you tell your friends—"

J. D. slammed the receiver in its cradle. (I want the new scene to be one of subtle irony, bitter humor, pathos. This is a major flowers-telephone-chimes cluster, contributing to what I call the story's charged image, a device for structuring and focusing all its elements.)

19. I wanted to give this story an atmosphere of mechanical menace—the door chimes that won't stop ringing, etc. Many other passages are meant to create this atmosphere in which everything goes wrong. I'm trying to create a mood of desperation, of depression and frustration, and to make

19. He slammed the door and locked it again. Standing on a chair, he rammed his fist against the electric-chimes mechanism that was fastened to the wall above the front door. The blow started the chimes going. He struck again and again, until the pain in his hand made him stop.

Reeling about the house searching for an object with which to smash the chimes, J. D. saw in his mind images from a Charlie Chaplin movie he had seen on the late show one night in the early years of television: Charlie entangled in modern machinery on an assembly line. The film moved twice

you feel it with
J. D.

20. Here, in the first
draft, a catering
service called J. D.,
offering to feed
guests after the fu-
neral. Furious, he
ripped the wire
from the wall. I cut
that passage as
being one unlikely
telephone call too
many.

21. I cut out "for his
dead family" be-
cause they are im-
plied by the context
and in the word
"remorse." In fic-
tion, language more
often connotes than
denotes meaning.
In my style, I try to
evoke rather than
literally state.

22. This line offers
a variation on
an earlier motif:

as fast in his head. He found no deadly
weapon in the house nor in the garage that
adjoined the house. Seeing the switch box,
he cut off the current.

20. Lying on the couch again, he tried to
relax. He thought of people passing, of more
people coming to offer their condolences,
of the flowers strewn like gestures of insanity in the yard. Carolyn would be shocked
at the stories she would hear of the flowers
in the yard; for until they all knew the truth,
it would appear to the neighbors that J. D.
had no respect, no love, felt no remorse for
his dead family.

21. He went out and gathered the flowers
into one overflowing armful and took them
into the house and put them in his leather
easy chair. Then he brought in the baskets,
urns and pots.

He had heard that lying on the floor relaxed tense muscles and nerves. He tried it.
He lay on the carpet, arms and legs sticking
straight out. After a few shuddering sighs,
he began to drift, to doze. He recalled the
funerals of some of his friends. Somewhat
as these people today had approached him,
he had approached the wives and families
of his departed friends. For the important
families, he had attended to insurance details
himself. How artificial, meaningless, ridicu-
lous, even cruelly stupid it all seemed now.

Coldness woke him. The room was black
dark. The cold odor of roses and lilies was
so strong he had to suck in air to breathe.
He rolled over on his belly and rose on his
hands and knees, then, holding onto the
couch, pulled himself up.

22. Weak and shivering, he moved across the
floor as though on a deck that heaved and
sank. When he pulled the cord, the drapes,

"Chimes. J. D. just stood there, letting the sound rock him like waves at sea." This image is not symbolic; it is simply a motif, a simile that evokes the quality of J. D.'s emotions. A contrast to this one is the motif of the astronaut and the man in the moon.

like stage curtains, opened on icy stars, a luminous sky.

None of the light switches worked. Then he remembered throwing the main switch in the garage. Using matches, he inched along until he found the switch.

Perhaps if he ate something, to get strength.

In the refrigerator, stacks of TV dinners. The pink stove gleamed in the fluorescent light of the kitchen. The buttons and dials, like the control panel of an airplane, were a hopeless confusion.

He was astonished that the first week in September could be so cold. Perhaps it had something to do with the hurricanes. Arctic air masses or something. What did he know of the behavior of weather? Nothing. Where was the switch to turn on the electric heat? He looked until he was exhausted. Perhaps he had better get out of the house for a while.

23. I try to avoid abstract statements such as this. The last part of the passage is totally abstract; there's nothing vivid or concrete to grasp hold of here, although I hope the context gives it some kind of power. "His hand on the ignition" is much more real to me, and if the abstraction works, that more concrete statement may in part be responsible. A further development of this statement comes in the next para-

23. Sitting behind the wheel, his hand on the ignition, he wondered where he could go. A feeling of absolute indecision overwhelmed him. The realm of space and time in which all possibilities lay was a white blank.

graph. Carolyn's dramatic speech a few lines later gives life to that abstract statement, I hope.

24. Sometimes a climactic speech extracted from a conversation can be very effective. This is the only speech quoted from the past, and the only words Carolyn (who is so important to the story) says. The speech is meant to suggest something about the meaning of J. D.'s experience, as well as summarizing her own. The speech would lose its effect if I were to quote everything that was said in the car on the way to the airport, including what the children said. It's selecting this one speech, isolating it, placing it, that makes it effective, makes it mean more, and, I hope, makes it more poignant. I want it to evoke her whole

As he sat there, hand on key, staring through the windshield as if hypnotized by the monotony of a freeway at night, he experienced a sudden intuition of the essence of his last moments with Carolyn. Ronnie and Ellen in the back seat, Carolyn

24. sat beside J. D., saying again what she had said in similar words for weeks and in silence for months, perhaps years, before that: "I must get away for a while. Something is happening to me. I'm dying, very, very slowly; do you understand that, Jay? Our life. It's the way we live, somehow the way we live." No, he had not understood. Not then. He had only thought, How wonderful to be rid of all of you for a while, to know that in our house you aren't grinding the wheels of routine down the same old grooves, to feel the pattern is disrupted, the current that keeps the wheels turning is off.

The telephone ringing shattered his daze. He went into the house.

life in a rush of in-
tuition. It further
suggests J. D.'s iso-
lation in that I don't
give his answer to
her statement.

Seeing the receiver on the floor, he realized that he had only imagined the ringing
of the phone. But the chimes were going.

25. The line is not too passive, but it might be more effective if I revise it now to read: "Only moonlight lay on the porch."

25. He opened the door. There was only moonlight on the porch. Then he remembered
striking at the chimes with his fist. Something had somehow sparked them off again.

26. I tried to fill the final paragraph with supercharged phrases that would reveal the theme in thematic language —but even with all this overt language, I do not clearly express the theme. It must emerge from your emotional and intellectual experience in reading the story.

26. As he stood on the threshold of his
house, the chimes ringing, he looked out
over the rooftops of the houses below, where
the rolling hills gave the development its
name. From horizon to horizon, he saw
only roofs, gleaming in moonlight, their
television aerials bristling against the glit-
tering stars. All lights were out, as though
there had been a massive power failure, and
he realized how long he must have slept.
He looked for the man in the moon, but the
moon appeared faceless. Then, with the
chimes filling the brilliantly lighted house at
his back, he gazed up at the stars; and as he
began to see Carolyn's face and Ronnie's
face and Ellen's face more and more clearly,
snow began to fall, as though the stars had
disintegrated into flakes,

27. "And he knew that he would never see his wife and children again" is the most stupid error I have ever made. This line ruined the story by making it obvious and sentimental and by

27. and he knew that he would never see his
wife and children again.

neatly tying up all its loose ends. By cutting this line I allow the reader to imagine the story's implications because the ending is more open.

Readers often fit stories into the contexts of their own lives. Sometimes they see, for their own reasons, an error before the writer does. A nurse once told me that she uses this story to teach students "the five classic stages of grief," but that she always omits the last line because it violates what she teaches.

Further Comment on "The Day the Flowers Came"

This was the conception I wanted to develop in the story: a series of bizarre coincidences suddenly converge upon a man and he is caught up in a swift, almost machinelike process that leaves him intuitively aware of his spiritual emptiness and he feels a kind of death-in-life.

As I started to write, I asked, Should I use the omniscient point of view, giving me access to all the characters wherever they are, past and present? No, that would scatter the focus. This is how the first paragraph would have sounded in the omniscient point of view: "One morning, in a house among thousands in a vast suburban complex, a man lay on his living room couch, in a drunken sleep. Voices on the television, which he had left on last night, woke him. He was confused. He heard a woman talking to him, then a man. Someone rang the front door bell. He got up, feeling pain in his head and eyes from the hangover." Maybe I should let J. D. or Bill or Carolyn tell it in the first person? I dismissed Carolyn because she is *perhaps* dead, and she would have no access to J. D.'s dilemma anyway. Bill wouldn't work because he would dilute the impact of the experience I wanted to put J. D. through; it would have to mean something in Bill's life somehow, and I saw no possibility of that.

This is how the first paragraph would have sounded in J. D.'s first-person voice: "When I opened my eyes that morning, I heard a woman's voice. Then a man was talking to me. Who were these people? I wondered. My head and my eyes hurt so bad I could hardly see the ceiling. Why was I on the couch? I saw an empty Jack Daniel's bottle on the coffee table and wondered why there were two glasses. The voices kept talking to me. 'Yes?' I asked. And then the front door bell rang." I decided that the reader must see J. D. receiving all the flowers and visitors, answering the phone, struggling with the kitchen appliances. If J. D. told the story himself, the reader would be inside him, looking out, listening to J. D. report on events that have already happened. I wanted the reader to watch J. D. become involved in events that are happening now. Also, I wanted the feeling at the end that J. D. is spiritually isolated from his fellow man, so he would not be telling his story to anybody.

And I wanted to describe his dilemma coldly. So I decided to use the third-person, central-intelligence method. I could then describe his actions in a staccato style, and describe his feelings in a rather cool, distant manner. So I chose a point of view and a style that would express the special quality of the experience I wanted to subject J. D. and the reader to. The effective use of point of view makes a greater demand on the writer's skills than any other technique.

My assumption was that anybody—and that means I was not conceiving a limited audience for this particular story—would experience fear, frustration, horror if one delivery after another of flowers came to his door, for a wife and children he didn't know were dead. To create this feeling in the reader, I knew that the events had to move straight ahead at a brisk pace. There's more action in this than in most of my stories. I tried to set up a rhythm of movement: action and repose, action and repose, fast and slow, a rhythmic blending of these contrasting kinds of experiences.

To sustain the pace, I had to make rapid transitions. The chimes and the telephone enabled me to mark one episode off from another. A pattern of action enhances the structure, contributes to coherence of form: I present a delivery of flowers, than a phone call, then another delivery of flowers, another phone call, a visit from a neighbor, another phone call, and this pattern of events is broken up by brief interludes in which J. D. struggles with the appliances in the house or tries to make sense of what's happening to him.

I try to create movement in the style, too, so that events are thrust forward quickly. The reader is not delayed while I passively describe events. I want the reader, caught up by the pace, to experience J. D.'s emotions and thoughts. But what a writer wants and what he gets is determined by the individual reader.

SELECTED LIST OF REVISION EXAMPLES

This is a list of most of the authors and their works which I have used to illustrate the process of revision. I have omitted those that would be too difficult for most readers to track down; for those who want to try, my *Writers' Revisions* (Scarecrow Press, 1981) offers bibliographical information with annotations for most of them. I have also omitted works that I have mentioned merely to illustrate a technique or to recommend generally; all such works are, however, listed in the index of authors and titles. Finally, I have included some works that I have not discussed in the text but that exist in two or more versions and are worth attention.

"See" references indicate items in the Bibliography that are especially helpful.

Agee, James. *A Death in the Family*. See Kramer.
Barth, John. Revised editions of the following Barth novels have appeared: *The End of the Road; The Floating Opera; Giles Goat-boy; The Sot-weed Factor*.
Bellow, Saul. For description of Bellow's revisions of his novels, see Fuchs.
Berry, Wendell. *A Place on Earth* (1967). Compare with 1983 revised version.
Boyle, Kay. "The Ballet of Central Park." See Kuehl.
Bradbury, Ray. *Dark Carnival* stories were revised for *October Country* edition.
Braine, John. *Room at the Top*. See revisions in his *Writing a Novel*.
Burgess, Anthony. *A Clockwork Orange*. Compare British and American editions; last chapter was cut from the American edition.
Butler, Samuel. *The Way of All Flesh*. See Hildick, *Word for Word* and *Writing With Care*.

Camus, Albert. *A Happy Death* prefigures *The Stranger*. Compare, any editions.

Cary, Joyce. *The Horse's Mouth*. See afterword by Andrew Wright in the Perennial Library edition (New York: Harper and Row, 1967). Many revisions. Compare with 1950 edition.

Cather, Willa. "Paul's Case." Compare versions in *The Troll Garden* and in *Youth and the Bright Medusa*.

Chandler, Raymond. *The Big Sleep*. See description of early versions in introduction by Philip Durham to *Killer in the Rain* (Boston: Houghton Mifflin, 1969), pp. vii–x.

Crane, Stephen. *The Red Badge of Courage*. Compare revised Norton edition, 1982, with any earlier edition.

Donleavy, J. P. *The Ginger Man* (1955). Compare with revised McDowell-Obolensky edition, 1958. See also the Delacorte Press 1965 "complete" edition.

Eliot, George. *Middlemarch*. See Hildick, *Word for Word* and *Writing with Care*.

Faulkner, William. *Absalom, Absalom!* See Langford.

———. "The Bear." Compare version in *Saturday Evening Post*, (CCXIV (May 9, 1942), pp. 30–31, 74, 76, 77, with version in *Go Down, Moses*, pp. 191–331.

———. *Flags in the Dust* (1973). Compare with cut version, *Sartoris* (1929).

———. *Light in August*. See Regina K. Fadiman, *Faulkner's "Light in August"* (Charlottesville, Va.: University of Virginia Press, 1975).

———. *Requiem for a Nun*. See Polk.

———. *Sanctuary* (1931). Compare with first version, published in 1981 (Random House). See Langford.

———. *The Sound and the Fury* (1929). Compare 1984 corrected text (Random House) with any earlier edition.

———. ""That Evening Sun Go Down." Originally in *American Mercury*, XXII (March 1931), pp. 257–65; Compare with "That Evening Sun" version, in *Collected Stories of William Faulkner* and elsewhere.

———. *Uncollected Stories*. Collection edited by Joseph Blotner (New York: Random House, 1979). Blotner describes revisions Faulkner made as he turned portions of novels-in-progress into stories or incorporated stories into novels.

Fielding, Henry. *Joseph Andrews* and *Shamela*. See the edition edited by Sheridan Baker, (New York: Thomas Y. Crowell, 1972); revisions are noted in margins.

Fitzgerald, F. Scott. "Babylon Revisited." Originally in *Saturday Evening Post*, CCIII (February 21, 1931), pp. 3–5, 82–84. Compare with version in *Taps at Reveille*.

———. *"The Great Gatsby:" A Facsimile of the Manuscript*, edited by Matthew J. Bruccoli, (Washington, D.C., Microcard Editions Books, 1973). Compare with any edition of the novel.

———. *Tender Is the Night*. See Cowley.

———. *The Last Tycoon*. See Bruccoli; see Cowley.

———. *This Side of Paradise*. See James L. W. West.

Flaubert, Gustave. See Steegmuller, who discusses revisions Flaubert made in *Madame Bovary* and provides Flaubert's scenario.

Fowles, John. *The Magus* (1965). Compare with 1977 revised version.

Gardner, John. *Resurrection* (1966). Compare with 1974 revised paperback version.

Graham, Sheilah. "Beloved Infidel." For F. Scott Fitzgerald's revision of Graham's story, see Graham.

Greene, Graham. *The Heart of the Matter* (1948). Compare with 1978 Penguin edition version.

Hannah, Barry. *Geronimo Rex*. Compare with "The Crowd Punk Season Drew," *Intro #1*, 1968.

Hardy, Thomas. *The Return of the Native*. See Riverside edition. (Boston: Houghton Mifflin, 1967); see also Paterson.

———. *Tess of the D'Urbervilles*. See Hildick, *Word for Word* and *Writing with Care*.

———. *Jude the Obscure*. See Bobbs-Merrill edition, 1972, introduction.

Hawkes, John. "The Nearest Cemetery." Compare with novel version, *Second Skin*; see Kuehl.

Hawthorne, Nathaniel. *The Scarlet Letter*. See introduction to 1967 Lippincott edition.

———. *The House of the Seven Gables*. See note on the text in 1964 Riverside edition, Houghton Mifflin publisher.

Heller, Joseph. "Catch-18," *New World Writing #7* (New American Library, 1955). Compare with first chapter of *Catch-22*, any edition.

Hemingway, Ernest. *A Farewell to Arms*. See Reynolds.

James, Henry. He revised all his novels for the 1912 New York complete works edition.

———. *The Ambassadors*. See "Editions and Revisions," 1964 Norton edition.

———. *The American*. Compare first with New York edition, 1912.

———. *Daisy Miller*. See Hildick, *Writing with Care*.

————. "Four Meetings," *Scribner's Monthly*, XV (November 1877). Compare with revised version reprinted in any collection.

————. *Lady Barberina and Other Tales: Benvolio, Glasses, and Three Essays*. Herbert Ruhm, ed. (New York: Universal Library, Grosset and Dunlap, 1961). Revisions shown.

————. *The Portrait of a Lady*. See Hildick, *Word for Word* and *Writing with Care*.

————. *The Princess Casamassima*. See Crowell edition, 1976; revisions discussed in introduction by Terry Comito.

————. *Roderick Hudson*. Compare first with New York edition, 1912.

————. *Watch and Ward*. Compare with New York edition, 1912.

Jones, James. *The Pistol*. See Kuehl.

Joyce, James. *Ulysses*. Compare with facsimile of manuscript, introduction by Harry Levin, published by Philip H. and A. S. W. Rosenbach foundation, 1975.

————. *Ulysses*. See Random House edition, 1986, edited by Hans Walter Gabler; revisions described in "Afterword."

————. *Stephen Hero* (1963). Compare with *A Portrait of the Artist as a Young Man*, corrected edition; see Anderson.

Lawrence, D. H. There are three versions of the Lady Chatterlly story: *The First Lady Chatterley, John Thomas and Lady Jane*, and *Lady Chatterley's Lover*. See any editions.

————. *The White Peacock*. See Hildick, *Word for Word*.

————. "Odour of Chrysanthemums." To compare versions, see Cushman, and see Hildick, *Word for Word*.

————. *The Rainbow*. See Ross, and see Hildick, *Word for Word*.

————. *Women in Love*. See Ross.

Madden, David. "The Day the Flowers Came," *The Shadow Knows*. Compare with revised version in Madden, *Revising Fiction*.

————. "The Creative Process: Author's Commentary on Revising 'No Trace,' " *Studies in the Short Story*, Virgil Scott and David Madden, eds. 5th ed. (New York: Holt, Rinehart, and Winston, 1980), pp. 299–310.

————. "Performing 'The Singer,' " *Dramatics* 50 (September-October 1978), pp. 23–32. Revisions described.

Mailer, Norman. *The Deer Park*. See Mailer's "The Last Draft of *The Deer Park*," *Advertisements for Myself*.

Malamud, Bernard. "Idiots First." See Kuehl; see Virgil Scott and David Madden, eds., *Studies in the Short Story* (New York: Holt, Rinehart & Winston, 1980), pp. 258–81.

Melville, Herman. *Billy Budd, Sailor.* See the 1962 University of Chicago Press edition, edited by Harrison Hayford and Merton M. Sealts, Jr., revisions shown.

Moore, George. *Confessions of a Young Man.* See the edition edited by Susan Dick (Montreal and London: McGill-Queen's University Press, 1972); revisions shown.

———. *Esther Waters.* See appendix of 1963 Riverside edition (Houghton Mifflin).

Morris, Wright. "The Ram in the Thicket," *Collected Short Stories* (1986). Compare with *Man and Boy* (1951).

———. *The Home Place* New York: Charles Scribner's Sons, 1948. Compare pp. 132–35 with "Privacy as a Subject for Photography," *Magazine of Art*, XLIV (February 1951), pp. 51–55.

Nabokov, Vladimir. "Tyrants Destroyed." Compare with *Bend Sinister*, any edition.

O'Connor, Flannery. "Geraniums." Compare with "Judgment Day," a completely revised version. See both in *Complete Stories.*

———. "You Can't Be Poorer Than Dead." Compare with first chapter of *The Violent Bear It Away.*

O'Connor, Frank. "Guests of the Nation." Compare version in *Collected Stories* (1981) with revision in *Stories by Frank O'Connor*, 1956 Vintage edition.

Roth, Philip. *Letting Go.* See Kuehl.

Steinbeck, John. "The Chrysanthemums." Originally in *Harper's Magazine*, CLXXV (October 1937), pp. 513–19; compare with version in *The Long Valley* (1938).

Sterne, Laurence. *A Sentimental Journey Through France and Italy by Mr. Yorick.* See edition edited by Gardner D. Stout, Jr., (Berkeley and Los Angeles: University of California Press, 1967); revisions shown.

Thackeray, William M. *Vanity Fair.* See note on the text in Modern Library edition (1950).

Twain, Mark. *The Mysterious Stranger.* See Gibson.

Vidal, Gore. *The City and the Pillar* (1948). Compare with revised edition, 1965.

Vleit, R. G. Compare *Solitudes* (1977) with later version *Soledad* (1986).

Warren, Robert Penn. "Proud Flesh." Play version of *All the King's Men*; see Kuehl.

Welty, Eudora. Compare "From the Unknown." with published version, "Where is the Voice Coming From?" in Kuehl, *Creative Writing and Rewriting.*

West, Nathanael. *Miss Lonelyhearts*. To compare the novel with the published short-story versions, see William White. "Nathanael West: a Bibliography." *Studies in Bibliography* 11 (1958): 207–24.

Wolfe, Thomas. *The Complete Short Stories* (New York: Charles Scribner's Sons, 1987). Compare "The Angel on the Porch" with *Look Homeward, Angel*; compare "No Door" with the version in *From Death to Morning* (1935).

Woolf, Virginia. *To the Lighthouse*. Compare with *Virginia Woolf, "To the Lighthouse": The Original Holograph Draft*, Susan Dick, ed. (Toronto: University of Toronto Press, 1982).

———. *Mrs. Dalloway*. See Hildick, *Word for Word*.

———. *The Voyage Out*. See DeSalvo.

———. *The Waves*. Compare with T. W. Graham, ed., *Virginia Woolf's "The Waves": The Two Holograph Drafts*. (Toronto: University of Toronto Press, 1976).

SELECTED LIST OF EXEMPLARY FICTION

The works in this list illustrate techniques discussed in the text. Others are cited in the text and listed in the index.

"Learning to write may be a part of learning to read," says Eudora Welty. "For all I know, writing comes out of a superior devotion to reading" ("Some Notes on Time in Fiction"). And William Faulkner stressed what every instructor of creative writing stresses fervently: "Read, read, read. Read everything—trash, classics, good and bad, and see how they do it. Just like a carpenter who works as an apprentice and studies the master." Even Faulkner, the most innovative of major American writers, read to "see how they do it." "Read! You'll absorb it. Then write."

Jane Austen, *Pride and Prejudice*
James Baldwin, "Sonny's Blues"
Djuna Barnes, *Nightwood*
Emily Brontë, *Wuthering Heights*
James M. Cain, *The Postman Always Rings Twice*
Albert Camus, *The Stranger*
Anton Chekhov, "Gooseberries"
Joseph Conrad, *Lord Jim*
Charles Dickens, *Bleak House*
Ralph Ellison, *Invisible Man*
William Faulkner, *The Sound and the Fury*
F. Scott Fitzgerald, *The Great Gatsby*
Gustave Flaubert, *Madame Bovary*
Ford Madox Ford, *The Good Soldier*
E. M. Forster, *A Passage to India*

William Gaddis, *The Recognitions*
William Goyen, *The House of Breath*
Ernest Hemingway, *The Sun Also Rises*
Henry James, *The Ambassadors*
James Joyce, *A Portrait of the Artist as a Young Man*
Franz Kafka, "In the Penal Colony"
Carson McCullers, *The Heart Is a Lonely Hunter*
Katherine Mansfield, "Miss Brill"
Herman Melville, *Moby-Dick*
Wright Morris, *The Field of Vision*
Katherine Anne Porter, "Flowering Judas"
Jules Romains, *The Death of a Nobody*
J. D. Salinger, *The Catcher in the Rye*
Evelyn Scott, *The Wave*
Gertrude Stein, "The Good Emma"
Laurence Sterne, *Tristram Shandy*
William Styron, *Lie Down in Darkness*
Michel Tournier, *The Ogre*
Mark Twain, *The Adventures of Huckleberry Finn*
Robert Penn Warren, *All the King's Men*
William Carlos Williams, "The Use of Force"
Thomas Wolfe, *Look Homeward, Angel*
Virginia Woolf, *To The Lighthouse*

BIBLIOGRAPHY

This bibliography includes notebooks, journals, diaries, novel outlines, letters, autobiographies, interviews, and prefaces by fiction writers and critical articles and books. Many of the works are discussed or cited in the text; some are not.

Wallace Hildick's *Writing with Care* and *Word for Word* and John Kuehl's *Creative Writing and Rewriting*, written for writers, are the three most useful books on revision. They led me to many examples, though I have made my own use of these examples. There is no substitute for consulting Hildick's and Kuehl's books directly. Unfortunately, they are out of print, except for *Word for Word*, the best of Hildick's. I urge the reprinting of Kuehl's book.

Allott, Miriam. *Novelists on the Novel*. New York and London: Columbia University Press, 1959.

Anderson, Chester. Criticism and notes in James Joyce, *A Portrait of the Artist as a Young Man*. New York: Viking Press, 1968. Corrected, definitive text.

Bach, Peggy. "The Searching Voice and Vision of Mary Lee Settle." *The Southern Review*, Vol. 20, no. 4, Autumn, 1984, pp. 842–50.

Beckson, Karl, and Arthur Ganz. *A Reader's Guide to Literary Terms: A Dictionary*. New York: Noonday Press, 1960.

Bellamy, Joe David, ed. *The New Fiction: Interviews with Innovative America Writers*. Urbana, Ill.: University of Illinois Press, 1974.

Booth, Wayne C. *The Rhetoric of Fiction*. Chicago: University of Chicago Press, 1961.

Bowen, Elizabeth. "Notes on Writing a Novel." In James E. Miller, ed., *Myth and Method: Modern Theories of Fiction*. Lincoln, Neb.: University of Nebraska Press, 1960.

Braine, John. *Writing a Novel*. New York: McGraw-Hill, 1974.

Brooks, Cleanth, and Robert Penn Warren. "Fiction and Human Experience: How Four Stories Came to Be Written." *Understanding Fiction*. New York: Appleton-Century-Crofts, 1943 (1959), pp. 526–643.

Bruccoli, Matthew J. *The Last of the Novelists: F. Scott Fitzgerald and "The Last Tycoon."* Carbondale, Ill.: Southern Illinois University Press, 1977.

Buckler, William E. *Novels in the Making.* Boston: Houghton Mifflin, 1961.

Cain, James M. Preface to *Three of a Kind.* New York: Alfred A. Knopf, 1941.

Camus, Albert. *Notebooks 1935–1942* and *Notebooks 1942–1951.* Edited and translated, with annotations, by Justin O'Brien. New York: Alfred A. Knopf, 1963, 1965.

Cassill, R.V. *Writing Fiction*, 2nd ed. Englewood Cliffs, N J.: Prentice-Hall, 1975.

Conrad, Joseph. *Joseph Conrad on Fiction.* Edited by Walter F. Wright. Lincoln, Neb.: University of Nebraska Press, n.d.

Cowley, Malcolm, ed. *Three Novels of F. Scott Fitzgerald (The Great Gatsby, Tender Is the Night, The Last Tycoon).* New York: Charles Scribner's Sons, 1953. Contains Fitzgerald's notes for *The Last Tycoon*, pp. 134–63.

Cushman, Keith. *D. H. Lawrence at Work.* Charlottesville, Va.: University of Virginia Press, 1978.

DeSalvo, Louise A. *Virginia Woolf's First Voyage: A Novel in the Making.* London: Macmillan, 1980.

Dostoevsky, Fyodor. *The Notebooks for "The Brothers Karamazov."* Edited and with an introduction by Edward Wasiolek. Chicago: University of Chicago Press, 1971.

———. *The Notebooks for "Crime and Punishment."* Edited and with an introduction by Edward Wasiolek. Chicago: University of Chicago Press, 1967.

———. *The Notebooks for "The Idiot."* Edited and with an introduction by Edward Wasiolek. Chicago: University of Chicago Press, 1967.

———. *The Notebooks for "The Possessed."* Edited and with an introduction by Edward Wasiolek. Chicago: University of Chicago Press, 1968.

———. *The Notebooks for "A Raw Youth."* Edited and with an introduction by Edward Wasiolek. Chicago: University of Chicago Press, 1969.

du Maurier, Daphne. *Myself When Young: The Shaping of a Writer.* Garden City, N.Y.: Doubleday, 1977.

Eliot, T. S. "Hamlet and His Problems." *Selected Essays*. New York: Harcourt, Brace, 1932 (1950, 1960).

Ellison, Ralph. *Shadow and Act*. New York: Random House, 1953, 1964.

Empson, William. *Seven Types of Ambiguity*. Charlottesville, Va.: University of Virginia Press, 1975.

Faulkner, William. *Faulkner in the University: Class Conferences at the University of Virginia, 1957–58*. Edited by Frederick L. Gwynn and Joseph L. Blotner. New York: Vintage Books, 1965.

Fitzgerald, F. Scott. *The Crack-up*. New York: New Directions, 1945.

Flaubert, Gustave. *Selected Letters*. Translated and edited by Francis Steegmuller. New York: Books for Libraries Press, 1971.

Ford, Ford Madox. *Joseph Conrad: A Personal Remembrance*. London: Duckworth, 1924.

Forster, E. M. "Pattern and Rhythm." *Aspects of the Novel*. New York: Harcourt, Brace, 1927.

Fuchs, Daniel. *Saul Bellow: Vision and Revision*. Durham, N.C.: Duke University Press, 1984. Descriptions of revisions of Saul Bellow's works.

Gardiner, Dorothy, and Katherine Sorley Walker. *Raymond Chandler Speaking*. Boston: Houghton Mifflin, 1962.

Gardner, John. *On Moral Fiction*. New York: Basic Books, 1978.

———. *The Art of Fiction*. New York: Vintage Books, 1985.

———. *On Becoming A Novelist*. New York: Harper & Row, 1983.

Gass, William. *Fiction and the Figures of Life: Essays & Reviews*. New York: Alfred A. Knopf, 1971.

———. "The Ontology of the Sentence, or How to Make a World of Words." *The World Within the Word*. New York: Alfred A. Knopf. 1978.

———. "And." In Allen Wier and Don Hendrie, Jr., eds., *Voice Lust: Eight Contemporary Fiction Writers on Style*. Lincoln, Neb: University of Nebraska Press, 1985.

Ghiselin, Brewster. *The Creative Process*. Berkeley: University of California Press, 1952.

Gibson, William. *Mark Twain: "The Mysterious Stranger" Manuscripts*. Berkeley: University of California Press, 1969.

Gide, André. *The Journal of André Gide*. Translated, selected, and edited by Justin O'Brien. 4 vols. New York: Alfred A. Knopf, 1947–51.

———. "Journal of *The Counterfeiters*." *The Counterfeiters*. New York: Alfred A. Knopf, 1951.

Glasgow, Ellen. *A Certain Measure: An Interpretation of Prose Fiction.* New York: Harcourt, Brace, 1943.

Gordon, Caroline, and Allen Tate. *The House of Fiction.* New York: Charles Scribner's Sons, 1950.

Graham, John, interviewer, and George Garrett, ed. *The Writer's Voice: Conversations with Contemporary Writers.* New York: William Morrow, 1973.

Graham, Sheilah. *College of One.* New York: Viking, 1967.

Graves, Robert, and Allen Hodge, eds. *The Reader Over Your Shoulder: A Handbook for Writers of English Prose.* New York: Macmillan, 1943.

Gundell, Glenn, ed. *Writing—from Idea to Printed Page: Case Histories of Stories and Articles Published in "The Saturday Evening Post."* New York: Doubleday, 1949.

Hall, Donald, ed. *The Modern Stylists: Writers on the Art of Writing.* New York: The Free Press, 1968.

Harris, Mark. "Easy Does It Not." *The Living Novel.* New York: Macmillan, 1957.

Hayman, David. "From *Finnegans Wake*: A Sentence in Progress," *Publications of the Modern Language Association* 73 (1958): 136–54.

Hemingway, Ernest. *A Moveable Feast: Sketches of the Author's Life in Paris in the Twenties.* New York: Charles Scribner's Sons, 1964.

Herring, Philip F., ed. *Joyce's Notes and Early Drafts for "Ulysses."* Charlottesville, Va.: University of Virginia Press, 1977.

Hildick, Wallace. *Thirteen Types of Narrative.* New York: Clarkson N. Potter, 1970.

———. *Word for Word.* New York: W. W. Norton, 1965.

———. *Writing with Care.* New York: David White, 1967.

Hulme, T. E. "Romanticism and Classicism." *Speculations.* New York: Harcourt, Brace, 1924.

Humphrey, Robert. *Stream of Consciousness in the Modern Novel.* Berkeley: University of California Press, 1954.

James, Henry. *The Art of the Novel.* With introduction by R. P. Blackmur. New York: Charles Scribner's Sons, 1934.

———. *The Notebooks of Henry James.* Edited by F. O. Matthiessen and Kenneth. B. Murdock. Chicago: University of Chicago Press, 1981, Phoenix edition.

Josephson, Matthew. *Zola and His Time.* Garden City, N.Y.: Garden City Publishing Company, 1928. See "Zola's Techniques: The Methods and Plans," pp. 523–49.

Kramer, Victor A. *"A Death in the Family* and Agee's Projected Novel." *Proof* 3. Columbia, S. C.: University of South Carolina Press, 1973, pp. 137–54.

Kronenberger, Louis, ed. *Novelists on Novelists: An Anthology*. Garden City, N.Y.: Anchor Books, 1962.

Kuehl, John. *Creative Writing and Rewriting: Contemporary American Novelists at Work*. New York: Appleton-Century-Crofts, 1967. Also published as *Write and Rewrite*, Meredith Publishing Co.

Langford, Gerald. *Faulkner's Revisions of "Absalom, Absalom!"* Austin, Texas: University of Texas Press, 1971.

———. *Faulkner's Revisions of "Sanctuary."* Austin, Texas: University of Texas Press, 1972.

Liddell, Robert. *Some Principles of Fiction*. London: Jonathan Cape, 1953.

———. *A Treatise on the Novel*. London: Jonathan Cape, 1947.

Lubbock, Percy. *The Craft of Fiction*. New York: Viking Press, 1957.

Macauley, Robie, and George Lanning. *Technique in Fiction*. New York: Harper & Row, 1968.

MacShane, Frank. *The Life of Raymond Chandler*. New York: E. P. Dutton, 1976. See pp. 68–69.

McCarthy, Mary. "Settling the Colonel's Hash." *On the Contrary*. New York: Noonday Press, 1961.

McCormack, Thomas, ed. *Afterwords: Novelists on Their Novels*. New York: Harper & Row, 1969.

McCullers, Carson. *The Mortgaged Heart*. Edited by Margarita G. Smith. Boston: Houghton Mifflin, 1971.

Madden, David. "The Craft of Writing and Rewriting the Short Story." Tape recording. Jeffrey Norton, two cassettes. 100 minutes (#23610/236511). Uses "The Day the Flowers Came" for examples, with a dramatic reading.

———. *The Poetic Image in Six Genres*. Carbondale, Ill.: Southern Illinois University Press, 1969.

———. *A Primer of the Novel: For Readers and Writers*. Metuchen, N.J.: Scarecrow Press, 1980.

———. *Writer's Revisions*. Metuchen, N.J.: Scarecrow Press, 1981.

Mailer, Norman. *Advertisements for Myself*. New York: G. P. Putnam's Sons, 1959.

Mann, Thomas. "The Making of *The Magic Mountain*." *The Magic Mountain*. New York: Alfred A. Knopf, 1961.

———. *The Genesis of a Novel*. Translated by Richard and Clara Winston. London: Secker & Warburg, 1961. Describes writing of *Doctor Faustus*.

Mansfield, Katherine. *The Journal of Katherine Mansfield*. Edited by John Middleton Murry. New York: Alfred A. Knopf, 1930.

Marrs, Suzanne. "The Making of *Losing Battles*: Plot Revision." *Southern Literary Journal*, XVIII (Fall 1985), pp. 40–49.

Matthiessen, F. O. "The Painter's Sponge and Varnish Bottle." *Henry James: The Major Phase*. New York: Oxford University Press, 1944. See pp. 152–86.

Maugham, W. Somerset. *The Summing Up*. New York: Literary Guild, 1938.

———. *A Writer's Notebook*. Garden City, N.Y.: Doubleday, 1949.

Mirrielees, Edith Ronald. *Story Writing*. Preface by John Steinbeck. New York: Viking Press, 1939; rev. ed., 1962.

Moffett, James, and Kenneth R. McElheny. *Points of View*. New York: New American Library, 1966.

Morris, Wright. *About Fiction*. New York: Harper & Row, 1975.

———. *Earthly Delights, Unearthly Adornments*. New York: Harper & Row, 1978.

———. "One Day." *Afterwords*. Edited by Thomas McCormack. New York: Harper & Row, 1969.

———. "Made in U.S.A." *The American Scholar*, XXIX (Autumn, 1960), 483–94.

Muir, Edwin. *The Structure of the Novel*. New York: Hogarth Press, 1929.

Nemerov, Howard. *Journal of the Fictive Life*. New Brunswick, N.J.: Rutgers University Press, 1965.

Nims, John Frederick. *Western Wind*. New York: Random House, 1974.

Nin, Anaïs. *The Novel of the Future*. New York: Macmillan, 1968.

O'Connor, Flannery. *Mystery and Manners: Occasional Prose*. New York: Farrar, Straus & Giroux, 1969.

O'Connor, Frank. *The Lonely Voice*. New York: World Publishing Company, 1963. A special anthology edition: New York: Bantam Books, 1968.

———. *The Mirror in the Roadway: A Study of the Modern Novel*. New York: Alfred A. Knopf, 1956.

O'Faolain, Sean. *The Short Story*. New York: Devin-Adair, 1951.

Orwell, George. "Why I Write." *Decline of the English Murder*. Harmondsworth, Middlesex, England: Penguin Books, 1965.

Paterson, John. *The Making of "Return of the Native."* Berkeley: University of California Press, 1963.

Perkins, Maxwell. *Editor to Author: The Letters of Maxwell Perkins*. Selected and edited, with commentary and an introduction, by John Hall Wheelock. New York: Charles Scribner's Sons, 1950.

Phillips, Larry W. *Ernest Hemingway on Writing*. New York: Charles Scribner's Sons, 1986.

————. *F. Scott Fitzgerald on Writing*. New York: Charles Scribner's Sons, 1986.

Poe, Edgar Allan. "The Philosophy of Composition." *The Portable Poe*. New York: Viking Press, 1973.

Polk, Noel. *Faulkner's "Requiem for a Nun."* Bloomington: Indiana University Press, 1981.

Porter, Katherine Anne. "Notes on Writing." *New Directions 1940*. New York: New Directions, 1940.

Read, Herbert. *English Prose Style*. Boston: Beacon Press, 1955.

Reynolds, Michael S. *Hemingway's First War: The Making of "A Farewell to Arms."* Princeton, N.J.: Princeton University Press, 1976.

Robbe-Grillet, Alain. *For a New Novel: Essays on Fiction*. New York: Grove Press, 1965.

Romains, Jules. Introduction to *The Death of a Nobody*. New York: Alfred A. Knopf, 1944 (1911).

Ross, Charles L. *The Composition of "The Rainbow" and "Women in Love."* Charlottesville, Va.: University of Virginia Press, 1979.

Roth, Philip. *Reading Myself and Others*. New York: Farrar, Straus & Giroux, 1975.

Scholes, Robert, and Robert Kellogg. *The Nature of Narrative*. New York: Oxford University Press, 1966.

Scholes, Robert, and Richard M. Kain, eds. *The Workshop of Daedalus: James Joyce and the Raw Materials for "A Portrait of the Artist as a Young Man."* Evanston, Ill.: Northwestern University Press, 1965.

Schorer, Mark. "Fiction and 'Analogical Matrix' and "Technique as Discovery." *The World We Imagine*. New York: Farrar, Straus & Giroux, 1968.

Scott, Evelyn. Preface to *Bread and a Sword*. New York: Charles Scribner, 1937.

Settle, Mary Lee. "The Search for Beulah Land." *The Southern Review*, Vol. 26, No. 1, Winter 1988, p. 13–26.

Steegmuller, Francis. *Flaubert and Madame Bovary*. Rev. ed. Chicago: University of Chicago Press, 1950.

Stein, Gertrude. *Lectures in America*. Boston: Beacon Press, 1957.

Steinbeck, John. *Journal of a Novel*. New York: Viking Press, 1969, 1972.

Stevick, Philip, ed. *Anti-Story: An Anthology of Experimental Fiction*. New York: The Free Press, 1971.

————. *The Chapter in Fiction*. Syracuse, N.Y.: Syracuse University Press, 1970.

————. *The Theory of the Novel*. New York: The Free Press, 1967.

Strunk, William, and E. B. White. *The Elements of Style*. New York: Macmillan, 1959.

Tate, Allen, and Caroline Gordon. *The House of Fiction*. 2nd ed. New York: Charles Scribner's Sons, 1950, 1960.

Trumbo, Dalton. *Night of the Aurochs*. New York: Viking Press, 1979. One third of his unfinished novel, with synopsis and notes for the rest, pp. 97–218.

Wallace, Irving. *The Writing of One Novel (The Prize)*. New York: Simon and Schuster, 1968.

Watkins, Floyd C., and Karl F. Knight, eds. *Writer to Writer: Readings on the Craft of Writing*. Boston: Houghton Mifflin, 1966.

Welty, Eudora. "On Place on Fiction." *The Eye of the Story: Selected Essays and Reviews*. New York: Random House, 1977.

————. "Words into Fiction." *Southern Review*, I (1965), pp. 543–53.

West, James L. W. *The Making of "This Side of Paradise."* Philadelphia: University of Pennsvlania Press, 1983.

West, Ray B. *The Art of Writing Fiction*. New York: Thomas Y. Crowell, 1968.

Wharton, Edith. *A Backward Glance*. New York: Appleton Century, 1934.

————. *The Writing of Fiction*. New York: Charles Scribner, 1925.

Wolfe, Thomas. *The Notebooks of Thomas Wolfe*. Edited by Richard S. Kennedy and Paschal Reeves. Chapel Hill, N.C., The University of North Carolina Press, 1970.

————. "The Story of a Novel." *The Thomas Wolfe Reader*. Edited by Hugh Holman. New York: Charles Scribner's Sons, 1962. About *Look Homeward, Angel*.

Woolf, Virginia. *The Common Reader*. New York: Harcourt, Brace, 1925.

————. *The Letters of Virginia Woolf, Volume One: 1888–1912*. Edited by Nigel Nicolson and Joanne Trautman. New York: Harcourt, Brace, Jovanovich, 1976.

————. *A Writer's Diary*. New York: Harcourt, Brace, 1953, 1954.

Writers at Work. Paris Review Series, nos. 1–7. New York: Viking Press, 1959–86.

AUTHORS AND TITLES INDEX

KEY WORD INDEX

The key (italicized) word for the question is given, followed by the name of the section in parentheses; not alphabetized are the names of the sections (see main table of contents).

312

Ⓟ Plume

WRITE TO THE TOP

(0452)

☐ **MAGIC WRITING: A Writer's Guide to Word Processing by John Stratton with Dorothy Stratton.** If you are a writer thinking about switching to a word processor, this complete guide will tell you in words you will understand how to choose, master, and benefit from a word processor. Plus a computerese-English dictionary and glossary.
(255635—$12.95)

☐ **WRITING ON THE JOB: A Handbook for Business & Government by John Schell and John Stratton.** The clear, practical reference for today's professional, this authoritative guide will show you how to write clearly, concisely, and coherently. Includes tips on memos, manuals, press releases, proposals, reports, editing and proofreading and much more.
(255317—$9.95)

☐ **THE WRITER'S GUIDE TO MAGAZINE MARKETS: NONFICTION by Helen Rosengren Freedman and Karen Krieger.** 125 top magazines describe the kinds of non-fiction articles they look for—and publish. Included are tips on the best way to prepare and submit your manuscript; the uses of an agent; guidance from writers who've successfully sold pieces; how to negotiate financial terms and rights; awards; grants and contests; plus a glossary of publishing terms and much, much more.
(257964—$9.95)

☐ **THE WRITER'S GUIDE TO MAGAZINE MARKETS: FICTION by Karen Krieger and Helen Rosengren Freedman.** Complete in-depth information on the kinds of short stories 125 top magazines seek—and publish. If you are a short story writer and want to be published, this is the book you owe it to yourself and your work to read.
(257956—$9.95)

Prices slightly higher in Canada.

Buy them at your local bookstore or use this convenient
coupon for ordering.

NEW AMERICAN LIBRARY
P.O. Box 999, Bergenfield, New Jersey 07621

Please send me the books I have checked above. I am enclosing $_____(please add $1.50 to this order to cover postage and handling). Send check or money order—no cash or C.O.D.'s. Prices and numbers are subject to change without notice.

Name_____

Address_____

City_____State_____Zip Code_____

Allow 4-6 weeks for delivery.
This offer is subject to withdrawal without notice.